INDIVIDUAL DIFFERENCES

INDIVIDUAL DIFFERENCES:
Normal and Abnormal

MICHAEL W. EYSENCK

A volume in the series
Principles of Psychology

Series Editors
Michael W. Eysenck
Simon Green
Nicky Hayes

LEA LAWRENCE ERLBAUM ASSOCIATES, PUBLISHERS LEA
Hove (UK)   Hillsdale (USA)

Lawrence Erlbaum Associates Ltd., Publishers
27 Palmeira Mansions
Church Road
Hove
East Sussex BN3 2FA
UK

British Library Cataloguing in Publication Data

A catalogue record for this book is available from the British Library

ISBN 0-86377- 256-0 (hbk)
ISBN 0-86377- 257-9 (pbk)
ISSN 0965-9706

Cartoons by Sanz
Subject index compiled by Sue Ramsey
Cover design by Stuart Walden and Joyce Chester
Printed and bound by BPC Wheatons Ltd., Exeter

To my son, Willie, with love

Acknowledgements

As always, I am very grateful to my wife, Christine, and to our three children, Fleur, Willie, and Juliet, for their support. By general agreement with the family, they take it in turns to have books dedicated to them. Even though a book published as recently as 1990 was dedicated to Willie, I have been writing so many books that already it is his turn again to have another dedicated to him!

Michael W. Eysenck

Contents

Introduction 1

O ne of the most obvious things that we notice in our everyday lives is that people differ markedly from each other. Some people are optimistic—others are pessimistic; some people are very sociable and friendly—others are cold and distant. For rather obscure reasons, psychology only began to consider individual differences in a systematic way towards the end of the nineteenth century. The starting point was the work of Charles Darwin (1859). He proposed the theory of evolution, which emphasised the importance of individual differences from the perspective of biology. In particular, Darwin argued that it was mainly those members of a species who were best adapted to their environment who would succeed in the struggle for existence (i.e. "survival of the fittest"). Sir Francis Galton (1883) was impressed by Darwin's views, and proposed that individual differences were of as much relevance to the human species as to other species.

Although human beings differ from each other in numerous ways, some of those ways are clearly of more significance to psychology than others. Foot size and eye colour are presumably of little or no relevance as determinants of behaviour (although foot size may matter to professional footballers!), whereas personality appears to play a major role in influencing our behaviour.

The structure of this book

There is reasonable agreement that the two main aspects of individual differences of interest to psychologists are intelligence and personality, both of which are discussed in this book.

Intelligence

Intelligence is basically concerned with individual differences in the ability to think and to reason, but should probably be broadened out to include creativity and more practical forms of intelligence. Difficult and controversial issues in research on intelligence include:

- How many factors of intelligence are there?
- What is the nature of these factors?
- What is the relative importance of heredity and environment in determining individual differences in intelligence?

All of these issues are discussed in Chapter 2.

Personality

Personality is dealt with in Chapters 3 and 4. According to what we call factor theories, the central focus of personality research is on individual differences at the emotional and motivational level. Only those aspects of emotion and motivation which are long-lasting are of concern to factor theorists, so that transient moods and desires are not regarded as forming part of human personality. Factor theories of personality are discussed in Chapter 3.

One of the limitations of the factor theory approach to personality is that individual differences in *cognitive processes* and structures are de-emphasised. Another limitation is that factor theories of personality have generally had only a modest impact on our understanding and treatment of mental disorders. A small group of theorists have tried to avoid these limitations: they have proposed theories which are basically cognitive in nature, and they have all been associated with the development of new forms of clinical therapy. Their respective theoretical and clinical contributions are discussed in Chapter 4.

Psychopathology

The first part of this book is mainly concerned with individual differences as they occur in the normal population. However, there are some people whose behaviour is so different from that of most other people that they are believed to be suffering from some form of psychological disorder. The study of such people forms the basis of *abnormal psychology* or *psychopathology*. The second part of the book takes a detailed look at individual differences from the perspective of psychopathology. There are clear links between the two parts of the book in that normal individuals with certain kinds of personality are more likely than most people to suffer from psychological disorders at some point in their lives. The links between normal personality and psychopathology are spelled out in the theories of George Kelly, Carl Rogers, and Albert Bandura (Chapter 4).

A key issue in abnormal psychology concerns the distinction between normality and abnormality:

- How do we decide that a certain individual's behaviour is abnormal?
- If psychiatrists argue that an individual is abnormal and pin a psychiatric label on him or her, does this tend to make it more difficult for that individual to recover?
- Because what is regarded as abnormal varies from one society to another, does this mean that the very notion of abnormality is entirely arbitrary?

These (and other) tricky questions are addressed in Chapter 5, which ⟩ *classification* · is also concerned with the issue of the categorisation of mental disorders. ⟩ It is often thought that a crucial first step in treatment is to identify the psychological disorder from which the patient is suffering. It has proved extremely difficult to devise a classificatory system that has reasonable reliability and validity, and many experts argue that mental disorders cannot appropriately be classified in the same sort of way as physical disorders. The most widely used classificatory systems are discussed at some length.

Chapter 6 provides a detailed analysis of some of the major forms of psychopathology. The disorders considered include many that we often hear discussed in everyday life, such as schizophrenia, depression, anxiety disorders, personality disorders, and childhood disorders. The pattern of symptoms associated with each disorder is considered, and so are the factors responsible for the development of the disorders. It is known that genetic factors, adverse life events, and so on, contribute to many forms of psychopathology. So far, however, it has generally not been possible to identify the mechanisms determining how these factors have their effects.

Treatment

Finally, in Chapter 7, the most important methods of treatment are discussed. In approach, these methods vary considerably. For example, ✳ behaviour therapy is based on the assumption that maladaptive behaviour is the problem, and so treatment should involve "correcting" that behaviour. In contrast, *psychoanalysis* (which is the best-known form of psychotherapy) is based on the view that treatment should focus on uncovering major unresolved conflicts within the unconscious mind and on providing the patient with "insight" into those conflicts. It is obviously very important to compare these different forms of therapy. Somewhat surprisingly, all the major methods of treatment are of approximately ⟵ equal effectiveness. However, they differ as to which psychological disorders they are able to treat most effectively.

2 Intelligence and intelligence testing

What is intelligence?

Psychologists have not been able to agree among themselves on a definition of the elusive concept of *intelligence*. In spite of its elusiveness, however, those who are good at abstract reasoning, problem-solving, and decision-making are often seen as more intelligent than those who are poor at those mental activities. As Thorndike (a behavioural psychologist working in the early 1900s) pointed out, intelligence can be thought of as "the quality of mind...in respect to which Aristotle, Plato, Thucydides, and the like differed most from Athenian idiots of their day."

Of particular importance to intelligence appears to be the ability to think or reason with partially novel information. Many unintelligent people can display apparently remarkable abilities if they are processing information with which they are extremely familiar. For example, there are *idiots savants* (i.e. mentally handicapped individuals who are nevertheless highly accomplished in some ways) who can do things such as calculating the answer to 465 × 399 in their heads in a few seconds or rapidly working out the day of the week on which 22nd March 1975 fell. Idiots savants have often spent hundreds or thousands of hours in developing strategies to perform such feats, and appear quite dull in most other ways. In essence, when deciding whether an individual's behaviour is intelligent, we need to consider how much training lies behind his or her performance.

Probably the greatest controversy about the definition of intelligence concerns its breadth. Intelligence certainly includes the ability to reason, but:

- Does it also include creative thinking?
- Is there musical intelligence?
- Can someone who is sensitive to the needs and attitudes of others be said to possess social intelligence?
- Are individuals who are "street-wise" (in the sense that they are very skilful at finding ways of furthering their own ends) necessarily intelligent?

Unfortunately, as we will see in this chapter, there are no definite answers to any of these questions. However, there is no doubt that opinions have changed during the course of the twentieth century.

Intelligence was originally defined rather narrowly as thinking, reasoning, and problem-solving ability. In contrast, most contemporary psychologists accept that the notion of intelligence is broader than that, and encompasses skills (e.g. street-wisdom; social intelligence) that are valued by the culture or society in which one lives. For example, Sternberg (1985) defined intelligence as "mental activity directed toward purposive adaptation to, and selection and shaping of, real-world environments relevant to one's life" (p. 45). The contemporary view has the advantage that it makes intelligence more variegated, interesting, and relevant to everyday life than did traditional views.

The great majority of psychologists are willing to accept that there is such a thing as intelligence. However, there is evidence to suggest that intelligence may be much less important in everyday life than is sometimes believed to be the case. For example, 8000 mentally retarded individuals who were inducted into the US Army were investigated. Most of these individuals had an intelligence quotient ("IQ"—a measure of general intellectual functioning) that was substantially below the population average of 100. The median (i.e. middle value) IQ of those who made a satisfactory adjustment to military life was 72, compared with a median IQ of 68 for those who did not. An implication is that well-adjusted behaviour depends to only a very modest extent on an individual's level of intelligence.

As well as doubts about its practical usefulness, some psychologists have questioned whether the concept of "intelligence" has much theoretical value. For example, Howe (1990a; b) argued that intelligence does not have any explanatory value. According to Howe (1990b), "For the important task of helping to discover the underlying causes of differing levels of performance, there is no convincing evidence that the concept of intelligence can play a major role. So far as explanatory theories are concerned, the construct seems to be obsolete" (p. 499).

Why did Howe (1990b) reach this pessimistic conclusion? He argued that statements such as "Tom is better at solving most kinds of problems than John because he is more intelligent", merely describe a state of affairs without explaining it. While there is a grain of truth in this, Howe's views appear to be over-simplified. As Kline (1991) has pointed out, tests of intelligence have proved to be reasonably successful in predicting how well different individuals will fare in their future study of subjects about which they know nothing at the time of testing. Such successful predictions can hardly be regarded as merely providing redundant descriptions of behaviour.

We will discuss various other ways in which the concept of "intelligence" is of explanatory value later in the chapter. However, two examples can be given here. It's possible to imagine that the level of each individual's abilities depends crucially on the amount of time he or she has devoted to each ability (e.g. those who have devoted a lot of time to swimming generally have more swimming ability than those who have not). If the time spent on an activity were the prime determinant of ability, then one would expect that an individual who was very good at some abilities would be rather poor at others (because he or she would not have enough spare time to devote to them). In fact, individuals tend to be either good or poor across a wide range of abilities. This suggests the existence of a rather general capacity which most psychologists call "intelligence".

The second example concerns a hypothetical situation in which two new companies are being set up. One company recruits only those people with IQs of 130 and above, and the other company recruits only those with IQs of 70 and below. If intelligence does not exist, then presumably the two companies would be equally likely to succeed. In fact, much of the evidence discussed later in this chapter makes it clear that the prospects would be much brighter for the former company because, generally, intelligence does have an impact on real-world success.

Intelligence testing

Much of the history of research into intelligence has been taken up with attempts to produce satisfactory tests of intelligence. This emphasis is illustrated by the well-known saying that, "Intelligence is what intelligence tests measure." Although it has sometimes seemed that too much attention has been paid to the details of intelligence-test construction, and not enough to theoretical analyses of intelligence, it is indisputable that intelligence can only be investigated properly when adequate measures are available.

The first person to produce a rudimentary test of intelligence was Sir Francis Galton in the late nineteenth century. His pioneering efforts were very impressive, but too many of the tests he devised measured simple skills such as sensory abilities. In other words, he failed to assess the more complex *cognitive skills* which are of the essence of intelligence. Indeed, some psychologists argue that Galton's tests were so primitive that he should not be regarded as the originator of the intelligence test. Such psychologists generally credit the Frenchman Alfred Binet with having devised the first proper measure of intelligence. At the beginning of the twentieth century he was asked to devise an intelligence test that would allow mentally retarded children to be identified at as young an age as possible. The reason for this was that such children could be given special educational facilities to remedy their mental retardation.

Binet and his associate Simon responded to the challenge. In 1905 they produced a wide range of tests which measured comprehension, memory, and various other psychological processes. This led to numerous later test formulations that followed the tradition established by Binet and Simon. Among the best-known are the Stanford-Binet test produced at Stanford University in 1916; the Wechsler Intelligence Scale for Children; and, in the 1970s, the British Ability Scales.

These, and other tests are designed to measure several different aspects of intelligence. For example, many contain vocabulary tests in which individuals are asked to define the meanings of various words. The tests also often include problems based on analogies (e.g. "Hat is to head as shoe is to ——"), and tests of spatial ability (e.g. "If I start walking northwards, then turn left, and then turn left again, what direction will I be facing?").

In spite of the differences among these major intelligence tests, they all share important similarities. They all have accompanying manuals which spell out in detail how the test should be administered. This is important, because the wording of the instructions given by the tester often makes a difference to the tested person's score. The major intelligence tests are also alike in that they are *standardised tests*. Standardisation of a test involves giving it to large, representative samples of the age groups covered by the test, so that the significance of an individual's score on the test can be evaluated by comparing it against the scores of other people.

Performance measurement

With most standardised tests, it's possible to obtain several measures of an individual's performance. These measures are mostly of a relatively specific nature (e.g. arithmetic ability or spatial ability), but the best-known measure is the very general IQ or *intelligence quotient*, which was mentioned earlier. This reflects performance on all of the sub-tests contained in an intelligence test, and is thus regarded as an overall measure of intellectual ability.

There are various ways in which the intelligence quotient can be calculated. What used to be the most popular method defined the intelligence quotient as follows: mental age divided by chronological age × 100. Chronological age is simply the actual age of the child taking the test, and mental age is the age at which the average child performs at the same level as the child taking the test. Thus, for example, if a child does as well as the average seven-year-old on the test, then his or her mental age is seven years, regardless of his or her actual or chronological age. An average child will, of course, have a mental age which is the same as his or her chronological age, and thus an IQ of 100. Bright children will have a mental age which is greater than their chronological age, and thus their IQs will be greater than 100. The opposite will be true of dull children, who have IQs of less than 100.

There are some dubious aspects associated with this method of calculating IQ. For example, a child of four needs a mental age *one* year ahead of his or her actual age in order to have an IQ of 125. The same child at the age of twelve needs a mental age *three* years ahead of chronological age to keep the same IQ. An IQ of 125 only means the same in such different circumstances if we are willing to assume that intellectual development proceeds in a steady fashion from year to year—and that is probably a mistaken assumption.

The problems associated with calculating IQ on the basis of the discrepancy between mental age and chronological age have led to the introduction of a less controversial method of assessing IQ. The basic notion is that an individual's performance on an intelligence test is compared only against the scores obtained by other children of his or her age in the standardisation sample. More specifically, most intelligence tests are devised so that the overall scores are normally distributed. The normal distribution is a bell-shaped curve in which there are as many scores above the mean as below it (see the figure opposite). Most scores cluster reasonably close to the mean, and there are progressively fewer scores as you move away from the mean in either direction. The spread of scores in a normal distribution is usually indicated by a statistic known as the *standard deviation*. In a normal distribution, 68% of the scores fall within one standard deviation of the mean or average, 95% fall within two standard deviations, and 99.73% are within three standard deviations. These characteristics of normal distributions can be used to express an individual's IQ as a *standard score*. This is based on the number of standard deviations above or below the mean of his or her age group that an individual's score lies.

Intelligence tests are typically designed to have a mean of 100 and a standard deviation of approximately 16. Therefore, an IQ of 116 represents a standard score of +1.0, and means that the individual is more intelligent than 84% of the population (50% fall below the mean, and a further 34% between the mean and one standard deviation above it). In summary:

1. An intelligence test must be given in the same way and with the same instructions to everyone who takes it.
2. The test needs to be standardised by administering it to large, appropriate samples, so that the meaning of any individual's score can be ascertained.

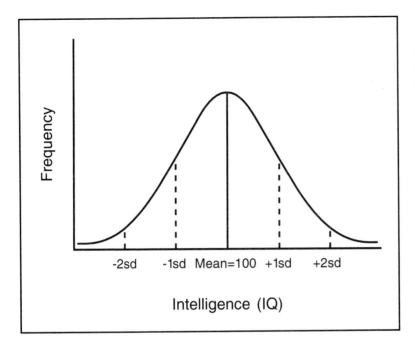

Frequency

-2sd   -1sd Mean=100 +1sd   +2sd

Intelligence (IQ)

3. The comparison of an individual's score against those of the standardisation sample yields a broad measure (the IQ) together with more specific scores.
4. In addition, as we discuss in the following sections, intelligence tests require other characteristics (in particular, reliability and validity) in order to qualify as satisfactory measuring instruments for intelligence.

So far we have emphasised the notion that intelligence tests are used to provide a single broad score known as the IQ. However, it is generally found that those with high IQs do not perform well on all of the tests within an intelligence-test battery, and those with low IQs do not perform poorly on every test. As a consequence, tests are usually constructed so that it is possible to obtain measures of various abilities (e.g. numerical; spatial; reasoning; perceptual speed). It is argued that we can obtain a more accurate assessment of an individual's intelligence by considering the profile of his or her perform-ance across these abilities rather than by focusing exclusively on the IQ. There have been theoretical disagreements as to which abilities should be assessed; these disagreements are considered later in this chapter.

Reliability

One of the requirements of a good test of intelligence is that it is reliable—i.e. the test provides consistent and replicable measurement. If, for example, an individual obtains an IQ of 125 when taking an intelligence test on one occasion and then, a short time later, obtains an IQ of 95 when re-taking the same test, then the test is clearly unreliable and cannot be an adequate measure of something as relatively unchanging as intelligence. Performance on an unreliable test is affected by such changeable factors as the motivation or mood of the person taking it.

Reliability is generally assessed by means of the *test–retest method*. All that happens is that a group of people take the same test on two separate occasions. Their scores on the two occasions are then correlated with each other. The higher the resultant correlation coefficient (the measure of the relationship between the two scores), the greater is the reliability of the test. Reliability can also be assessed by the *equivalent forms method*: two equivalent forms of the same intelligence test are used, both of which are given to the same group of people at about the same time. For example, the Stanford-Binet intelligence test has two forms (L and M) which correlate approximately +0.90 with each other (this correlation coefficient indicates a very satisfactory degree of reliability). A final way of assessing reliability is by a modified version of the equivalent-forms method known as the *split-half method*. An intelligence test can be divided into two halves (e.g. all the odd items vs. all the even items), with the two halves being correlated with each other to assess reliability.

Which method of assessing reliability is to be preferred? It's difficult to answer this because the three methods suffer from different disadvantages. The equivalent-forms method is complicated to use, because it is very time-consuming to construct strictly comparable or equivalent intelligence tests. The same problem applies to a lesser extent to the split-half method. The use of the test–retest method has the drawback that when subjects are given the test for the second time, they may remember some of the answers they gave on the first administration, and this can produce a spuriously high reliability coefficient. In addition, there can be quite large practice effects that result from re-taking an intelligence test with which the subjects are already familiar.

In spite of the problems with assessing reliability, all the methods indicate that most of the standard intelligence tests possess satisfactory reliability. Test–retest reliability, equivalent-forms reliability, and split-half reliability all produce reliability correlation coefficients of approximately +0.90. Because perfect reliability would be represented by a correlation coefficient of +1.0, the obtained coefficients mean that scores are rather consistent.

Validity

Although reliability is one of the necessary requirements of an adequate intelligence test, it is by no means the only one. An intelligence test must also be valid—i.e. it must measure what it claims to measure. It is entirely possible that an intelligence test could be highly reliable but invalid, because it provided consistent measurement of some characteristic other than intelligence.

There are basically four ways of attempting to assess the validity of a test:

1. Content validity
   - face
   - factorial
2. Empirical validity
   - predictive
   - concurrent
3. Test validity
4. Construct validity.

Content validity involves considering the types of items contained within the test. There are two kinds of content validity, known as face validity and factorial validity. Face validity simply refers to whether or not the content of the test appears to be relevant. For example, a test of mathematical ability which included a vocabulary test would clearly have rather low face validity. Factorial validity is more complex. In essence, a statistical technique known as *factor analysis* is used to assess the number and nature of the different abilities or factors contained within a test. If all of the items dealing with mathematics are found to form a factor which differs from the factors formed from the other items in the test, then it seems reasonable to argue that these items measure mathematical ability. This factorial approach is discussed in more detail later in this chapter.

The most direct approach to validity is known as *empirical validity*. The basic idea is that we would expect highly intelligent individuals to be more likely than less intelligent ones to achieve certain criteria (e.g. doing well at school; passing A-levels; obtaining a university degree). Performance is correlated on an intelligence test with whatever criterion has been selected. *Predictive validity* is involved if the criterion measure is obtained after the test has been administered, whereas *concurrent validity* is involved if information about the criterion is available at the time the test is administered.

The major difficulty with empirical validity is that nearly all the criteria which have been used are clearly affected by several other factors apart from intelligence level. For example, academic success at school undoubtedly depends in part on intellectual ability, but it also depends on motivation, the personality characteristics of the child, the amount of parental encouragement, and so on. It follows that if scores on an intelligence test failed to correlate at all with academic success at school, then we would conclude that the test was invalid. In practice, intelligence test scores typically correlate approximately +0.5 or 0.6 with school or college performance. This is usually highly significant statistically, and indicates a reasonably strong relationship between the two measures. Although this suggests that most intelligence tests possess some validity, it does not permit a more definite conclusion. The reason that correlations between test and criterion are not higher may either be because of poor validity of the test or because the criterion is too vague.

A very simple approach to validity is known as *test validity*. This involves correlating scores on a new intelligence test with one or more well-established tests of intelligence. If a well-established test has been shown to have satisfactory reliability and validity, then a new test which correlates highly with that test is also likely to be a valid measuring instrument.

A final approach to validity is known as *construct validity*. If a psychologist has a theory which incorporates intelligence as a hypothetical *construct*, then the validity of an intelligence test can be assessed by testing some of the predictions of the theory. For example, suppose that a theorist argued that the speed with which simple verbal material (e.g. words) could be processed was an important skill underlying verbal ability. The theory (and the validity of a test of verbal ability) could be investigated by comparing speed of verbal processing of high and low scorers on the test of verbal ability. If the prediction were confirmed, then this would suggest that the theory might be correct and the test valid. However, if the prediction were not confirmed, then it would not be clear whether the theory or the test (or both) was at fault. The construct validity approach to the assessment of the validity of intelligence tests has not been widely used, but will probably become more popular in the future as an increasing number of explanatory theories of intelligence are put forward.

Heredity vs. environment

One of the most controversial issues surrounding the topic of intelligence is the relative importance of heredity and environment in determining adult levels of intelligence. This issue has generated a lot of research, but many psychologists argue that it is essentially meaningless. The Canadian psychologist Donald Hebb pointed out many years ago that asking whether intelligence is determined more by heredity or by environment is like asking whether the area of a field is determined more by its length or by its width: both are absolutely indispensable. However, it is still possible to ask the question whether the differences in the areas of several fields are due more to their different lengths or their different widths. If we apply that logic to intelligence, this means that it may make sense to ask whether differences in intelligence among individuals occur mainly because these individuals differ in terms of heredity or because they differ in terms of their experience or environment.

One of the initial problems that has to be faced by anyone attempting to investigate the heredity–environment issue is that experimental control is lacking. It is not possible ethically to manipulate heredity in a systematic fashion by a programme of breeding, and it is also not feasible to achieve much control over the environment in which children develop. In addition, we cannot assess accurately an individual's genetic potential (known as the *genotype*), because all that we can measure directly are the observable characteristics (known as the *phenotype*). To add to the catalogue of complications, there is no consensus regarding which aspects of the environment are of greatest importance for the development of intelligence, and it is no easy matter to provide adequate measures of something as complex as environmental impact. Finally, there is the problem of measuring intelligence. Most researchers assess intelligence by obtaining IQs from standard intelligence tests. This is a reasonable approach if IQ is a good measure of intelligence, but many theorists would deny that it is. At the very least, as was discussed earlier, IQ has the limitation that it ignores specific abilities in favour of providing a single very general measure of intelligence.

At this point, you may feel that it is impossible to establish the relative roles of heredity and environment in affecting intelligence. Although it is certainly difficult to do so, there are various possible ways of tackling the issue. For example, it is known that the closer the familial relationship between two people, the greater on average is their genotypic similarity. The two words "on average" are important. This is because genetic theory argues that although children will tend to have genotypes resembling those of their parents, there is some chance that their genotypes will be very different. As far as environmental factors are concerned, it seems very reasonable to claim that two children who are brought up together in the same family will usually experience more similar environments than two children brought up in different families. Because we can make these generalisations about heredity and environment, the appropriate conclusion is that we should be able to make at least some headway in our attempts to assess the influence of these factors on intelligence.

Twin studies

When we consider the real world, we discover that individuals who are likely to have similar genotypes also tend to be exposed to similar environments. Thus, siblings usually resemble each other genotypically more than cousins, but they are likely to have more similar environments (i.e. the same family home). If, as is typically the case, siblings are more similar than cousins in intelligence, it is extremely difficult to decide whether the genotypic or the environmental similarity is more important.

However, nature does provide us with some particularly revealing cases, and these are made use of in the twin-study approach. Identical twins (technically known as *monozygotic twins*) derive from the same fertilised ovum, and thus possess essentially identical genotypes. In contrast, fraternal twins (known as *dizygotic twins*) derive from two different fertilised ova, and so their genotypes are no more similar than those of two ordinary siblings. If heredity is an important determinant of intelligence, then we would expect to discover that identical twins are more alike than fraternal twins in intelligence. However, it appears to be the case (as Gross, 1992, pointed out) that monozygotic twins are more likely than dizygotic twins to be treated in the same way. This means that both environmental and genetic similarity are greater in monozygotic twins than in dizygotic twins, so that greater similarity of intelligence in monozygotic than dizygotic twins could result from heredity, or environment, or both.

The degree of similarity in intelligence shown by pairs of twins is usually reported in the form of correlation coefficients. In essence, the scores of the two members of each twin pair are correlated, and related to the differences in scores between pairs. A high positive correlation indicates that the twins involved tend to be reasonably similar in intelligence. A review of over 50 studies was prepared by Erlenmeyer-Kimling and Jarvik (1963). The average correlation coefficient for identical twins reared together was +0.87, compared to +0.53 for fraternal twins reared together. This difference might result from the greater genetic similarity of monozygotic twins. However, it might also result from the greater environmental similarity for monozygotic than for dizygotic twins. For example, it is certainly true that identical twins tend to spend more time in each other's company than do fraternal twins, and they are also more likely to have the same friends. It should also be noted that the correlation coefficient for monozygotic twins should approach the maximum possible value of +1.00 if heredity is the only determinant of intelligence. The fact that the figure is rather below that means that environmental differences between monozygotic twins are affecting intelligence, and thus indicates a definite influence of environment on intelligence.

Additional evidence relevant to the heredity–environment issue comes from the rather small number of identical twins who were separated in early life and then reared apart. Such twins are especially important because (at least in principle) we have a clear distinction between very similar heredity within each pair, and dissimilar environment. Thus, if heredity is of major importance, such twins should have very similar measured intelligence, whereas if environment is of primary importance, there should be little or no similarity in intelligence. According to Erlenmeyer-Kimling and Jarvik (1963), who based their work on the evidence available at that time, the average correlation coefficient for these twins is +0.75. This is somewhat lower than the corresponding figure for identical twins reared together, but higher than the figure for fraternal twins reared together. However, it should be noted that this figure for identical twins brought up apart includes the data of Burt (1955). These data are almost certainly fraudulent, and so the "true" figure for identical twins brought up apart is somewhat less than the one quoted by Erlen-meyer-Kimling and Jarvik (1963). More specifically, of the studies other than the one reported by Burt (1955), the lowest correlation coefficient reported was +0.62 and the highest was +0.77.

If heredity were all-important, then the correlation coefficient for monozygotic twins brought up apart should approach +1.00. The fact that it is a long way below that indicates that environmental factors have a substantial impact on the measured intelligence of these twin pairs. In general, educational differences between monozygotic twins brought up apart appeared to be especially important in producing differences in IQ: large educational differences were associated with differences of up to 24 IQ points.

The most problematical aspect of studies on monozygotic twins brought up apart is that in many cases they were actually brought up in rather similar environments. This is important, because it means that environmental factors may contribute substantially to the observed similarity in intelligence of these twin pairs. In one of the largest studies, two-thirds of the pairs were in fact brought up in branches of the same family and the children attended the same school. Furthermore, many of the twin pairs spent the first few years of their lives together before being separated. In addition, there is what is known as *selective placement*: adoption agencies generally have a policy of trying to place infants in homes with similar educational and social backgrounds to those of their biological parents. All in all, it is clear that much of the general similarity in IQ within monozygotic twin pairs brought up apart is due to environmental factors. It is also clear that studying monozygotic twins brought up apart doesn't provide a straightforward way of assessing the relative contribution of heredity and environment to intelligence.

Fostering studies and extreme environments

There is another way of investigating the heredity–environment issue. This involves comparing intelligence in foster children who are brought up in the same family. These children are unrelated, and so should not resemble each other in intelligence if heredity is of prime importance. On the other hand, they are brought up together, and so environmentalists would expect them to be fairly similar in intelligence.

In fact, as Gleitman (1986) noted, the average correlation between foster children brought up together is approximately +0.2. This is much lower than the correlation of approximately +0.5 which is typically found when siblings brought up by their natural parents are compared for intelligence (see Gleitman, 1986). This evidence is consistent with that from twin studies in indicating a definite involvement of heredity in the determination of intelligence. However, the fact that there is usually a positive correlation between foster children brought up together suggests that environmental factors are also important. The importance of environmental factors is suggested by a further finding: foster children generally have higher IQs than their natural or biological parents, presumably because the environment provided by their foster parents has served to raise their measured intelligence.

There is also plentiful evidence that the environment can exert either a beneficial or an adverse effect on intelligence. Wheeler (1942) studied the members of an isolated community in Tennessee in the United States. This community gradually became more integrated into society as schools and roads were built, and communications with the outside world developed. The intelligence of the members of this community increased by 10 IQ points during the time that those environmental changes were occurring. In contrast, canal-boat children in England who received practically no formal schooling showed a progressive decrease in IQ as their years of isolation from society increased (Gordon, 1923).

To sum up, it has proved extremely difficult to assess the relative importance of heredity and environment in determining intelligence. Environmental factors can certainly have a considerable impact on individual differences in intelligence, and it is likely that genetic factors also play a part. It is worth noting that the relative importance of heredity and environment should not be regarded as fixed and unchanging. The environments experienced by children within Western societies probably tend

JUST AS HE WAS ABOUT TO LEAVE THE SHOP,
IGOR SPIED A BARGAIN, ... AND THE REST IS HISTORY . . . .

to be less dissimilar than those experienced by children in some other societies. For example, nearly all children in the United Kingdom receive at least eleven or twelve years of schooling, whereas large percentages of children in some other societies receive no schooling at all. The relevance of this to the heredity–environment issue is as follows: the more similar the environments are for individuals within a society, the greater will be the apparent impact of heredity in determining individual differences in intelligence. Indeed, if everyone were exposed to exactly the same environment, then all individual differences in intelligence would be due to heredity!

Group differences

The issue of the relative importance of heredity and environment becomes very sensitive politically when one considers the reasons for group differences in IQ. This is particularly true of differences in intelligence between whites and blacks in the United States, which are sometimes as great as 15 IQ points. This is an average figure, and it should be noted that approximately 20% of blacks have an IQ that is higher than that of the average white person. Most psychologists have favoured an environmentalist explanation of the group difference. However, Arthur Jensen (1969) argued that genetic differences might be responsible, and this led to considerable media interest in the issue and a huge amount of controversy.

Many researchers in this area have assumed implicitly or explicitly that white and black Americans form two distinct biological groups. In fact, that assumption is erroneous. There are actually marked variations within each group, and this considerably complicates the task of making sense of the data. Indeed, some experts believe that it invalidates the whole exercise.

Those theorists who favour an environmentalist explanation have usually focused on three main points:

- Most intelligence tests are culturally biased against blacks and other minority groups.
- Blacks are more likely than whites to grow up in deprived conditions which prevent them from realising their intellectual potential.
- Blacks are likely to experience prejudice and discrimination.

So far as the first point is concerned, it is certainly true that the great majority of intelligence tests have been devised by white, middle-class psychologists. As a consequence, it seems plausible to assume that blacks brought up in a very different culture would be disadvantaged by this cultural divide when taking an intelligence test. However, the evidence does not provide much support for this argument. The Stanford-Binet intelligence test was translated into what is known as "black English" (the dialect of English spoken by many black Americans). It was then administered orally to black children by black examiners. In spite of these efforts, the tested intelligence of the black children was essentially the same as when the test was given in its standard form (Quay, 1971). However, other studies have suggested that culturally biased tests can significantly reduce the performance of black individuals (see Gross, 1992).

There is much more support for the notion that environmental deprivation often holds back American blacks. Some studies (discussed by Loehlin, Lindzey, & Spuhler, 1975) have compared blacks and whites who were matched in terms of factors such as family income, occupational level, and family socio-economic status. When this was done, there was a substantial reduction in the difference between the mean IQs of blacks and whites, but whites generally still performed better than blacks. However, measures such as income and socio-economic status are very crude, and probably do not permit accurate assessment of the actual levels of environmental deprivation experienced by American blacks. In particular, there are numerous subtle forms of discrimination and prejudice which affect working-class black families, and which are probably present even in middle-class black families with high incomes.

More evidence of the importance of environmental factors was obtained by Scarr and Weinberg (1976). They studied 99 black children who were adopted by white, middle-class parents. The mean IQ of these black children who had the advantage of a reasonably privileged environment was 110, which is approximately 25 IQ points higher than the mean of all American blacks. Selective placement by the adoption agency may have played a part in producing the findings, but it is probable that the environmental advantage enjoyed by the black children was the major factor responsible for their high mean IQ.

In sum, it is not possible to be certain of the appropriate explanation of the difference in mean IQ between American whites and blacks. The extent of the environmental deprivation and discrimination experienced by blacks, and their impact on intellectual development, cannot be calculated with any precision. In terms of heredity, there is no direct way of comparing the genetic endowment of whites and blacks. If it were possible to have several pairs of identical twins, with one black and one white child in each pair, then more definitive evidence could be obtained. As it is, all that can be said with reasonable certainty is that environmental factors account for much of the lower IQ of blacks than of whites; it is possible that they account for all of the group difference in IQ.

Finally, it should be emphasised that research designed to investigate racial differences in intelligence poses important ethical issues. Extreme groups (e.g. the National Front) have used the findings to promote racial disharmony, which is of course totally unacceptable. In view of the ways in which the findings have been used for disreputable ends, there is much validity in the argument that this is an issue which would have been better left unexplored. However, since it has (regrettably) been explored, it is appropriate to evaluate the relevant research, inconclusive though that research has turned out to be.

Factor theories of intelligence

The first two psychologists to offer systematic theoretical accounts of intelligence were Francis Galton (1883) and Alfred Binet (e.g. Binet & Simon, 1905).

✗ Galton argued that intelligent individuals differ from unintelligent ones in that they possess more energy and are more sensitive to physical stimuli. His emphasis on low-level cognitive skills led him to devise simple tests of intelligence. In contrast, Binet stressed the relevance of high-level cognitive processes. In the words of Binet and Simon (1916), "To judge well, to comprehend well, to reason well, these are the essential activities of intelligence. A person may be a moron or an imbecile if he is lacking in judgement; but with good judgement he can never be either" (pp. 42–43). As a consequence of his theoretical views, Binet devised tests (e.g. solution of analogies; precis of a story) that were intended to assess high-level cognitive skills.

Most factor theorists have followed Binet rather than Galton, in that they have emphasised the role of high-level rather than low-level cognitive processes in intelligence. There is no doubt that many simple processes are involved in almost any intelligent piece of behaviour, but it doesn't necessarily follow that we can understand intelligence fully by focusing on those simple processes. For example, Shakespeare undoubtedly had an excellent vocabulary and a good grasp of grammar, but it would be ludicrous to claim that his literary genius can be explained by these low-level skills.

Factor analysis

Most of the early theories of intelligence after those of Galton and Binet were factor theories. This basic approach involves inferring the structure of intelligence from factor analyses of people's performance on intelligence tests. *Factor analysis* is too complex a topic to discuss fully here, but an outline will be provided.

The usual first step is to administer numerous tests (e.g. vocabulary; mental arithmetic) to a large number of individuals, and to obtain scores for each individual on each test. The inter-correlations among the tests are then entered into a correlation matrix (see example below). If two tests correlate highly with each other, this means that those people who perform well on one test tend to perform well on the other test, whereas those who perform poorly on one test usually do poorly on the other test. The basic assumption is that when tests correlate highly with each other, the reason

An example of a small correlation matrix showing the inter-correlations of five intelligence tests.

	TEST 1	TEST 2	TEST 3	TEST 4	TEST 5
TEST 1	—	0.85	0.82	0.10	0.14
TEST 2	0.85	—	0.79	0.07	0.14
TEST 3	0.82	0.79	—	0.17	0.03
TEST 4	0.10	0.07	0.17	—	0.05
TEST 5	0.14	0.14	0.03	0.05	—

is that the two tests measure approximately the same intellectual ability. In contrast, if two tests do not correlate with each other, then an individual's performance on one test is not predictive of his or her performance on the other test. In such a case, it is assumed that the two tests in question measure separate abilities.

Factor analysis makes use of the pattern of inter-test correlations in the correlation matrix to provide a mathematical account of the number of factors required to make sense of the inter-correlations. These factors are often regarded as corresponding to intellectual abilities, and are labelled in line with the contents of the tests that correlate most highly with each factor. The end result is that a large correlation matrix can be reduced to a relatively small number of factors, and the hope is that these factors help to reveal the structure of intelligence.

In spite of the apparent advantages of factor analysis, it does suffer from a number of significant limitations:

- Different methods of factor analysis tend to produce somewhat different factor solutions to a correlation matrix
- There is, in principle, an infinite number of factor solutions for any correlation matrix, and there is no consensus concerning ways of deciding which solution is optimal.
- It is usual to continue the factor analysis only until the main factors have been extracted, and thus to ignore rather small factors; although this is a reasonable procedure, there is likely to be a certain arbitrariness in deciding when to discontinue the factor analysis.
- Factor analysis has been compared to a sausage machine, in that what you get out of it depends on what you put into it in the first place. If, for example, no mathematical tests are administered to the subjects, then the subsequent factor analysis is most unlikely to produce a factor of mathematical ability.

In view of the ambiguities which surround factor analysis, it should come as no surprise to discover that there have been major disagreements among factor theorists concerning the number and nature of the factors that make up intelligence. These disagreements will be considered shortly. For the present, it is probably best to regard factor analysis as a tool that can offer guidelines about the intellectual abilities making up intelligence, but which is unable to provide definitive evidence.

Early factor theories

The first factor theory of intelligence was proposed by Charles Spearman in the early years of this century. According to his two-factor theory, individual differences in performance on a test are due to a *general factor* (which is common to all tests) together with a factor which is specific to that particular test. He referred to the general factor as "g", because he regarded it as a factor of general intelligence.

There are certainly good reasons for identifying a general factor of intelligence. It is usually found that nearly all the tests in an intelligence-test battery correlate positively with each other at least to some extent, and the general factor can be used to explain these positive correlations. However, the notion that the only other factors identifiable in intelligence-test performance are specific to individual tests no longer seems tenable, as there is overwhelming evidence for factors which are less general than "g" but more general than Spearman's specific factors.

An attempt to eradicate the deficiencies in Spearman's (1923) two-factor theory led Sir Cyril Burt and other British psychologists to propose a hierarchical theory of mental abilities. According to this theory, there is a general factor (as Spearman had claimed) which is common to all of the tests. In addition, there are a number of *group factors*, each of which is involved in the performance of some (but not all) of the tests in a battery. The group factors that seem to be most important include those relating to verbal, spatial, mechanical, and mathematical abilities. Highly specific factors limited to a single test can also be identified, according to hierarchical theorists, but are of much less theoretical interest than the general and group factors.

Spearman, Burt, and other British factor theorists typically made use of statistically independent factors (i.e. factors that do not correlate with each other). However, the American psychologist L.L. Thurstone (1938) argued that this was not the best way to proceed. He claimed that the data were more consistent with the idea that many factors of intelligence are correlated with each other. More specifically, his view was that the most appropriate criterion for choosing a factor solution is based on "simple structure". By simple structure, he meant that factors should correlate highly with some of the tests, but not at all with other tests. Thurstone found that it was easier to achieve simple structure if he used correlated factors rather than the independent or non-correlated factors preferred by Spearman and Burt.

Thurstone's approach to factor analysis led to his multiple-factor theory. In this theory, there are seven factors or "primary mental abilities":

1. spatial ability;
2. numerical ability;
3. memory;
4. verbal fluency;
5. perceptual speed;
6. inductive reasoning;
7. verbal meaning.

Despite the different theoretical approaches of Thurstone and the British theorists, it is clear that there are some resemblances between Thurstone's primary mental abilities and the group factors identified by Spearman and Burt. In addition, if a further factor analysis is carried out on the seven factors identified by Thurstone, then a very general factor resembling Spearman's "g" factor emerges.

Guilford's structure-of-intellect theory

J.P. Guilford (1967) proposed a much more ambitious theoretical model of the structure of intelligence than any of those that we have considered so far. He argued that one should distinguish among five types of mental operation—thinking; remembering; divergent production (involving original solutions to problems); evaluation; and convergent production (logical thinking leading to the correct solution). These mental operations produce six types of products: units; classes; relations; systems; transformations; and implications. Finally, there are four types of content that can be involved in processing: figural; semantic; behavioural; and symbolic. If each intellectual ability involves a particular mental operation, a particular product, and a specified content, then there are in theory $5 \times 6 \times 4$ intellectual abilities, giving a total of 120.

Although Guilford made a noble effort to come to grips with the complexities of human intelligence, his theory cannot be considered to be successful. First, his exclusive focus on rather specific factors meant that he ignored the fact that most of the tests he used correlated positively with each other. These positive inter-correlations point to the existence of much more general factors than those identified by Guilford. Second, it has never been demonstrated satisfactorily that there are 120 distinguishable intellectual abilities; indeed, the evidence indicates that the actual number is very considerably smaller.

Cattell's theory of crystallised and fluid intelligence

Raymond Cattell (1963) has made the interesting suggestion that the general factor of intelligence that has been emphasised in much of the literature really involves two conceptually separate types of intelligence. These types of intelligence are referred to as crystallised and fluid intelligence. Crystallised intelligence features on tests which involve the use of previously acquired skills and ways of thinking, whereas fluid intelligence is of use when the test requires new approaches and ways of thinking.

The distinction between crystallised and fluid intelligence emerged from factor analyses of test data, and it appears to have some validity. According to Cattell, fluid intelligence reaches its highest level earlier in life than does crystallised intelligence. Fluid intelligence declines with age, with the decline starting at about the age of 40 or even earlier. In contrast, crystallised intelligence shows little or no decline even in the later years. For example, there is no drop in performance on vocabulary tests in normal elderly people even at the age of 85 (Blum, Jarvik, & Clark, 1970).

There is another important difference between crystallised and fluid intelligence. Crystallised intelligence depends on the particular learning experiences of the individual, and thus is much influenced by environmental factors. In contrast, fluid intelligence depends to a greater extent on genetic influences (Cattell, 1963).

An overview of factor theories

Factor theories have been successful in many ways. In particular, they have shed valuable light on the *structure* of human intelligence. This is true in spite of the fact that there are important differences among factor theorists, as is illustrated by the enormous discrepancy between Thurstone's seven factors of intelligence and the 120 proposed by Guilford. In essence, most of the available evidence is consistent with a hierarchical model of intelligence with three levels:

1. At the top level, there is the general factor of intelligence first proposed by Spearman.
2. At the intermediate level, there are a number of group factors or primary mental abilities, some of which resemble those put forward by Thurstone.
3. Finally, at the lowest level, there are the specific or idiosyncratic factors associated with one test or a small number of tests, as was proposed by Spearman.

A specific version of this hierarchical model was proposed by Carroll (1986; see the figure opposite). He extensively re-analysed many of the factor-analytic findings we have discussed and concluded that the general factor of intelligence ("g") is at the apex of the hierarchy. At the middle level, there are the following seven factors: fluid ability (possibly identical

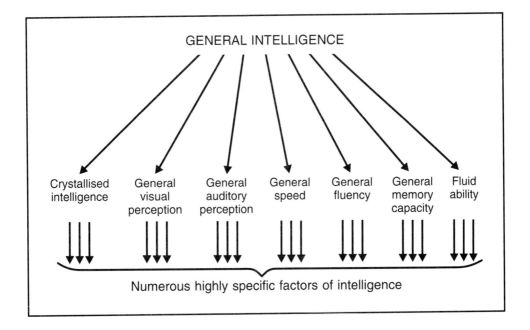

A three-level hierarchical model of intelligence (based on Carroll, 1986).

to g); crystallised intelligence; general visual perception; general auditory perception; general speed; general idea production or fluency; and general memory capacity. There are numerous highly specific factors at the bottom of the hierarchy, but there is little agreement about their nature.

The findings obtained by factor theorists have implications for psychological testing. Once a factor theorist has decided on the appropriate structure of intelligence, it follows that the tests included in an intelligence-test battery should be those that seem to be relatively "pure" measures of the various factors. Tests that correlate only modestly with the factors are rejected. In other words, the possession of a factor-based structural model provides the test constructor with a rational basis for including or excluding particular tests.

The main limitation of the factor-theory approach to intelligence is that, although it may provide a reasonable *description* of the structure of intelligence, it is rather uninformative so far as an *explanation* of the processes and mechanisms involved in intelligent behaviour is concerned. For example, suppose that we agree with Thurstone that there is a factor of numerical ability. It would be very useful to know precisely how those with high numerical ability differ from those with low numerical ability: is the crucial difference in the range of processes available, in the relevant knowledge possessed, or in the speed of processing? Such issues were simply not addressed in a systematic fashion by factor theorists.

Creativity.   Another limitation of most factor theories of intelligence is that little or nothing is said about the important quality of creativity (i.e. inventive, original, and innovative thinking and behaviour). One of the few exceptions is the work of Guilford, with his mental operation of divergent production. In essence, the difficulty is that it has not been possible to devise good tests of creativity.

Some of the best-known tests were devised by Guilford (1967), and include the Consequences Test, the Remote Associates Test, and the Unusual Uses Test. Here are some sample items:

- imagine all of the things which might possibly happen if all national and local laws were suddenly abolished (Consequences Test);
- find a fourth word which is associated with each of these words: rat, blue, cottage (Remote Associates Test); and
- name as many uses as you can think of for a brick (Unusual Uses Test).

Performance can be scored in terms of fluency (i.e. the number of answers provided) and/or the originality or unusual nature of the answers provided.

The problem with these and many other tests is that they do not really provide an assessment of the quality of the ideas produced. Someone can be highly original in the sense of producing unusual answers without those answers being of any great merit. It is for this reason that tests of creativity do not correlate highly with creative professional ability (see Kline, 1991). Some of the factors that are associated with creativity were uncovered by MacKinnon (1962) in a study of architects. The most creative architects generally had a fairly high level of intelligence combined with certain personality characteristics (e.g. unconventionalism; social sensitivity; non-defensiveness). Personality also emerged as important in a study of prominent British novelists, painters, playwrights, poets, and sculptors (Jamison, 1984). These creative individuals were much more likely than less creative individuals to have received treatment for depression or manic-depressive illness.

In summary, creative individuals tend to differ from non-creative ones in terms of their personality and a generally higher level of intelligence as conventionally assessed. Attempts to devise tests specifically to assess creativity have not proved very useful.

Idiots savants.   Idiots savants (mentally handicapped individuals who are nevertheless highly accomplished in some ways) apparently pose a problem for factor theories of intelligence. Factor theorists predict that most accomplished individuals will score rather highly on the general factor of intelligence, which is by no means the case with idiots savants. In other words, factor theorists expect in general that individuals who have high ability in some directions will have high ability in other directions, whereas idiots savants show a very large discrepancy between their apparently low general level of intelligence and their special skills. These skills are very diverse. However, the most common one is known as calendar calculating, in which the idiot savant can very rapidly and accurately answer questions such as the day of the week associated with a particular date, or the date corresponding to the tenth Thursday in the year 1921.

To what extent do the feats of idiots savants invalidate the factor theory approach? According to Howe (1989), "The contrasts observed in idiots savants between levels of ability at different skills are simply manifestations of something that is true of all people, namely that their different skills are to a large degree autonomous" (pp. 204–205). In other words, the implication is that there is no general factor of intelligence. This is probably overstating the case. In fact, idiots savants have simply compensated for their low level of general intelligence by investing a huge amount of time and effort in acquiring special skills. As Howe (1989) himself says, "The chances are that someone for whom calendars were a main interest in life, and who spent several hours every day thinking about them, would...end up retaining a very considerable amount of calendar information. Something of this kind probably takes place with most idiot savant calendar calculators" (p. 200). This suggests that idiots savants are interesting curiosities, but that their feats do not have any important implications for factor theories of intelligence.

Contemporary theories of intelligence

There have been two major developments in theorising about intelligence over the past 20 years or so. First, several theorists have attempted to provide detailed accounts of the processes involved in intelligent performance that were not provided by the factor theorists. *Cognitive psychologists* are interested in thinking, problem-solving, memory, and other mental activities, and they have generally focused on the processes involved. Thus, there are good reasons for assuming that it would be fruitful to amalgamate the factor analytic and cognitive approaches in order to achieve greater understanding of intelligence. The theories of Hunt (1978) and Sternberg (1985), discussed in the following two sections, are both based on that assumption.

Second, theorists have increasingly recognised that intelligence consists of more than the cognitive processing assessed by conventional intelligence tests. More specifically, the intelligent person is more skilful than the unintelligent person at handling the problems of everyday life. Although purely cognitive abilities are relevant, so are additional factors such as social intelligence and various "street-wise" skills. Sternberg (1985) proposed a well-known cognitive theory of intelligence, but also expanded it to extend the realm of intelligence beyond the purely cognitive. Another theory that attempts to broaden the scope of intelligence is that of Gardner (1983), which is discussed after those of Hunt and Sternberg.

Hunt's cognitive theory

Earl "Buzz" Hunt (e.g. 1978) is a cognitive psychologist who has carried out much research in an attempt to understand the cognitive processes underlying verbal intelligence. His basic assumption is that individuals who are high in verbal ability can gain access to lexical (i.e. relating to items of vocabulary) information in *long-term memory* more rapidly than those of low verbal ability. This extra speed of lexical access gives them an advantage in most verbal tasks.

This assumption was tested by Hunt, Lunneborg, and Lewis (1975). They presented their subjects with pairs of letters (e.g. AA, Aa, Ab) which could be the same or different either physically or in name. The two letters AA are the same both physically and in name, the two letters Aa are the same in name but not physically, and the two letters Ab differ both physically and in name. There were two rather different task conditions:

1. *Physical-match condition*: subjects had to decide rapidly whether each pair of letters was a physical match; this simple task does not require lexical access and so provides a measure of sheer speed of response.
2. *Name-match condition*: subjects had to decide as quickly as possible whether each pair of letters was a name match; this task is more difficult and requires lexical access.

Hunt et al. (1975) argued that subtracting the physical-match time from the name-match time would provide a good measure of lexical-access time, uncontaminated by the sheer speed of responding. They discovered that this lexical-access time correlated approximately -0.3 with verbal intelligence as assessed by tests—i.e. those high in verbal intelligence tended to have faster lexical access than those of lower ability (see the figure opposite). This suggests that speed of lexical access is relevant to verbal intelligence.

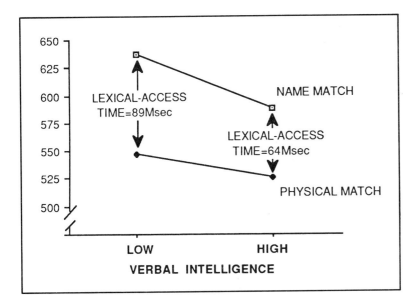

Hunt's approach was innovative, in that he was perhaps the first person to demonstrate clearly that the areas of cognitive psychology and intelligence can complement each other. However, there are doubts about the ultimate value of his contribution. The fact that the correlation between lexical-access time and verbal intelligence was only -0.3 means that there is much more to verbal intelligence than simply the speed with which lexical information can be accessed. As Sternberg and Frensch (1990) conclude, "almost any task will correlate at the 0.3 level with psychometric test scores if it involves any level of decision at all" (p. 70). In other words, it is not clear that lexical-access time is of particular importance in determining verbal intelligence.

Sternberg's triarchic theory

Robert Sternberg (1985) proposed a rather complex theory of intelligence, consisting of three separate subtheories:

1. *The componential subtheory*: this specifies the cognitive processes and structures involved in intelligence, and is concerned with the *internal world* of the individual.
2. *The contextual subtheory*: this deals with the use of cognitive processes in everyday life to cope with environmental demands; it is concerned with intelligence and the *external world* of the individual.

3. *The experiential subtheory*: this deals with the ways in which people handle the relationship between their internal and external worlds; it is concerned with intelligence and experience.

Componential subtheory.   Sternberg (1985) proposed that cognitive tasks should be analysed into their components, defining a component as "an elementary information process that operates upon internal representations of objects or symbols" (p. 97). An example of this componential approach is his analysis of analogical reasoning problems having the form "A is to B as C is to D" (e.g., "Hand is to foot as finger is to toe"). The subject's task is to decide whether the analogy is true or false. It is particularly important to consider analogical reasoning, because analogical reasoning performance has been found to correlate approximately +0.8 with the general factor of intelligence. That means that analogical reasoning performance provides a good measure of intelligence.

Careful analysis of the analogical reasoning task indicated that six components are involved in it. Five of these components must be used, and the sixth is optional. The components are as follows:

1. encoding the terms in the problem;
2. inference (discovering the rule relating A to B);
3. mapping (discovering the rule relating A to C);
4. application (making a decision as to what the fourth or D term should be, and comparing it against the actual fourth term supplied);
5. justification (the optional component which considers the accuracy with which the earlier components have been carried out); and
6. preparation-response.

Sternberg (1985) went on to examine the correlations between the speed with which each component was completed and various factors of intelligence. The highest correlation was between preparation-response and reasoning ability. This suggests that the last component involved in analogical reasoning is of particular importance in reasoning ability.

What is the precise relationship between factors of intelligence and the components of information processing identified by Sternberg? His claim is that there is a simple relationship between the two, with factors of intelligence being "constellations of components showing common patterns of individual differences." In other words, cognitive psychology and the information-processing approach can be used to clarify the processes and skills involved in reasoning ability, spatial ability, and so on.

Contextual subtheory. The contextual subtheory addresses the role of the prevailing socio-cultural context in defining what is considered intelligent behaviour. The factor theorists discussed earlier in the chapter tended to regard intelligence as something that is not affected by cultural factors. This view is almost certainly wrong. As several critics of factor theories and intelligence tests have argued, most of the tests which are used seem to have been devised with white, middle-class subjects from the Western world in mind. That is to say, the skills that are typically acquired by this group are assessed by intelligence tests, whereas some of the skills acquired by other groups (e.g. navigating by the stars) are ignored by most tests. According to Sternberg, intelligence is a relativistic notion which varies somewhat from one culture to another, and in the contextual subtheory he considers some of the the aspects of intelligence which are especially useful in living successfully in the prevailing culture. These aspects include social intelligence and practical intelligence.

"AH!..DR. TOPOFF I PRESUME... I READ YOUR THESIS ON 'INDIGENOUS IGNORANCE'... HIGHLY INACCURATE, BUT AMUSING NONETHELESS..."

An important ingredient of the contextual subtheory is tacit or street-wise knowledge. This is the knowledge which is not generally discussed or taught, but which is very useful when coping with any given situation. Wagner and Sternberg (1986) produced tests to assess tacit knowledge in business management and academic psychology. Scores on these tests correlated approximately +0.4 with the real-world success of business managers and academic psychologists as assessed by some relevant measures (e.g. performance ratings and merit pay rises for the managers; quality of institution and frequency of publication for the psychologists). As scores on the tests of tacit knowledge did not correlate with standard intelligence tests, it is clear that tacit knowledge is an aspect of intelligence which is quite different from the skills assessed by conventional tests of intelligence.

As the contextual subtheory emphasises the fact that intelligence is, at least in part, culturally determined, it may be wondered how cultural influences manifest themselves. Sternberg (1985) argued that the basic information-processing components themselves do not differ across cultures, but rather the relative emphasis placed on different components varies from one culture to another. For example, it could be argued that Western societies attach undue importance to verbal and numerical skills at the expense of more directly practical skills.

Experiential subtheory. The experiential subtheory deals with the ways in which an individual's experience mediates between his or her internal and external environments. More specifically, Sternberg (1985) argued that intelligence can be assessed at two stages of experience or practice with a given task:

1. when a task is relatively novel, and adaptation to novelty is required; and
2. when a task has already been practised extensively, and automatised processing is involved.

Tasks that are completely novel are unlikely to be good measures of intelligence. For example, confronting very intelligent five-year-old children with problems in calculus would be a pointless exercise. In contrast, relatively novel tasks enable intelligent individuals to bring relevant knowledge and skills to bear to a much greater extent than is the case with less intelligent individuals. Intelligence can also be assessed by automatised performance. Complex skills such as reading are possible only because many of the skills involved (e.g. word identification) have been automatised, thus freeing processing resources to attend to novelty (e.g. the particular meaning conveyed by the text being read). Thus, an individual with well-developed automatised information processes is at a great advantage when performing most complex tasks.

Sternberg's (1985) distinction between the ability to adapt to novelty and automatisation of processing resembles that of Cattell (1963) between fluid and crystallised intelligence. Fluid intelligence requires appropriate adaptation to novelty, and crystallised intelligence depends at least in part on automatised processing. Adaptation to novelty can be assessed in several different ways. For example, Sternberg (1982) investigated subjects' ability to think with new concepts such as "grue", meaning green until the year 2000 and blue after that date. Those subjects who had previously been found to be well able to cope with novelty performed best on this task.

Evaluation. In various ways, Sternberg's (1985) theory of intelligence is much more comprehensive in scope than most other theories of intelligence. First, he has managed to forge strong links between the areas of intelligence and of cognitive psychology, and has done so in a more extensive way than Hunt (1978). Second, whereas most other theorists have argued that intelligence is concerned either with the internal world of the individual (e.g. problem-solving; reasoning) or with the external world of the individual (e.g. dealings with the environment), Sternberg (1985) claimed that it is both. Third, Sternberg (1985) and Cattell (1963) are among the few theorists to consider seriously the relationship between experience and practice on the one hand, and intelligence on the other.

On the negative side, the triarchic theory is still in a rather early stage of development. For example, the ways in which the three subtheories relate to each other remain somewhat unclear. In addition, Sternberg (1985) has blurred the distinction between intelligence and personality. Sternberg (1985) himself admits that his theory "includes within the realm of intelligence characteristics that typically might be placed in the realms of personality or motivation" (pp. 54–55). For example, individuals who are "street-wise" generally possess valuable information that others don't, but they also tend to have certain personality characteristics (e.g. confidence; sociability). In other words, the contextual subtheory may actually combine the areas of intelligence and personality in a confusing mixture rather than providing a theory solely concerned with intelligence.

Gardner's theory of multiple intelligences

Howard Gardner (1983) argued that several essentially independent intelligences can be identified. An intelligence in Gardner's terms is regarded as "an ability or set of abilities that permits an individual to solve problems or fashion products that are of consequence in a particular cultural setting"

(Walters & Gardner, 1986, p. 165). In total, Gardner (1983) distinguished seven intelligences:

1. Logical-mathematical intelligence: as the name implies, this kind of intelligence is of special value in handling abstract problems of a logical or mathematical nature.
2. Spatial intelligence: this is used when deciding how to go from one place to another, how to arrange suitcases in the boot of a car, and so on.
3. Musical intelligence: this is used both for active musical processes such as playing an instrument or singing, and for more passive processes such as appreciating the music one hears.
4. Bodily-kinaesthetic intelligence: this is involved in the fine control of bodily movements in activities such as sport, ballet, and dancing.
5. Linguistic intelligence: this is involved in language activities on both the input (reading and listening) and the output (writing and speaking) sides.
6. Intrapersonal knowledge: this form of intelligence is concerned with sensitivity to one's own abilities and emotional states.
7. Interpersonal intelligence: this is involved in interacting with other people, and covers activities such as communication with, and understanding of, others.

How did Gardner (1983) identify these particular intelligences rather than others? His basic approach was to require any proposed intelligence to satisfy most of the following criteria:

- an identifiable set of crucial operations;
- a unique symbol system (e.g. language);
- selective impairment by brain damage has been studied;
- exceptional groups (e.g. musical prodigies) have been studied;
- cross-cultural studies have been conducted;
- there are data about its evolution;
- there is information about the development of the intelligence in normal and gifted groups; and
- there are psychological training studies demonstrating progressive improvement in the intelligence.

Gardner's (1983) theory of multiple intelligences appears to have important implications for intelligence testing. Most of the standard intelligence tests contain items which are relevant to linguistic, logical-mathematical, and spatial intelligence, but are not designed to assess musical, bodily-kinaesthetic, interpersonal, and intrapersonal intelligence. If one accepts Gardner's theoretical position, then nearly all the existing tests of intelligence are woefully inadequate.

How useful is the theory of multiple intelligences? There is undoubtedly some mileage in the notion that there are several rather separate collections of skills and aptitudes which approximate to the seven intelligences identified by Gardner (1983). It is particularly impressive that there is a wide range of different kinds of evidence supporting the existence of each of the seven intelligences. However, there are doubts as to whether they should all be regarded as intelligences in the sense of abilities that "are of consequence in a particular cultural setting." Deficiencies in linguistic, logical-mathematical, spatial, or interpersonal intelligence all have serious consequences for everyday life, but it is less clear that the same is true of musical or bodily-kinaesthetic intelligence. It is entirely possible for someone to have very low musical and bodily-kinaesthetic intelligence (e.g. to be tone-deaf and poorly co-ordinated) without it having any great effects on his or her ability to function effectively in most societies. In other words, perhaps musical and bodily-kinaesthetic intelligence (and perhaps intrapersonal intelligence) should not really be regarded as intelligences.

There are two other problems with Gardner's theory. First, he has focused on identifying the different varieties of intelligence and has not properly specified the processes involved in each type of intelligence. For example, a full understanding of musical intelligence would require a specification of how the strategies, processes, and so on, of those high in musical intelligence differ from those low in musical intelligence. Second, individuals who are high scorers on some intelligences tend to score highly on the other intelligences. That suggests that the seven intelligences are not entirely independent of each other in the way that Gardner (1983) suggested.

Summary: Intelligence and intelligence testing

- Much of the work which has been done on intelligence has related to the development of appropriate measuring instruments for assessing intelligence.
- In order for an intelligence test to be useful, it needs to fulfil various criteria. It should be reliable, in the sense that it provides a consistent measure of intelligence. It should also be valid, meaning that it actually measures intelligence rather than anything else. In addition, each test should be standardised (i.e. it should have been administered to large samples of the age groups covered by the test, so that it is possible to assess the meaning of the score obtained by any individual).
- The best-known measure obtained from intelligence tests is the so-called intelligence quotient or IQ. This is simply a reflection of an individual's overall performance on the intelligence test relative to other individuals of the same age. In addition to this general measure, it is usually also possible to extract more specific measures which provide information about that individual's abilities (e.g. verbal, mathematical, spatial).
- One of the major issues in the area of intelligence concerns the relative importance of heredity and environment in determining the level of intelligence. The issue is a complex one, and no definitive answers are available. However, the study of monozygotic or identical twins brought up apart is of particular value, because such twins have essentially the same genetic make-up but differing environments. Identical twins brought up apart tend to resemble each other in intelligence, but the fact that they are often brought up in similar environments makes it difficult to interpret this finding. Similar problems of interpretation beset studies of foster children. There is very strong evidence that environmental factors (e.g. parental influence; educational opportunities) are of major importance. In sum, the only reasonable conclusion is that intelligence is determined by both heredity and environment, although the relative importance of these two factors remains unclear.
- There has been much controversy about the reasons for group differences in intelligence, especially the difference between American whites and blacks. It is highly probable that environmental deprivation and racial discrimination play the major role in producing this difference. However, it remains unclear whether these factors explain all of the difference, or whether genetic differences are also involved.

- Most of the early theories of intelligence were based on factor analysis. Spearman identified a very general factor ("g") and numerous highly specific factors, whereas Thurstone proposed seven primary mental abilities which were neither very general nor very specific. Probably the most satisfactory factor theory is a hierarchical one which postulates three different levels: a general factor at the apex; fairly general mental abilities at the intermediate level; and highly specific factors at the lowest level.
- Although factor theorists made progress in identifying the structure of human intelligence, they had little to say about the processes underlying intelligent performance. Cognitive psychologists have attempted to remedy this situation. Factor theories of intelligence are also limited in that intelligence is regarded as consisting solely of a range of cognitive skills. Theorists such as Sternberg and Gardner have argued that the scope of intelligence is much broader, and encompasses each individual's dealings with his or her society. This argument led Gardner to postulate an interpersonal intelligence, and it led Sternberg to propose a triarchic theory of intelligence consisting of three subtheories: a componential subtheory (concerned with the internal world of the individual); a contextual subtheory (concerned with the external world of the individual); and an experiential subtheory (concerned with the inter-relationships between the internal and external worlds).
- Gardner has argued that there are several different intelligences, many of which are not assessed by traditional intelligence tests. He has amassed a wide range of evidence to substantiate this argument. However, some of the intelligences seem much less important than others, and it is not clear that the intelligences are all independent of each other.

Further reading

A good historical review of theories of intelligence is provided by R.J. Sternberg and P.A. Frensch (1990) Intelligence and cognition, in: M.W. Eysenck (Ed.), *Cognitive psychology: An international review* (Chichester: Wiley). Intelligence testing is discussed reasonably thoroughly by H. Gleitman (1987) in *Basic psychology* (Second Edition) (London: Norton). Contemporary theoretical views on intelligence are to be found in R.J. Sternberg (1985), *Beyond IQ: A triarchic theory of human intelligence* (Cambridge: Cambridge University Press) and in P. Kline (1991), *Intelligence: The psychometric view* (London: Routledge).

3 Personality: Factor theories

What is personality?

The concept of *personality* is one that has been defined in several ways in the history of psychology. However, a definition that captures much of what psychologists mean by personality was provided by Child (1968), who described it as "more or less stable, internal factors that make one person's behaviour consistent from one time to another, and different from the behaviour other people would manifest in comparable situations" (p. 83). This definition is rather broad, because it includes intelligence as an aspect of personality. Many theorists argue that the term "personality" should be restricted to emotional and motivational factors, but others (e.g. Raymond Cattell) would extend it to include intelligence.

As Hampson (1988) pointed out, the four key words in Child's definition are "stable", "internal", "consistent", and "different". The whole notion of personality is based on the assumption that it is relatively stable or unchanging over time. Moods or emotional states may change dramatically over shortish periods of time, but personality does not. Because personality is internal, it cannot be equated with external behaviour. Instead, we use behaviour (e.g. restlessness; lack of eye contact) to draw inferences about the underlying personality. If personality is moderately stable over time, and if personality determines behaviour, then it follows that any given individual will behave in a reasonably consistent fashion on different occasions. Finally, those who study human personality are basically interested in individual differences. They assume that there are considerable individual differences in personality, and that these differences will be revealed by different ways of behaving in a given situation (e.g. in a social group, extraverted people will talk more than introverted people).

It's extremely important to note that explanations for individual differences in behaviour can take many forms. Suppose, for example, that I am friendly with Thomas, but Christopher is not. One possible explanation is that my inherited personality makes me more extraverted and sociable than Christopher. Another possible explanation is that Thomas has been more friendly and rewarding to me than to Christopher, and this is why I like him more than Christopher does. Yet another possible explanation is that Thomas reminds me of someone I used to like very much, and that is why I like Thomas. The crucial point to note is that these different explanations are not mutually exclusive: there may be some validity in all these explanations, each one of which is based on considering the same phenomenon from different perspectives. In other words, each explanation may capture part of the truth. The same is the case for the various theories of personality we will be discussing.

There are several very different approaches to personality that have been adopted over the years. We will focus in this chapter on those theorists who have made use of factor analysis to identify what they claim are the major personality traits or dimensions. Alternative theoretical positions are discussed in Chapter 4.

Traits and types

We have seen that personality can be regarded as consisting of stable internal factors. The next issue to consider is how these factors should be conceptualised. Several possible kinds of factors have been proposed over the years, including:

- instincts
- goals
- desires
- beliefs
- motives
- attitudes
- motivational states.

However, most personality theorists have argued that personality consists of a number of *traits*, which have been defined as "broad, enduring, relatively stable characteristics used to assess and explain behaviour" (Hirschberg, 1978, p. 45). The inclusion of the word "broad" is crucial. Smiling, on its own, could not form the basis of a personality trait, because it is too narrow, but smiling, talkativeness, participation in social events, and so on, could together underlie a personality trait such as "sociability".

Personality theorists of the past often used to identify *personality types* rather than traits. In essence, type theorists assume that all individuals can be allocated to one of a relatively small number of types or categories. An example of a type theory is the simple version of the astrological theory of star signs, according to which everyone belongs to one of 12 personality types as a function of when they were born within the year. Another example comes from the Ancient Greeks, some of whom claimed that there were four major personality types: melancholic, sanguine, choleric, and phlegmatic. The most obvious difference between the type and trait approaches is that possession of a type is regarded as all-or-none (i.e. an individual is or is not a member of a type), whereas individuals can possess a trait such as sociability in varying degrees. More specifically, most theorists have assumed that traits are normally distributed in the population, which means, taking for example the trait of sociability, that most people have a moderate level of sociability, with a small number being either very unsociable or very sociable. This notion of trait theorists that most people have non-extreme personalities can be contrasted with the type theorist's emphasis on allocating individuals to relatively extreme categories.

Which of these two approaches to personality is to be preferred? Most contemporary trait theories of personality (e.g. those of Cattell and H.J. Eysenck) are based on the trait approach, and there are good reasons for favouring the trait over the type approach. First, the contention of type theorists that the allocation of individuals to a few categories provides an adequate account of personality seems improbable, in that it signally fails to capture the complexity of human personality. For example, it is difficult to agree with the Ancient Greeks that there are only four major kinds of personality. Second, our everyday experience indicates that most people have non-extreme personalities, and this view is supported by personality research. Most traits have been found to be normally distributed, and this supports a trait approach over a type-based approach.

In order to avoid subsequent confusion, it should be noted that H.J. Eysenck has drawn a somewhat different distinction between traits and types. He argues that traits and types differ in their level of generality, with types being more general than traits. In more technical terms, he defined a type as a collection of correlated traits. Thus, for example, extraversion is regarded as a personality type consisting of a number of related traits such as sociability, liveliness, activity, assertiveness, and sensation-seeking.

Personality assessment

Personality is inferred from behaviour, and personality theorists have developed four major forms of behavioural measures in their attempts to assess personality:

1. questionnaires;
2. ratings;

3. objective tests; and
4. projective tests.

The most common way of assessing personality is by means of *self-report questionnaires*. This method requires people to decide whether various statements about their thoughts, feelings, and behaviour are true or not. For example, one of the questions might be, "Do you tend to be moody?". The questionnaire approach has the advantage of being quick and easy to administer. It also has the advantage that the individual presumably knows more about himself or herself than do other people.

The second form of personality assessment is by means of *ratings*. What happens here is that observers produce ratings of other people's behaviour. Typically, the raters are given a list of different kinds of behaviour (e.g. "initiates conversations"), and they then rate their ratees (i.e. those being rated) on those aspects of behaviour. Obviously, the more different situations in which the raters observe the ratees, the more valid their ratings are likely to be.

The third form of personality assessment involves the use of *objective tests*. More than 400 objective tests exist, but what they have in common is that they measure behaviour under laboratory conditions in such a way that the subjects do not know what the experimenter is looking for. For example, asking subjects to blow up a balloon until it bursts is a measure of timidity, and the speed at which subjects can read backwards assesses rigidity.

The fourth form of personality assessment is by means of *projective tests*. The essence of a projective test is that the subject is given a rather unstructured task to perform, such as making up a story to fit a picture or describing what can be seen in an inkblot. The underlying rationale of projective tests is that people confronted by such unstructured tasks will reveal their innermost selves.

Any useful method of personality assessment needs to possess two important qualities: reliability and validity. The reliability of a personality test refers to its consistency of measurement (e.g. whether an individual's score on a personality test is similar on two separate occasions). In contrast, validity refers to the extent to which the test measures what it is supposed to measure. There are various forms of validity, of which the most important are *predictive validity* and *construct validity* (which are also important with respect to intelligence: see Chapter 2). Predictive validity refers to the extent to which scores on a personality test predict something in real life (e.g. does a test of sociability predict the number of dates a student has?). In contrast, construct validity is more theoretically based, and involves testing theoretical predictions about the relationship between a personality trait and several aspects of behaviour.

Self-report questionnaires

Because the self-report questionnaire is by far the most often used method of personality assessment, it will be discussed at greater length than the other methods. Three of the best-known personality questionnaires are the following:

1. the Minnesota Multiphasic Personality Inventory (MMPI);
2. Cattell's Sixteen Personality Factor (16PF) Test; and
3. the Eysenck Personality Questionnaire (EPQ).

The MMPI was published in 1940. It was designed to assess the similarity between the personality characteristics of an individual subject and those of various psychiatric groups. As a consequence, the ten scales which form the MMPI all have a psychiatric feel about them:

- hypochondria
- depression
- conversion hysteria
- psychopathic deviate
- masculinity–femininity
- paranoia
- neurosis
- schizophrenia
- hypomania
- introversion.

The items belonging to these scales were selected simply because they discriminated between patients with the relevant diagnosis and other patients. For example, if depressed patients tended to answer "yes" to a question such as "Do you prefer apricot jam to marmalade?", whereas other patients answered "no", then that item would form part of the depression scale in spite of there being no obvious reason why it should discriminate between depressed and other patients.

The MMPI also contains a number of scales designed to check that the answers on the ten major scales are reasonably accurate. One such scale is a lie scale containing items such as "Once in a while I laugh at a dirty joke." It is assumed that there is only likely to be one honest answer to such items, and anyone who consistently fails to give the expected answers is lying. There is another scale containing bizarre statements such as "There are persons who are trying to steal my thoughts and ideas." Even psychiatric patients rarely agree with such statements, and so their frequent endorsement by a subject indicates that his or her answers are suspect.

There are two main weaknesses with the MMPI. First, the designers of the test relied heavily on the assumption that the psychiatric diagnoses they used (e.g. depression; schizophrenia) were valid. In view of the general unreliability and low validity of psychiatric diagnoses, this is a dubious assumption. If the diagnoses were lacking in validity, then many of the items do not properly belong to the scale to which they have been assigned. Second, although it is claimed that there are ten separate scales, there is actually a fair amount of overlap in terms of what different scales are measuring. For example, most of the scales can be regarded, at least in part, as measuring neuroticism or emotionality (see Eysenck & Eysenck, 1985).

The 16PF and the EPQ will be discussed further when we deal with the theories of personality proposed by Raymond Cattell and H.J. Eysenck. In essence, it is claimed for both tests that they assess the most important factors of personality. The 16PF allegedly provides scores for 16 different personality traits (see below).

In contrast, the EPQ provides measures of a much more modest three personality factors. These are introversion–extraversion; neuroticism–stability; and psychoticism–normality.

Personality factors in the 16PF.

Factor	Characteristics	Factor	Characteristics
A	Reserved vs. outgoing	L	Trusting vs. suspicious
B	Less intelligent vs. more intelligent	M	Practical vs. imaginative
C	Affected by feelings vs. emotionally stable	N	Forthright vs. shrewd
E	Humble vs. assertive	O	Placid vs. apprehensive
F	Sober vs. happy-go-lucky	Q1	Conservative vs. experimenting
G	Expedient vs. conscientious	Q2	Group-dependent vs. self-sufficient
H	Shy vs. venturesome	Q3	Casual vs. controlled
I	Tough-minded vs. tender-minded	Q4	Relaxed vs. tense

Apart from the substantial difference in the number of personality factors measured by the 16PF and the EPQ, there are other major differences between the tests. In part, this is because Cattell regards the scope of personality as being broader than does Eysenck. As a consequence, the 16PF contains scales measuring aspects of individual differences (e.g. intelligence; social attitudes) which Eysenck does not believe form part of personality *per se*. Another difference is that Cattell argues that the abnormal personality differs qualitatively (i.e. in kind) from the normal personality, and the 16PF is designed primarily for use within normal populations. In contrast, Eysenck claims that there are no qualitative differences in personality between normal and abnormal populations, and so the EPQ is of relevance to both populations.

The 16PF and the EPQ both possess good *test–retest* reliability, with correlations of approximately +0.80 to 0.85 being obtained over relatively short time periods. So far as validity is concerned, the EPQ is reasonably satisfactory, as is discussed later. However, there are grave doubts about the 16PF. There is overwhelming evidence that the 16PF does not, in fact, contain anything like 16 different personality factors. A very thorough investigation of the questionnaire was carried out by Howarth and Browne (1971), who administered it to a total of 567 subjects. They managed, by means of factor analysis, to identify only ten different factors in the 16PF. This led them to conclude that "the 16PF does not measure the factors which it purports to measure" (p. 117).

Some problems with assessment of questionnaires   There are a number of fairly obvious problems which beset most questionnaires. It is usually relatively easy for anyone completing a personality questionnaire to fake his or her responses. Faking most commonly takes the form of *social desirability response set*, which is the tendency to respond to questionnaire items in the socially desirable fashion. Thus, for example, the socially desirable answer to the question "Do you tend to be moody?", is clearly "no" rather than "yes".

One way of reducing, or eliminating, the effects of social desirability response set is to make use of the method of forced choice keying. In essence, the person answering the questionnaire is required to choose either one or other of a pair of items that have been carefully matched for social desirability. The Edwards Personal Preference Schedule is an example of a personality questionnaire constructed using forced choice keying.

An alternative way of approaching social desirability effects is to attempt to detect their existence by means of an appropriate lie scale. Lie scales (such as the ones in the MMPI and the EPQ) often consist of items where the socially desirable answer is rather unlikely to be the true answer (e.g. "Do you ever gossip?"; "Do you always keep your promises?"). If someone answers most of the questions on the lie scale in the socially desirable direction, then it is assumed that they are faking their responses. Of course, this is unfair on the small minority of genuinely saintly people in the population!

Another problem with questionnaire assessment is known as *acquiescence response set*. It is defined as the biased tendency to select "yes" as the response to the items contained within a personality questionnaire. One way of assessing acquiescence response set is to select the questionnaire items carefully. If, for example, one wants to measure trait anxiety, then half of the items can be written so that a "yes" answer is indicative of high anxiety, with the remaining items being written so that a "no" answer reflects high anxiety. Anyone who consistently answers "yes" to both groups of items is obviously demonstrating acquiescence response set.

Most personality questionnaires possess reasonably good reliability or consistency of measurement. The most frequent method of assessing their reliability is based on test–retest reliability, in which the same test is administered to the same group of people on two separate occasions. Unless there is a very long time interval between the two testing occasions, individuals typically obtain similar scores on each test administration.

So far as validity is concerned, one of the most direct approaches is known as *consensual validity*. This involves correlating subjects' questionnaire responses with ratings made by external observers who are relatives, friends, or acquaintances of the subjects completing the questionnaire. The correlations between self-report questionnaire data and observer ratings are often as high as +0.50, which suggests that many questionnaires possess at least moderate validity.

There is another approach to validity which can sometimes be used. If we have a questionnaire which measures a personality dimension such as trait anxiety (a measure that assesses individual differences in susceptibility to anxiety across a wide range of situations), then we can ask whether there are groups in the population who are either very high or very low in trait anxiety. In this particular case, it is reasonable to assume that patients with a psychiatric diagnosis of, say, generalised anxiety disorder, will tend to be rather high in trait anxiety. In practice, such patients as a group score considerably above average on all the standard tests of trait anxiety (cf. Watson & Clark, 1984); this suggests that the tests are valid.

Ratings

The use of observers' ratings of other people's behaviour has the obvious advantage that it avoids some of the problems associated with self-report questionnaires. In particular, the problem that people filling in a questionnaire may distort their responses in order to present a favourable impression does not apply to observers' ratings.

However, ratings pose problems of their own. First, the items of behaviour which are to be rated may be interpreted somewhat differently by different raters. For example, an item such as "behaves in a friendly way towards others" might be thought to imply much more interaction with other people by a very sociable rater than by an unsociable one. Second, most raters are likely to observe other people in only some of the situations in which they find themselves in everyday life. Someone who appears relatively distant and aloof when observed at work may relax and be extremely friendly outside the work environment. The partial view which a rater has of his or her ratees may obviously lead to inaccurate assessment of the ratees' personalities.

In spite of the limitations of using ratings as a method of assessing personality, there is reasonably good evidence that they do possess some validity. One method of gauging this is *consensual validity*, which was discussed earlier in this chapter. In one form of consensual validity, raters fill in a personality questionnaire as they believe the ratees would fill it in, and then these guessed responses are compared with those actually made when the ratees complete the same questionnaire in the standard self-report form. The ratee filling in the questionnaire has access to information (e.g. his or her secret thoughts and desires) which is denied to external raters, but nevertheless the correlations between the questionnaire scores of raters and ratees are often around +0.40 or +0.50 (see Eysenck & Eysenck, 1985). As the biases inherent in ratings and self-report data are quite different, it is probably fair to assume that the similarity between these two methods of personality assessment occurs because they are both valid.

Some of the strongest evidence that ratings and self-report questionnaires produce broadly comparable findings has been obtained by Cattell (e.g. Cattell & Kline, 1977). He discovered that several personality traits, such as self-confident vs. guilt-prone, tough-minded vs. tender-minded, and submissiveness vs. dominance, were present in both rating and self-report data.

Of course, ratings need to be reliable as well as valid if they are to be regarded as a satisfactory way of assessing personality. The reliability of personality ratings is usually measured by comparing ratings of the same ratees by two or more raters. Reliability is generally reasonably high when assessed in this way.

Objective tests

The common feature of all objective tests is that they involve the careful assessment of some aspect of behaviour under controlled conditions. The behaviour which is assessed can extend to the physiological. For example, Eysenck and Eysenck (1967) argued that introverts are more sensitive physiologically than extraverts. They discovered that introverts produced more saliva than extraverts when lemon juice was placed in their mouths, presumably because of the greater physiological sensitivity of the introverts.

There are obvious advantages associated with the use of objective tests. For one thing, they are usually free from the problems of deliberate distortion that can affect self-report questionnaires. It is unlikely that many subjects given the lemon-drop test would guess that their level of extraversion was being assessed. Even if they did, it is doubtful whether they could wilfully alter the flow of saliva. Further, objective tests are also free of the major problem with ratings—the limited knowledge of the ratees possessed by the raters.

In spite of these advantages, there are various substantial problems with objective tests. It is sometimes difficult to know exactly what any given objective test is measuring, and the results are often much affected by apparently minor changes in procedure. For example, the lemon-drop test correlates with introversion–extraversion when one kind of lemon juice is used but not when a different kind is used. Even when objective tests are used in exactly the same form on two separate occasions, test reliability is often rather disappointing.

Raymond Cattell has probably made greater use of objective tests than any other personality theorist. He has carried out several major studies designed to address the issue of whether the personality traits revealed by objective tests are the same as those found in questionnaire and rating data. The findings are rather complex. However, in general there is rather good agreement between the personality factors in questionnaire data and those in rating data, but objective tests seem to be assessing rather different aspects of personality. This pattern of results raises the question of exactly what is being measured by objective tests. It is probably fair to say that it is sometimes not possible to provide a clear answer to that question.

Projective tests

We saw earlier that self-report questionnaires suffer from the limitation that people can usually guess reasonably accurately what the socially desirable response is, and this opens up the possibility of systematic lying. In addition, such questionnaires are necessarily concerned only with those aspects of thinking and behaviour of which the individual is consciously aware.

According to several theorists of a psychoanalytic persuasion, the way to get round these problems is to make use of projective tests. If, for example, someone is asked to say what they can see in an inkblot, they do not know what the socially desirable answer might be. Instead, each inkblot provides a vague stimulus onto which the individual allegedly "projects" his or her deep-seated concerns and emotions. It is perhaps for this reason that projective tests have been used mostly with psychiatric patients rather than normal groups.

The two best-known and most used projective tests are the Rorschach Inkblot Test, introduced by the Swiss psychologist Hermann Rorschach in 1921, and the Thematic Apperception Test, developed by Henry Murray (Morgan & Murray, 1935). The standard form of the Rorschach test involves presenting ten inkblots, and asking the subject to suggest what each inkblot might represent. Afterwards, the person conducting the test asks the subject to indicate which part of the blot formed the basis for each of his or her responses.

The interpretation of the meaning of a subject's responses to the ink-blots is based on three aspects of those responses: content; location; and determinants. Content refers to the nature of what is seen by the subject, location refers to the part of the blot that is used to produce the response, and determinants are the characteristics of the inkblot (e.g. colour; form) that determine the choice of response. The interpretation of a subject's responses is a complicated matter and is essentially subjective (i.e. dependent on the judgement of the person administering the test). However, information about location and determinants is generally regarded as being more important than the content of the responses. Some sample interpretations are given by Gleitman (1986): "Using the entire inkblot is said to indicate integrative conceptual thinking, whereas the use of a high proportion of small details suggests compulsive rigidity. A relatively frequent use of the white space...is supposed to be a sign of rebelliousness and negativism" (p. 618).

In contrast to the Rorschach test, the main emphasis with the Thematic Apperception Test (or TAT) is on content. The subject is presented with a number of pictures, and is asked to say what is happening, what led up to the situation depicted, and what will happen subsequently. These stories are interpreted in a rather flexible and subjective fashion, taking the individual's case history into account. The object is to identify his or her major underlying motives and conflicts.

In spite of the popularity of projective tests, they generally possess rather low reliability and validity. The unstructured nature of the Rorschach and the TAT appears to encourage subjects to respond to these tests rather differently on separate occasions, and this means that the tests are unreliable. The situation is equally bleak as far as validity is concerned. According to evidence discussed by Zubin, Eron, and Shumer (1965), the Rorschach test possesses very little predictive or construct validity. For example, although it is claimed that creativity is indicated by numerous human movement responses, eminent artists do not produce more of such responses than an ordinary group of individuals. Interestingly, whereas most Rorschach experts argue that location and determinants are more informative than content, the evidence suggests that content possesses more validity than the other two measures.

Why do Rorschach experts continue to believe that their test provides useful information? The most plausible reason is that the subjective nature of the interpretation of Rorschach responses allows information from the patient's case history to colour that interpretation. It may be this information from the case history that gives the Rorschach such validity as it possesses. This view is supported by the finding that clinical psychologists can infer a patient's personal characteristics just as well from the case history as from the case history plus the Rorschach test information (e.g. Kostlan, 1954). However, it should be noted that Holley (1973) developed an objective and reliable scoring system (called G analysis) for the Rorschach test. G analysis has been used to discriminate reasonably well among the Rorschach test performances of depressives, schizophrenics, and normal individuals.

The situation with the TAT is very similar. It does not appear to tell clinical psychologists much more than the information about a patient contained in the case history (e.g. Winch & More, 1956). However, there is evidence that the TAT may be of somewhat more value than the Rorschach. When attempts have been made to create a particular motive state (e.g. hunger by means of food deprivation), then the subsequent TAT stories have tended to incorporate information about the appropriate motive.

Why are projective tests relatively unsuccessful? First, the unstructured nature of these tests means that the responses produced by the subjects may be determined by their current moods or concerns rather than by deep-rooted characteristics. Second, the very subjective nature of the interpretation of responses on projective tests means that much depends on the expertise of the person carrying out the interpretation. Non-expert interpretation will reduce the validity of the tests, and the subjectivity of interpretation reduces their reliability.

Factor theories of personality

One of the most important issues that personality theorists have to consider is the number and nature of the traits which together form human personality. There are various methods that could be used in order to determine the structure of personality. However, the most frequently used method is factor analysis. As we saw in Chapter 2, factor analysis has been employed on patterns of correlations among intelligence-test items to produce a manageable number of factors of intelligence. Precisely the same procedure can be used with the personality information obtained from questionnaires, from rating data, or from objective-test data. In essence, items or measures which correlate highly with each other are regarded as belonging to the same underlying trait or factor, whereas those which fail to correlate reflect different traits.

Several factor theories of personality have been proposed over the years. However, the two best-known and most influential are those of Raymond Cattell and H.J. Eysenck, and our discussion will deal mainly with those theories. Before embarking on that discussion, it's worth considering some of the limitations of the factor analytic approach. First, factor analysis cannot possibly do more than reveal the factors contained within the items that are analysed. If, for example, no items dealing with sociability are included in the factor analysis, then a factor of sociability will not emerge from the factor analysis.

Second, the results of a factor analysis should not be regarded as providing the basis for a theory of personality. Factor analysis is merely a statistical technique and, as such, it can do no more than suggest guidelines for subsequent theory and research. If a personality trait is to be regarded as important, then factor-analytic evidence is not sufficient. What is also needed is evidence that that trait is of significance in everyday life.

Third, factor analysis involves making a number of essentially arbitrary decisions. The number and nature of the factors or traits extracted from any given set of data depend to quite an extent on decisions concerning the precise form of factor analysis to be carried out on the data. One important decision relates to the number of factors to be extracted. Extracting too many factors leads to an unnecessarily complicated picture, whereas extracting too few produces an unrealistically simple solution. As we will see, Cattell has erred on the side of extracting too many factors, whereas Eysenck has done the opposite.

Another important decision concerns the issue of whether it is permissible for two factors or traits to be correlated with each other. In *orthogonal solutions*, the factors are all uncorrelated with each other, so that knowing an individual's score on one trait provides no basis for predicting his or her score on a second trait. In contrast, *oblique solutions* permit the various factors to correlate with each other. Eysenck favours the use of orthogonal solutions, whereas Cattell prefers oblique solutions. These differences in approach help to explain why Cattell's 16PF assesses 16 traits, whereas the EPQ meaures only three.

In summary, factor analysis applied to personality assessment data produces a set of personality traits or factors. However, one cannot be sure that all these traits are of real-life significance purely on the basis of factor analysis, and it is possible that there are major personality traits which do not emerge from any given factor analysis. In essence, factor analysis can provide no more than suggestive evidence about the structure of human personality.

Cattell's trait theory

One of the most difficult matters for personality theorists is to try to ensure that they include all the major personality traits in their theory. Probably the most thorough attempt to produce an exhaustive personality theory was that of Raymond Cattell. He argued that the words in the English language provide useful information about the main personality traits, because any important aspect of individual differences would be represented by some relevant words. This line of reasoning led him to make use of the work of Allport and Odbert (1936). They uncovered a grand total of 18,000 words in the dictionary which were of relevance to personality, 4500 of which are used for personality description. These 4500 words were reduced to 160 trait words by eliminating synonyms and removing unfamiliar words. Cattell (1946) then added 11 traits from the personality literature, producing a total of 171 trait names which were claimed to cover almost everything of importance in the personality sphere.

Cattell was still left with an unwieldy number of potential traits. Accordingly, he made use of the findings from several previous rating studies to identify traits which tended to correlate highly with each other. It was argued that such traits were all basically similar to each other, and reflected a single underlying trait or variable. By this means, Cattell was left with 35 variables which were then examined in further rating studies. These studies suggested to Cattell that there are approximately 16 factors in rating data—or, in Cattell's terminology, life (L) data.

The indefatigable Cattell then decided to investigate the personality factors to be found in questionnaire (Q) and objective test (T) data. His initial assumption was that L, Q, and T data would all give rise to essentially the same personality traits. In fact, as mentioned earlier, although factor analyses of ratings or life data and questionnaire data produced rather similar factors, the factors emerging from objective test data were rather different. Questionnaire research led to the development of the 16PF, which was described earlier in the chapter.

It will be remembered that Cattell deliberately looked for personality factors that were correlated with each other. Even a casual inspection of the factors contained in the 16PF (see the table on p. 43) suggests that several of his factors are measuring rather similar aspects of personality. For example, we would generally regard someone who is:

1. affected by feelings (Factor C)
2. shy (Factor H)
3. suspicious (Factor L)
4. apprehensive (Factor O)
5. controlled (Factor Q3) and
6. tense (Factor Q4)

as being anxious. It is possible to make use of the inter-correlations among the original 16 primary or first-order factors to produce a smaller number of orthogonal or uncorrelated second-order factors. The most important of these second-order factors are anxiety, which arises out of the six inter-correlated first-order factors mentioned above, and exvia–invia, which is formed out of Factor A (outgoing), Factor F (happy-go-lucky), Factor H (venturesome), and Factor Q2 (group-dependent). The second-order factor of exvia–invia closely resembles Eysenck's introversion–extraversion factor.

Cattell (e.g. Cattell & Child, 1975) has gone on to argue that personality consists not only of the way we do things (assessed by tests of temperament and ability), but also of the reasons why we do things (i.e. motivation). When he investigated motivational strength via objective tests, he discovered that three main dimensions emerged from the factor analysis of the scores. Interestingly enough, there was some resemblance between these three dimensions and the Freudian concepts of id (basic instincts), ego (conscious cognitive system), and superego (conscience). As Hampson (1988) expressed Cattell's position, "Motivation consists of three components: id interest (I want), ego interest (I choose to want) and superego (I ought to want)" (p. 65).

Cattell used the term *ergs* to refer to the basic goals of motivation. These ergs have biological roots, and include sex, food-seeking, and gregariousness. Although these ergs are found in all cultures, the ways in which they are satisfied (termed *sentiments* by Cattell) vary considerably from one culture to another. There are complex relationships between ergs and sentiments. One sentiment can satisfy more than one erg (e.g. a dinner party satisfies the goals of food-seeking and gregariousness), and each erg can be satisfied in more than one way. The various connections between ergs and sentiments form a *dynamic lattice*.

Cattell's theory—an assessment. How fruitful is Cattell's theoretical approach? On the positive side, he has made a concerted effort to identify the major traits of personality. In particular, his view that we can have particular confidence in the importance of those traits that are found in a number of different kinds of data (e.g. ratings and questionnaires) is entirely reasonable, and he has done more than anyone else to study personality systematically in several different ways.

On the negative side, the major problem is that Cattell has not been successful in his aim of identifying the main personality factors. In essence, he was over-ambitious in believing that it was possible to discover approximately 16 traits, because many of these traits or factors are almost bound to be rather weak and difficult to replicate (i.e. obtain repeatedly). We have already seen that there are far fewer than 16 traits in the 16PF (cf. Howarth & Browne, 1971), and it also appears that Cattell has exaggerated the number of traits to be found in rating data. Several researchers (e.g. Norman, 1963) have discovered that there are five strong, replicable factors in Cattell's rating scales rather than the 15 or so claimed by Cattell.

The fact that Cattell failed to produce an adequate set of personality traits has serious implications for his entire approach. A theory which provides an inaccurate description of personality traits is unlikely to work at the level of explaining the nature of those traits. Thus, it must be concluded that Cattell's theory does not form a firm basis for the future.

Eysenck's trait theory

Eysenck agrees with Cattell that factor analysis is a useful tool to use in order to discover the structure of human personality. However, they disagree on the relative importance of rather specific first-order factors and more general second-order factors. Cattell has always emphasised first-order, oblique (or correlated) factors, because he argues that it is at this level that the most informative description of personality is possible. In contrast, Eysenck claims that second-order, orthogonal (or uncorrelated) factors are preferable because first-order factors are often so weak that they cannot be discovered consistently. The fact that it has proved almost impossible to confirm the existence of 16 different first-order factors in the 16PF suggests that there is some substance to this viewpoint.

Eysenck's (1944) initial attempt to make use of factor analysis to identify the major orthogonal factors involved a sample of 700 patients suffering from neurotic disorders. Psychiatrists' ratings on 39 rating scales could be accounted for reasonably well by the two factors or traits of *neuroticism–stability* and *introversion–extraversion*. Those high in neuroticism are more tense and anxious than those who are low in neuroticism, and extraverts are more sociable and impulsive than introverts. Scores on the neuroticism factor were relevant to the severity of neurotic disorder, whereas scores on the extraversion factor distinguished between two major forms of neurosis (anxiety and hysteria). Those patients suffering from hysteria were much more extraverted than those suffering from anxiety.

A considerable amount of subsequent research on normal and psychiatric groups has amply confirmed the importance of the factors of neuroticism and extraversion. It has also suggested the existence of a third major trait or factor known as *psychoticism–normality*. Those who score high on psychoticism tend to be rather aggressive, hostile, and uncaring. The psychoticism dimension can be regarded as the individual's predisposition to psychotic breakdown (psychosis—i.e. severe mental derangement), and it is noteworthy that psychotic patients such as schizophrenics have high psychoticism scores.

Although Eysenck used rating data in his early studies, he subsequently developed a series of personality questionnaires to assess his main personality traits. The Eysenck Personality Inventory (EPI) measures introversion–extraversion and neuroticism–stability, and the Eysenck Personality Questionnaire (EPQ) measures those two factors and also psychoticism–normality. As assessed by the EPQ, these three factors are all relatively uncorrelated or orthogonal, so that knowing an individual's score on one factor does not allow prediction of his or her scores on the other factors.

According to Eysenck, his three factors are very broad, and can be regarded as types or "superfactors". Each of these factors consists of a cluster of more specific traits such as the ones investigated by Cattell. Thus, for example, sociability and impulsivity are two of the traits forming part of introversion–extraversion.

In spite of this, you may very well feel that much of the richness of human personality is left out of Eysenck's approach, and in a sense you would be right. However, many aspects of personality can be understood as involving *combinations* of two (or even all three) of his personality dimensions. Thus, for example, although the EPQ does not provide a direct measure of the trait of "cheerfulness", it is probable that those who are high in extraversion and low in neuroticism tend to be reasonably cheerful, whereas those who are both introverted and high in neuroticism are low in cheerfulness.

Bases of the three "superfactors". Where do the personality dimensions of extraversion, neuroticism, and psychoticism come from? According to Eysenck (e.g. Eysenck & Eysenck, 1985), individual differences in these dimensions are due in large measure to heredity. Some of the strongest support for this view has come from twin studies. If heredity is important, then monozygotic or identical twins (who have essentially the same heredity) should resemble each other more in personality than do dizygotic or fraternal twins, who are no more alike in terms of heredity than ordinary siblings. In a study by Shields (1962), he reported that the correlation between identical twins brought up together was +0.38 for neuroticism and +0.42 for extraversion, in contrast with correlations of +0.11 for neuroticism and -0.17 for extraversion between fraternal twins. Somewhat surprisingly, identical twins brought up apart were even more similar in personality than those brought up together, producing correlations of +0.53 for neuroticism and of +0.61 for extraversion. As these twins were brought up in completely different environments, it is only through heredity that they could have similar personalities.

Eysenck (1967) proposed a theory of the physiological bases of the personality dimensions of introversion–extraversion and neuroticism. According to this theory, introverts have a chronically higher level of *cortical arousal* (i.e. activity in the brain) than extraverts because of greater activity in a part of the brain known as the ascending reticular activating system. It may be that introverts often show better *conditioning* than extraverts because their high level of cortical arousal means that their nervous systems form the necessary associations more readily.

If one assumes that people prefer an intermediate level of arousal, then it would be expected that under-aroused extraverts would seek stimulation, whereas over-aroused introverts would avoid stimulation. This makes sense in terms of the observed behaviour of introverts and extraverts. Extraverts spend much more of their time than introverts socialising with others and behaving impulsively, whereas introverts adopt a more cautious and reserved approach to life.

So far as neuroticism is concerned, Eysenck (1967) proposed that the *autonomic nervous system* is involved. More specifically, he argued that neuroticism depends on activity within the *visceral brain*, which consists of the hippocampus, amygdala, cingulum, septum, and hypothalamus. The notion that those high in neuroticism have a relatively active autonomic nervous system is consistent with the finding that they report many more physiological symptoms (e.g. rapid heart rate; indigestion) than those low in neuroticism.

There is reasonable support for the view that introverts are more cortically aroused than extraverts. Some of this support comes from studies of *electroencephalography* (EEG—i.e. brain-wave activity). This literature was reviewed by Gale (1983), who considered 33 studies reporting a total of 38 experimental comparisons. Extraverts were significantly less cortically aroused than introverts in 22 comparisons, whereas introverts were significantly less aroused than extraverts in five comparisons; introverts and extraverts did not differ in the remaining 11 cases. Thus, introverts are generally more cortically aroused than extraverts, but there are obviously some situations in which that is not the case.

There is much less support for the notion that groups high and low in neuroticism differ in physiological activity in the visceral brain. Fahrenberg (1987) reviewed the evidence, and concluded that there are no consistent psychophysiological differences between the two groups. This produces a somewhat paradoxical situation in that those high in neuroticism report many more physiological symptoms than those low in neuroticism, but there are no corresponding differences in actual physiological activity. Perhaps those low in neuroticism are simply less attentive to their physiological functioning, and this leads them to underreport physiological symptoms.

Eysenck's theory—an assessment. How useful is Eysenck's personality theory? The descriptive theory which identifies the major factors or dimensions of personality is very successful. It's probably true to say that extraversion and neuroticism (and to a lesser extent psychoticism) are the most important factors of personality. This can be seen by considering in detail other theorists' personality questionnaires. For example, Saville and Blinkhorn (1981) administered the EPI and the 16PF to a very large group of subjects. They discovered that the 16PF can be regarded largely as measuring extraversion and neuroticism. When the impact of extraversion and neuroticism was removed statistically from the 16PF, most of what was left consisted of factors of intelligence—e.g. tough- vs. tendermindedness, and conservatism vs. radicalism. Many theorists would argue that such factors generally are not directly relevant to personality at all, with the two examples belonging to the area of social attitudes.

In spite of the value of his descriptive theory, Eysenck's explanatory theory of the physiological basis of personality is considerably less successful. Some progress has been made in establishing the physiological foundation for introversion–extraversion, but the basis of both neuroticism and psychoticism remains very unclear. In other words, we know that genetic factors are involved in determining an individual's level of extraversion, neuroticism, and psychoticism, but we know very little about the ways in which these genetic factors actually influence the physiological system.

Gray's trait theory

Jeffrey Gray (1973; 1982) has proposed a modified version of Eysenck's theory. The basis of Gray's theory is that there are separate reward and punishment systems in the brain, and that these systems are important in the development of personality. In essence, he argued that there is one personality dimension with stable extraversion at the low end and neurotic introversion at the high end (see below). This is an *anxiety* dimension and it corresponds to individual differences in susceptibility to *punishment*. There is another personality dimension, which is known as *impulsivity*. It runs from stable introversion at the low end to neurotic extraversion at the high end. This dimension corresponds to individual differences in susceptibility to *reward*.

One of the implications of Gray's theoretical position is that introverts differ from extraverts in part because neurotic introverts are especially susceptible to punishment, whereas neurotic extraverts are especially susceptible to reward. This contrasts with Eysenck's view that introverts generally condition better than extraverts. Support for Gray's predictions was obtained by Nagpal and Gupta (1979). They used a verbal operant conditioning task, in which the effects of reward (praise for correct responses) and punishment (electric shock for errors) on the tendency to produce certain kinds of responses were assessed. There were four personality groups: neurotic introverts, neurotic extraverts, stable introverts,

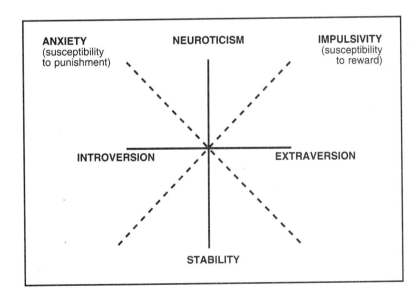

Gray's personality theory, which represents a modification of H.J. Eysenck's theory (based on Gray, 1973).

and stable extraverts. As predicted, reward produced more verbal conditioning for neurotic extraverts than for the other three groups, whereas punishment was most effective with the neurotic introverts.

Gray (1982) has been particularly successful in his attempt to uncover the physiological basis of the anxiety dimension. It appears that individuals high and low in trait anxiety differ in the functioning of the behavioural inhibition system, which consists of the septo-hippocampal system, its monoaminergic afferents from the brain stem, and its neocortical projection in the frontal lobe. There is considerable evidence from both animal and human studies to indicate the crucial role played by the behavioural inhibition system in anxiety.

In summary, the hypothesis that reward and punishment systems provide the fundamental basis for individual differences in personality is a very powerful one. Apart from anything else, it helps to explain why it is that anxious individuals experience more intense negative emotional mood states than non-anxious ones, and why impulsive individuals experience more intense positive emotional mood states than non-impulsive individuals (cf. Tellegen, 1985). However, most of the research supporting Gray's (1982) theoretical position has been carried out on animals, and so it is difficult to assess the ultimate value of his approach.

Structure of personality: Compromise

The factor-analytic approaches of Cattell and Eysenck are the best-known in the field of personality. However, there are other theorists who have provided influential views on the structure of human personality, and who have offered a compromise between the 16(+) personality traits of Cattell and the three traits of Eysenck.

Of particular importance is the work of Norman (1963). Small groups of students all rated each other on several of Cattell's trait rating scales. The rating data were then submitted to a factor analysis, and five personality factors emerged. These factors were as follows:

1. extraversion (e.g. talkative; sociable);
2. agreeableness (e.g. good-natured; co-operative);
3. conscientiousness (e.g. responsible; tidy);
4. emotional stability (e.g. calm; composed); and
5. culture (e.g. artistically sensitive; imaginative).

What is especially impressive about Norman's (1963) five-factor model of the structure of personality is the amount of subsequent evidence that has supported it. Several rating and self-report studies have produced five-factor solutions resembling the one proposed by Norman (1963) (see

Digman,1990, for a review). For example, McCrae and Costa (1985) had subjects rated on 80 scales by a number of people who knew them well factor analysis produced the following five factors:

1. extraversion (vs. introversion);
2. agreeableness (vs. hostility, jealousy);
3. conscientiousness (similar to will to achieve);
4. neuroticism (vs. stability); and
5. openness (similar to intelligence or intellect).

There are fairly obvious overlaps between these five factors and some of those proposed by Cattell and Eysenck. The extraversion and neuroticism factors are essentially the same as those postulated by Eysenck. In addition, low agreeableness and high conscientiousness or will to achieve are ingredients within Eysenck's psychoticism factor. So far as Cattell's 16PF is concerned, his factors of being affected by feelings (Factor C), shy (Factor H), suspicious (Factor L), apprehensive (Factor O), and tense (Factor Q4) all have relevance to the neuroticism factor; reserved (Factor A) and happy-go-lucky (Factor F) relate to the extraversion factor; while expedient vs. conscientious (Factor G) relates to the conscientiousness factor, and so on.

How is this impressive consistency of factors across numerous studies to be explained? According to Goldberg (1981), the five factors may correspond to the crucial information that we need to know about other human beings:

- "Will this person dominate me?" (extraversion)
- "Will I like this person?" (agreeableness)
- "Can I trust this person to do a good job?" (conscientiousness)
- "Is this person crazy?" (emotional stability); and
- "Is this person smart?" (culture).

Practical usefulness

One of the major goals of personality theorists is to propose theories of personality and methods of assessment which will have practical usefulness. There are many forms that such usefulness might take. However, because of space limitations, we will consider only occupational performance and anti-social behaviour.

Occupational performance. Personality tests such as Cattell's 16PF and the EPI have been used extensively in personnel selection. It has been assumed that many jobs will be performed well by people with certain personality characteristics and poorly by people with different characteristics. There is some support for this notion. For example, it might be expected that neurotic extraverts or impulsive individuals would make less successful bus drivers than stable introverts or non-impulsive individuals. This was strongly confirmed in a study of accident-prone and safe South African bus drivers (Shaw & Sichel, 1970).

Further striking evidence of the relevance of personality to occupational performance has been obtained in studies of pilots. Jessup and Jessup (1971) found that the EPI predicted success and failure among trainee pilots. The failure rate was 60% among the neurotic introverts but only 14% among the stable introverts. The importance of low levels of neuroticism to pilot success was further confirmed by Reinhardt (1970). He discovered that the best pilots in the United States Navy had a mean neuroticism score which was only approximately half that of the population at large. It is not surprising that high levels of neuroticism or anxiety are a disadvantage when it comes to a demanding and stressful job such as flying a plane.

One of the problems with using personality tests in personnel selection is that job applicants are likely to "fake good" when desirable job opportunities are at stake. As might be expected, job applicants often obtain lower neuroticism or anxiety scores but higher lie scale scores than those

FIVE MINUTES INTO THE OPERATION, HARVEY'S UNSUITABILITY FOR SURGERY BECAME RATHER APPARENT.

who complete questionnaires under more normal circumstances. They also sometimes score higher on extraversion. Of course, the high lie scale scores suggest that faking is occurring, but it is unfortunately not possible to know what the true scores should be.

Anti-social behaviour. Anti-social behaviour and crime depend to some extent on social factors such as deprivation, poverty, and broken homes. However, it has been suggested by some personality theorists (e.g. Eysenck & Eysenck, 1985) that personality may play a part in determining whether any given individual will behave in an anti-social or criminal fashion. Eysenck (1977) argued that criminality is deviant behaviour that tends to be exhibited by those high in neuroticism and psychoticism. He also argued that extraverts are more likely than introverts to become criminals because extraverts' poor conditioning ability inhibits their acquisition of social rules and a conscience.

Eysenck and Eysenck (1985) reviewed the evidence. In essence, there is some tendency for those who commit anti-social and criminal behaviour to be high in psychoticism, neuroticism, and extraversion. However, none of the associations between personality dimensions and anti-social or criminal behaviour is strong, and the links between extraversion and criminality and between neuroticism and anti-social behaviour are either weak or non-existent.

The relationship between personality and criminality has also been examined by Cattell. For example, Cattell, Eber, and Tatsouka (1970) administered the 16PF to 800 prisoners. They discovered that the prisoners were expedient (low Factor G), affected by feelings (low C), sober rather than happy-go-lucky (low F), unassertive (low E), casual (low Q3), apprehensive (high O), and imaginative (high M). However, all seven of these links between personality and criminality were rather weak, and many of them have proved difficult to replicate.

One of the reasons why findings in this area have proved disappointing is because those who behave in an anti-social or criminal way cannot plausibly be regarded as forming a homogeneous group. For example, the type of person who becomes a counterfeiter and devotes hundreds of hours of meticulous work to the production of high-quality fake banknotes is unlikely to resemble the type of person who carries out bank raids with a sawn-off shotgun. In other words, there may be no such thing as the "criminal personality".

Evaluation. Personality theories and tests have been found to be of some usefulness in predicting those who will perform successfully in various occupations and those who will behave in an anti-social or criminal fashion. However, personality generally emerges as a factor of rather modest importance. Why should this be so?

First, most personality tests possess no more than moderate validity, and so it is not possible to assess personality with any great degree of accuracy. Second, there are undoubtedly numerous environmental factors which influence occupational performance and the decision to become a criminal. It is difficult to identify these environmental factors as precisely as one would like, but it is probable that their cumulative impact is much greater than that of personality.

Situationism

Mischel (1968) argued that the lack of cross- situational consistency in behaviour invalidates the trait approach to personality. He proposed social learning theory as an alternative approach (as did Bandura, 1962; see Chapter 5), and this theoretical approach subsequently became known as *situationism*. Situationism is in essence a *behaviourist* approach, in that it is based on the assumption that behaviour is determined very largely by environmental factors. There is no place within strict situationism for any internal personality factors such as traits.

How can individual differences in the response to a given situation be accounted for by the situationist approach? According to Mischel (1968), everyone has encountered a rather different set of situations, and so their learning experiences are unique. These differences in experience and in learning mean that the response to a given situation will vary from one person to another. This account was developed by Mischel (1973), who was concerned to explain in more detail how past experience influences present behaviour. He argued that an individual's experiences affect his or her information-processing strategies. These strategies influence the way in which a situation is perceived or interpreted (e.g. as a threat or a challenge), and this interpretation then determines the response to the situation.

How useful is the situationist approach? On the positive side, there are many situations in which behaviour is determined by the situation rather than by personal characteristics. For example, nearly everyone stops their car at a red light and behaves in a respectful fashion during a church service. However, there are numerous situations (e.g. being in your own room; being in a park) in which the situation itself imposes relatively few constraints on behaviour, and where there is considerable scope for individual differences in personality to manifest themselves.

The situationists claim that behaviour is determined by the current situation. If that is correct, then the way an individual responds to a given situation on one occasion should resemble his or her response to the same situation on another occasion. As expected, consistency of behaviour in this sense is generally fairly high (Mischel, 1968).

In spite of the successes of situationism, it does not provide an adequate basis for understanding individual differences in behaviour. The fact that the situation plays an important role in determining behaviour does not mean that personality traits can be ignored. By analogy, the area of a field is determined in part by its length, but it is determined to an equal extent by its width. As we will see in the next section, contemporary interactionist theorists argue that the situation and the person must both be considered if individual differences in behaviour are to be accounted for.

There are other problems with social learning theory and the situationist approach in general, but we will consider only one of them here. It is a major assumption of the situationists that the environment rather than heredity determines behaviour. It is impossible within this approach to account for the rather similar personality characteristics and behaviour of monozygotic or identical twins brought up apart.

It should be noted as a final point that the controversy between trait theorists and situationists and social learning theorists is in some ways an artificial one. The goal of trait theorists is to provide a general understanding of individual personality at the emotional and motivational levels, whereas the situationists have as their goal the detailed prediction of behaviour. The substantial differences in their goals help to explain the different views of the two groups of theorists.

Interactionism

Several theorists (e.g. Bowers, 1973; Endler & Edwards, 1978) have argued that the best way of resolving the controversy between trait theorists and situationists is by means of *interactionism*. According to this approach, the person, the situation, and their interaction are all important determinants of behaviour. Since the notion of "interaction" is of crucial importance to this theoretical approach, it will be discussed in some detail. Consider the question "When do people experience a high level of anxiety?". One answer might be that individuals who have anxious personalities (i.e. high trait anxiety) will experience much anxiety. Another answer is that exposure to a stressful situation will create a high level of anxiety.

Personality in the form of trait anxiety and situational failure stress have both been found to influence experienced or self-reported state anxiety (Hodges, 1968). However, as is shown overleaf, a more complicated effect was discovered. More specifically, although a stressful situation did increase experienced anxiety, this was much more the case

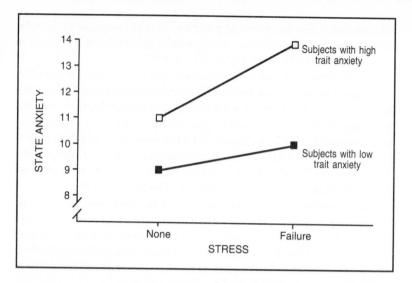

An interaction between trait anxiety and stressfulness of the situation (based on Hodges, 1968).

for those subjects high in trait anxiety than for those low in trait anxiety. Such a pattern of results, in which the effect of one variable (i.e. a stressful situation) depends on another variable (i.e. trait anxiety) is known as an interaction effect.

The study by Hodges (1968) suggests that the interactionists may be correct in their contention that the person, the situation, and their interaction all need to be considered. More detailed evidence was provided by Bowers (1973), who averaged the findings from 11 studies in terms of the percentage of the variance accounted for by each of these three factors. In essence, the higher the percentage of the variance accounted for by a given factor, the greater the importance of that factor in influencing perform-ance. Bowers (1973) discovered that on average, the person accounted for 12.71% of the variance, the situation for 10.17%, and the interaction between person and situation for 20.77%.

These findings suggest that the interaction between person and situation is generally a more important determinant of performance than either persons or situations on their own. They could be interpreted as indicating the superiority of an interactionist approach over the rival trait and situationist approaches. However, there are various reasons for not accepting this conclusion:

1. The figures for the percentage of the variance accounted for by the various factors vary considerably as a function of the range of persons and situations sampled: average percentages are thus almost meaningless.

2. If we consider studies in which the interaction between some measured personality characteristic and the situation was assessed, a rather different picture emerges. Sarason, Smith, and Diener (1975) found, across 138 experiments, that the situation accounted on average for 10.3% of the variance, personality for 8.7% of the variance, and the interaction between the two for only 4.6% of the variance.
3. The distinction between person and situation is not always clear-cut. For example, individuals with an extraverted personality choose to spend much more of their time in social situations than do introverts, so that personality characteristics can determine the situations in which people place themselves.
4. To a greater extent than is generally realised, trait theories tend to involve an interactionist perspective. For example, it is obvious that individual differences in trait anxiety will be more apparent in anxiety-provoking situations than in relaxing situations.

How useful is the interactionist approach to personality? It is certainly important to consider the person, the situation, and their interaction, although this basic approach had been proposed by several theorists well before the recent upsurge of interest in interactionism. It is also true that the interactionist approach has proved valuable in accounting for the effects of anxiety and stress on performance (e.g. Endler & Edwards, 1978). On the negative side, however, although most interactionist studies provide evidence of the importance of interactions between personality and situations, they fail to explain the processes responsible for producing those interaction effects. More importantly, there is the difficulty that an almost limitless number of interaction effects is possible. We may discover that trait anxiety interacts with situational stress, but we may then discover that this interaction is found among women but not men, at some times of day but not at others, and so on. The existence of such complicated interaction effects makes it very difficult for anyone to make theoretical sense of them.

Beyond interactionism: Constructivism

The main focus of this chapter has been on factor theories of personality. Such theories—even those which adopt an interactionist perspective— emphasise the notion that personality depends ultimately on biology and genetic inheritance. The greatest weakness with this entire theoretical approach is that it is too narrow, ignoring much of the complexity of human interaction. As Hampson (1992) pointed out:

> The danger with biological perspectives is that one may wrongly assume that everything of psychological importance can be captured at the various levels of physical inquiry. In fact, humans are unique because of consciousness and culture, and these are eminently non-physical phenomena...Humans are less controlled by genetic blueprints than any other animal, so complex human behaviour will never be adequately explained by genetics.

Hampson (1988; 1992) has proposed a constructivist approach, according to which interpersonal interactions play a key role in the development of personality. When you meet someone, you generally have some awareness of the impression you make on that person, and you also form an impression of the other person. The other person, in similar fashion, will be aware of the impression he or she makes and will form an impression of you. The personality you display in a given situation is determined at least in part by all of these factors, and not simply by your inherited personality. Of particular importance, the way in which you behave in an interpersonal situation is determined to a large extent by the behaviour and attitudes towards you displayed by the other person or people.

Evidence of the impact that someone else's behaviour can have was obtained in a study using an interview situation, in which participants were asked questions designed to produce either extraverted or introverted behaviour. A sample extraverted question is "What would you do if you wanted to liven things up at a party?", and a sample introverted question is "What things do you dislike about loud parties?". As predicted, participants who had behaved in an extraverted fashion in the interview rated themselves afterwards as more extraverted than those who had behaved in an introverted fashion. Raters agreed with the participants' assessment of their own personalities.

Even more striking evidence of how our behaviour and personality are influenced by other people was obtained in another study. Subjects were led to believe that another person either liked or disliked them. Those subjects who thought the other person liked them behaved in a much friendlier way than those subjects who believed themselves disliked: they revealed more about themselves, used a more positive tone of voice, had a more positive general attitude, disagreed less, and expressed dissimilarity less. Thus, it seems that our behaviour and personality are moulded to some extent by the views that we believe others hold about us.

Summary: Personality—factor theories

- Personality is generally regarded as referring to stable internal factors which underlie consistent individual differences in behaviour. These internal factors are usually called traits, and it is assumed that individuals differ in terms of the extent to which they possess any given trait.
- In contrast, some theorists have preferred to classify individuals into different types or categories, it being assumed that membership of a given type is all-or-none. The trait approach is much more plausible than the type approach.
- Personality can be assessed in at least four different ways. First, and most popularly, there are self-report questionnaires such as the MMPI and the 16PF. Second, there are ratings made by observers. Third, there are objective tests, in which behaviour is observed under controlled conditions without the subject realising that his or her personality is being measured. Fourth, there are projective tests, in which it is not clear to the test taker what is being assessed. In general terms, self-report questionnaires and ratings tend to be reasonably reliable and valid, whereas objective tests and projective tests provide less satisfactory measures of personality.
- One way of working out the structure of personality is by applying factor analysis to self-report or rating data. Prominent factor theories based on this approach are those of Cattell and Eysenck. Cattell has claimed that 16 different personality factors can be identified in self-report questionnaire data, but the evidence indicates that no more than about 8–10 can be obtained consistently. Eysenck has focused on three major independent factors of personality: introversion–extraversion; neuroticism; and psychoticism. There is strong evidence that genetic factors play a role in producing individual differences in each of these factors, but it has proved very difficult to establish the ways in which these genetic factors influence physiological functioning.
- Gray has proposed a theoretical approach which resembles that of Eysenck. He argued that there is an anxiety dimension (similar to neuroticism) which corresponds to individual differences in susceptibility to punishment, and an orthogonal impulsivity dimension (similar to extraversion) corresponding to individual differences in susceptibility to reward.
- One of the greatest problems with factor theories of personality is that they appear to assume that individuals will display more cross-situational consistency than they actually do. This led Mischel and other theorists to propose situationist theories, in which the emphasis is on the role of the situation rather than personality in determining behaviour. It is true that the situation is an important determinant of behaviour, but the situationist approach is much too narrow.

- A superior approach is that of interactionism, in which it is assumed that behaviour is determined jointly by personality and by the situation. One of the main limitations of most interactionist approaches is that the ways in which personality and situation interact are not usually specified in any detail.
- The constructivist approach has gone beyond the factor theory approach. It is claimed that personality is in part a construction or creation which evolves as a function of our interactions with others. Our personality depends not only on what we have inherited, but also on the expected and actual behaviour and attitudes of other people towards us.

Further reading

There are several books on personality. One which may be strongly recommended is S.E. Hampson (1988), *The construction of personality* (London: Routledge). It is very readable and full of interesting ideas. A more difficult but more comprehensive book is N. Brody (1988), *Personality: In search of individuality* (London: Academic Press). Eysenck's approach to personality is dealt with very thoroughly in H.J. Eysenck and M.W. Eysenck (1985), *Personality and individual differences: A natural science approach* (New York: Plenum). For those who want a relatively brief overview of the factor theory approach to personality, the following can be recommended: P. Kline (1992), The factor structure in the fields of personality and ability, in: A. Gale and M.W. Eysenck (Eds.), *Handbook of individual differences: Biological perspectives* (Chichester: Wiley).

Cognitive approaches to personality 4

Although the factor theory approach has historically been the dominant one in personality research, there are several other approaches that are of major importance. In this chapter, we will be considering three of these: the theories of George Kelly, Carl Rogers, and Albert Bandura. In contrast to the factor theorists discussed in Chapter 3, these three theorists all agreed that it was important to consider cognitive processes when addressing the issue of individual differences in personality. They also agreed that learning experiences were crucial in the development of personality, and disagreed with the factor theorists' emphasis on the role of genetic factors in determining individual differences in personality.

What is perhaps the most important point of agreement among Kelly, Rogers, and Bandura is the notion that an understanding of human personality and of how it develops can be of immense value when it comes to providing treatment for patients suffering from mental disorders. Many disorders occur as a result of experiences which cause problems with personality and its development, and a knowledge of personality facilitates the task of diagnosing the clinical patient's condition and proposing remedial action. In other words, there can be closer links between the study of normal human personality and abnormal psychology than appeared from the work of the factor theorists.

In spite of the similarities among the three theorists discussed in this chapter, it will rapidly become clear that there are also major dissimilarities. For example, at a very general level, Kelly and Rogers both favoured *phenomenology* (according to the phenomenological approach, considerable significance should be attached to people's reports of their direct experience of themselves and of the world around them). In contrast, Bandura rejects the phenomenological standpoint, and instead argues for a more objective and behaviour-focused approach to personality and to clinical treatment.

Kelly's personal construct theory

George Kelly (1905–1966) was a major theorist who had a rather idiosyncratic view of human nature. According to him, people have a great interest in being able to predict what is going to happen in the future. As a consequence, people will change their ways of looking at the world in order to be in a position to anticipate the future more accurately. In Kelly's (1955) own words, "A person's processes are psychologically channelized by the ways in which he anticipates events" (p. 46).

We can understand more clearly what Kelly was driving at here by drawing an analogy with the behaviour of a scientist. A scientist forms hypotheses about the world in the hope that these hypotheses will increase his or her ability to predict events. If the hypotheses are not successful, then the scientist changes them in order to provide a better account of the world. In similar fashion, individuals change their ways of thinking about other people and situations until they feel confident in their ability to predict the future. As Kelly (1955) expressed it, "Let us..., instead of occupying ourselves with man-the-biological-organism or man-the-lucky-guy, have a look at man-the-scientist" (p. 4).

According to Kelly (1955), we can understand an individual only when we know how he or she construes (i.e. interprets the meaning of) the world. This is determined by the system of personal constructs which the individual has developed over the years in his or her efforts to make sense of the world. In essence, an individual's personality is defined by the particular personal construct system possessed by that individual.

The Role Construct Repertory Test

In view of his theoretical concerns with the ways in which people construe the world, it was obviously important for Kelly to have some way of assessing an individual's constructs. The major instrument that he devised for this purpose is the Role Construct Repertory Test, which is often referred to simply as the Rep Test. Anyone wanting to use the test has first of all to draw up a Role Title List. This is a list of roles or figures that are believed to be of importance to all those subjects who will be given the test: mother, good friend, or a well-liked teacher are examples of appropriate roles. The person being tested then selects specific individuals to fill each of the designated roles.

After the testee has selected the individuals to fill the roles and to be rated, the tester chooses three of them. The person being tested is asked to indicate some way in which two of the individuals are alike but different from the third. For example, the testee might say, "My mother and my good friend are both easy-going, whereas a teacher I liked was strict." This would identify:

1. easy-going/strict as a construct;
2. easy-going as the *similarity pole* of the construct; and
3. strict as the *contrast pole* of the construct.

This exercise is repeated several times with different sets of three individuals being chosen each time. It is hoped by these procedures to identify the major constructs that an individual uses in his or her attempts to make sense of the world.

It should be emphasised at this point that the Rep Test is very flexible, and has been used in a variety of forms other than the one described. For example, a common variant is known as the "repertory grid". This involves a grid or network of horizontal and vertical lines in which the columns represent people and the rows represent personal constructs. Individuals can then be rated in terms of the personal constructs. Another variant is to examine an individual's constructs in some major area of life (for example, marriage). In this case, the similarity and difference judgements would be based on elements of relevance to that area of life (e.g. children; sex; housework). The ways in which the Rep Test is used are limited only by the ingenuity of the person administering the test.

Rep Test results. Detailed examination of the results of the Rep Test suggests that personal constructs vary in terms of their significance. On the one hand, there are *core constructs* which are of fundamental importance to the individual, and on the other there are *peripheral constructs* which can be changed without any major implications for the core structure. Constructs appear to be hierarchically organised. *Superordinate constructs* (e.g. good/bad) are towards the top of the hierarchy and include other constructs within their context, whereas *subordinate constructs* (e.g. likes sport, or likes holidays) are towards the bottom of the hierarchy and are included in the contexts of superordinate constructs.

One of the obvious limitations of the Role Construct Repertory Test is that it measures only those constructs of which the individual is consciously aware. Kelly (1955) accepted that there are preverbal constructs which are used by the individual even though he or she does not have the language to express them. He also accepted that one end of a construct might not be accessible to the conscious mind; such constructs were said to be "submerged". In spite of his recognition of the existence of preverbal and submerged constructs, Kelly did not really develop any effective methods of studying them.

As we will see later, the Rep Test has been used primarily in clinical settings. However, it can be used to shed light on individual differences in personality in normal groups. For example, the test provides information about an individual's cognitive complexity–simplicity. Those who are high in cognitive complexity have a richly differentiated and hierarchically structured set of personal constructs, whereas those who are low in cognitive complexity do not. Bieri (1955) discovered that cognitively complex individuals were significantly more accurate than cognitively simple individuals when given the task of predicting the behaviour of others. He also found that they were better at identifying differences between themselves and other people.

Other differences have been discovered between those high and low in cognitive complexity. In one study (Mayo & Crockett, 1964), subjects were presented with information about a person which was inconsistent with the other information they had available. Those low in cognitive complexity tended simply to ignore the inconsistent information, whereas those high in cognitive complexity adjusted their impressions of the person to incorporate the apparently inconsistent information.

An individual's personal construct system can determine how he or she responds to threat. According to Kelly (1964), threat "is the threshold between confusion and certainty, between anxiety and boredom. It is precisely at this moment when we are most tempted to turn back" (p. 141). Threat leads us either to produce a comprehensive change in our basic construct structure or to retreat to old constructs. Individual differences in response to threat were examined by Tobacyk and Downs (1986) in a study of music students who were faced by an examination in front of a music jury. They were asked to rate themselves in general terms, and also to rate themselves in the specific case of performing poorly on the music examination with respect to 40 central constructs (e.g. competent–incompetent) on a Threat Index.

It was argued that the examination would be most threatening for those students for whom failure would produce the largest change in the personal construct system. As predicted, the students predicting the largest effects of failure on their self-constructs showed the greatest increase in anxiety as the date of the examination drew closer.

Clinical applications

On the face of it, Kelly's (1955) personal construct theory seems so heavily cognitive in its orientation that it is not clear how much relevance it has for the understanding of emotionally disturbed individuals suffering from various forms of mental illness. In fact, however, Kelly (e.g. 1955; 1964) claimed that various deficiencies in the personal construct system are typically associated with abnormal behaviour.

Problems are likely to occur if an individual uses his or her constructs to make predictions in ways involving either excessive *tightening* or *loosening*. In tightening, the same predictions are made almost regardless of the particular circumstances. Tightening may be characteristic of patients who behave in compulsive ways. In loosening, the predictions are very erratic and inconsistent. Bannister and Fransella (1966) investigated loosening in thought-disturbed schizophrenics (schizophrenics typically suffer from problems with attention, thinking, social relationships, emotion, and motivation, and have at least a partial loss of contact with reality; see Chapter 6). They found that these patients showed much less consistency in repeated ratings of photographs than did other groups such as non-thought-disturbed schizophrenics, neurotics, depressives, and normals. The implication is that at least part of the problem of being a thought-disturbed schizophrenic is having excessive loosening.

Problems can also arise if an individual's constructs are either excessively *permeable* (i.e. capable of being penetrated) or excessively *impermeable*. An extremely wide range of stimuli is admitted into permeable constructs, whereas no new stimuli gain access to impermeable constructs. Similarly, the construct system will not function well if there is either excessive *constriction* or *dilation*. Constriction occurs when the construct system is made excessively narrow in order to reduce the possibility of inconsistencies being detected. This may characterise the cognitive structure of depressed patients. Dilation, which involves attempts to broaden the scope of the construct system, is found in manic patients (*mania*: a state of irrational elation).

The essence of clinical treatment within the context of Kelly's theoretical approach is to produce changes in the patient's personal construct system so that he or she can predict more accurately what is going to happen, and so be more in tune with the environment. The possibility of beneficial change is increased:

1. if the therapist provides an easy-going atmosphere in which new constructs can be "tried on for size" without the patient feeling embarrassed or threatened;
2. if the therapist endorses the new constructs that the patient is considering;
3. when the patient attempts to deal with, and to resolve, new situations.

The therapist himself or herself represents a new element, and can lead the patient to question his or her current set of constructs.

In practice, Kelly used a number of different therapeutic techniques. One of his favoured techniques was *fixed-role therapy*. In essence, the therapist uses his or her knowledge of the patient to produce a description of a new person, and the patient then tries to behave as if he or she were that person. The intention is that playing such a role will produce substantial alterations to the personal construct system. Not surprisingly, most patients find it rather difficult to pretend to be someone else, and so the therapist plays a key role in facilitating the process. As Kelly (1955) made clear, the therapist must constantly "play in strong support of an actor—the client—who is continually fumbling his lines and contaminating his role" (p. 399).

Critical evaluation

As Pervin (1989) pointed out, "For Kelly, listening to what the person has to say and taking it at face value—paying attention to content for its own sake, rather than as a symbol for some underlying meaning—became important" (p. 482). Many of the strengths and limitations of Kelly's approach to personality and to therapy stem from this adherence to phenomenology. This approach has the great merit of being very direct. It also has the advantage that exploring how an individual construes or interprets the world does provide some insight into his or her personality. On the negative side, the reliance on verbal reports of experience means that cognitive processes of which there is no conscious awareness are not assessed. There are also potential problems of deliberate distortion (e.g. people may attempt to provide socially desirable responses on the Rep Test rather than truthful ones). Within Kelly's approach, it is extremely difficult to do anything other than accept at face value what testees say on the Rep Test.

Kelly's (1955) theory has the advantage over the factor theories of personality discussed in Chapter 3 that individual differences in cognitive processing and structure are considered in detail. However, it has the disadvantage that many aspects of emotion and motivation receive very little theoretical attention. According to Kelly (1955), people strive to develop and expand their personal construct systems and to increase the accuracy of their predictions about the world. Although there is probably a grain of truth in that notion, it nevertheless seems like a rather threadbare account of the numerous biological and other motivational forces which influence human behaviour.

Another limitation of personal construct theory is that there is a sad lack of detail about many of the processes allegedly involved in the development and use of constructs. For example, the origins of an individual's construct system are obscure, as are the processes determining which construct will be selected as the best predictor in a given situation.

Rogers' phenomenological theory

Carl Rogers (1902-1987) devoted much of his working life to the search for improved methods of treating clinical patients. This search led him to develop what he called "client-centred therapy" (Rogers, 1951). However, he also became increasingly interested in personality. He recognised that some of his ideas about his patients' problems and about appropriate forms of treatment contained within them the seeds of a theory of personality. At a very general level, the approach favoured by Rogers corresponds fairly closely to that of Kelly. Both theorists subscribed to phenomenology, according to which an individual's direct experience is of crucial significance. In other words, we can understand other people best by focusing on their conscious awareness of themselves and of the world around them.

Self-concept

According to Rogers (1951; 1959), the concept of "self" is of fundamental importance. An individual's self-concept is mainly conscious, and consists of his or her thoughts and feelings about himself or herself both as an individual and in relation to others. According to Rogers, it would not be possible to engage in systematic study of any parts of the self that existed below the level of conscious awareness. There is an important distinction between the *self-concept* and the *ideal self*: the self-concept is the self as it is currently experienced, whereas the ideal self is the self-concept that an individual would most like to possess. Not surprisingly, happy people tend to have a much smaller discrepancy between their ideal self and their self-concept than is the case with those who are relatively unhappy.

One way in which it is possible to assess the self-concept and the ideal self is by means of what is known as the *Q-sort method*:

1. An individual is presented with a pile of cards, each of which contains a statement of personal relevance (e.g. "I am a friendly person"; "I am tense most of the time").
2. The individual's first task is to decide which statements best describe his or her own self, which statements are the next best in their descriptive power, and so on, right down to those state-

ments that are the least descriptive. (Sometimes the individual is constrained to place only a certain number of cards in each category in order to force him or her to make use of all of the available categories.)

3. Precisely the same procedure is followed with respect to the ideal self.
4. Finally, the experimenter calculates the amount of discrepancy between the two categorisations.

There are other ways in which the self-concept can be assessed. For example, it is possible to use the semantic differential. Concepts such as "my self" or "my ideal self" are rated on several seven-point scales, each extreme of which is defined by a pair of adjectives (e.g. good/bad; clever/stupid; active/passive). Another possibility is to use an adjective checklist. Each person is simply asked to indicate those adjectives that he or she feels are applicable.

There are some fairly obvious limitations associated with all of these ways of assessing the self-concept and the ideal self. First, the various methods cannot shed any light on those aspects of the self about which there is no conscious awareness. Second, the tests are open to deliberate distortion. For example, it is clearly more desirable to be a friendly rather than an unfriendly person, and so many unfriendly people might be inclined to pretend that the statement "I am a friendly person", is highly descriptive of themselves. Third, it is possible that people possess a number of different self-concepts, whereas the tests are designed to assess a single self-concept.

According to Rogers (1951; 1959), human motivation is largely devoted to the task of actualising (i.e. making real) needs and potentialities. Self-actualising has many aspects. However, the need for positive regard (the need to be liked and respected by other people) and the need for positive self-regard (the need to like and respect oneself) are of especial importance. The extent to which an individual is self-actualised can be assessed in various ways. For example, there is a 15-item questionnaire called the Index of Self-Actualisation, which measures self-esteem, self-acceptance, acceptance of one's emotional life, trust in interpersonal relations, and the ability to act in an independent fashion. The Index of Self-Actualisation appears to have some validity, because there is reasonable similarity between these self-report scores and the ratings provided by other people.

Personal development and self-concept. Rather optimistically, Rogers claimed that young children are naturally good at selecting those actions and experiences which are useful to them while at the same time avoiding harmful experiences. However, as children grow up, they are increasingly influenced by the values and attitudes of other people. As a consequence, children often incorporate other people's values into their own ways of thinking; this process is known as *introjection*. Such introjected values are called "conditions of worth", because they define the conditions necessary for us to experience positive self-regard. Thus, for example, a child might feel good about keeping his room tidy because tidiness is valued by his mother. An individual who accepts these conditions of worth is given what is known as "conditional positive regard".

As time goes by, we are all exposed to changing experiences of the self, and this should lead to corresponding changes in the self-concept. However, problems can arise when there is incongruence between an individual's real experiences and his or her self-perceptions. For example, a child who believes herself to be unaggressive finds herself behaving aggressively. One reaction to such incongruence is *distortion* (e.g. the child decides she was merely behaving assertively rather than aggressively). A more extreme reaction is *denial* of the existence of the experience. These processes of distortion and denial lead to incongruence, in which some of an individual's real experiences are not incorporated into the self-concept. In turn, incongruence makes the individual more vulnerable to threat, more anxious, and psychologically maladjusted.

How is incongruence to be avoided during the course of development? According to Rogers (1951; 1959), many problems arise because conditions

of worth are frequently provided by parents and others who offer only conditional positive regard. The way to become fully functioning and minimise incongruence is to be offered unconditional positive regard from important other people at an early age. This ideal state of affairs allows the individual to experience life without having his or her experiences distorted by the needs and values of others.

Some evidence in favour of this general theoretical approach was obtained by Coopersmith (1967), who carried out a large-scale study of the factors influencing development, and especially the growth of self-esteem. In order to assess self-esteem (which is related to actualisation), he made use of a 50-item Self-esteem Inventory. The major findings emerging from this study were summarised in the following way by Coopersmith (1967):

> The most general statement about the origins of self-esteem can be given in terms of three conditions: total or nearly total acceptance of the children by their parents; clearly defined and enforced limits; and the respect and latitude for individual actions that exist within the defined limits (p. 236).

A related important factor which helps to determine the development of the self-concept is *openness to experience*. Many experiences are threatening because they are inconsistent with our self-concept (e.g. "I am a friendly person, but I have just been rude to my neighbour"). Those who are open to experience acknowledge the inconsistency and change their self-concept accordingly (e.g. "I am a friendly person, but I find it difficult to be friendly to some people"). In contrast, as we will see later, a lack of openness to experience can play a part in the development of mental illness.

Client-centred therapy

The central assumptions underlying client-centred therapy are that incongruence plays a major role in the development of mental illness and that therapists should attempt to reduce their clients' levels of incongruence.

Some evidence that there is a link between incongruence and mental illness was obtained by Cartwright (1956). In a memory experiment, he found that subjects showed poorer recall of words that were not descriptive of themselves than of those that were self-descriptive; a phenomenon which could be regarded as an indication of incongruence. This tendency to have poor recall of non-self-descriptive words was more pronounced in poorly adjusted subjects who had either applied for therapy or who had received unsuccessful therapy, than it was in well-adjusted subjects.

Most clinical psychologists have argued that it is important to diagnose the mental illnesses from which their patients are suffering, and several different classificatory systems have been proposed (see Chapter 5). Rogers (1951; 1959) argued that there was little point in such diagnosis. However, he did feel that it was useful to distinguish the different ways in which patients seek to defend themselves when their experiences are inconsistent with their self-concept. One example is *rationalisation*, in which an individual distorts the interpretation of his or her own behaviour in order to make it consistent with his or her self-concept (e.g. "My behaviour looked bad, but it really wasn't my fault"). Another example is *fantasy*: an individual may fantasise about himself (e.g. "I am Napoleon"), and then deny or refuse to accept those experiences which refute the fantasy (e.g. "I can't speak French").

According to Rogers, the best way to reduce a client's incongruence is to provide a supportive environment in which he or she feels able to be open to experience. It thus follows that therapists who are

1. unconditional in positive regard,
2. genuine, and
3. empathic (i.e. understanding another person's feelings),

should be more effective in treating patients than therapists lacking some or all of those characteristics. Part of the reason for this is that therapists possessing these characteristics really listen to what their patients are telling them, rather than being unduly influenced by their own preconceptions. There is some evidence supporting the view that these characteristics are valuable in therapists. Truax and Mitchell (1971) reviewed several studies involving various methods of psychotherapy, and concluded that the most successful therapists tended to have these three characteristics. However, much of the recent evidence indicates that being unconditional in positive regard, genuine, and empathic are less important than was claimed by Rogers (e.g. Beutler, Cargo, & Arizmendi, 1986).

Although Rogers (1951) emphasised the importance of the personal qualities of the therapist in determining the success of therapy, the situation is actually rather more complicated. The therapist and the patient are in dynamic interaction with each other, and it may well be easier for the therapist to be unconditional in positive regard, empathic, and genuine with some patients than with others. Evidence that the behaviour and attitudes of the patient are important was reported by Fiske, Cartwright, and Kirtner (1964). Patients who at the first interview discussed their feelings and problems concerning important personal relationships were found to succeed considerably better in therapy than those patients who discussed their problems as if they were someone else's. In other words, the attitude of the patient may be much more important in determining the success of therapy than was acknowledged by Rogers.

Critical evaluation

Strengths.   Rogers has had a lasting impact on psychology in at least three different ways. First, his client-centred therapy has proved to be a reasonably effective form of treatment for a variety of mental disorders. However, it is probably more useful in the treatment of relatively mild disorders than of severe ones (Davison & Neale, 1990). Various other therapeutic procedures have developed out of client-centred therapy, of which encounter groups are probably the best-known example. In essence, participants in encounter groups are encouraged to examine their own feelings with great honesty, and to discuss them freely and openly with the other members of the group. Encounter groups have often produced a number of beneficial effects, but individuals who are rather disturbed or low in self-esteem may actually suffer adverse effects from participating (Kaul & Bednar, 1986).

Second, Rogers was one of the first therapists to provide detailed information about therapy sessions to other interested therapists and researchers. In many cases this information took the form of tape recordings of sessions. Such information is obviously extremely important if there is to be a proper understanding of therapeutic change. It also facilitates the task of evaluating the success of therapy. Rogers' contributions in this area were so great that Davison and Neale (1990) argued that "Rogers can be credited with originating the whole field of psychotherapy research" (p. 527).

Third, Rogers (together with Abraham Maslow, 1970) was a crucial figure in the development of *humanistic psychology*. Humanistic psychology is "concerned with topics that are meaningful to human beings, focusing especially upon subjective experience and the unique, unpredictable events in individual human lives" (Cartwright, 1979, pp. 5–6). With its emphasis on subjective experience rather than on behaviour, humanistic psychology represents a very different approach to psychology from that advocated by many other psychologists. Some of the disadvantages of relying on subjective experience are discussed in the next section, but much of value about an individual's personality can be learned from a careful consideration of their reports of their own experience.

Weaknesses.   A crucial characteristic of Rogers' approach was his reliance on phenomenology. As he expressed it: "To my way of thinking, this personal, phenomenological type of study—especially when one reads all of the responses—is far more valuable than the traditional 'hard-headed' empirical approach. This kind of study, often scorned by psychologists as being 'merely self-reports', actually gives the deepest insight into what the experience has meant" (p. 133). It would make the task of psychologists relatively easy if it were possible to obtain a complete understanding of other people simply by asking them to describe their experiences in a direct fashion. However, many psychologists doubt whether phenomenology is as useful an approach as was claimed by Rogers.

One of the major problems with phenomenology is that it is concerned only with those thoughts of which we have conscious awareness. There is much of importance lying below the level of awareness which cannot be accessed by the techniques favoured by Rogers. In addition, because we can have no direct independent evidence of how another individual experiences life, it is entirely possible for people to report their experiences in a deliberately distorted fashion. Most psychologists would argue that the study of behaviour is of value in attempting to understand others, but Rogers argued that it was of considerably less relevance than experience.

One of the other weaknesses with Rogers' theoretical approach concerns his treatment of motivation. According to Rogers (1959), people are primarily motivated towards actualisation or realisation of their potential: "It should be noted that this basic actualising tendency is the only motive which is postulated in this theoretical system." In view of the fact that our behaviour is influenced by a large number of different biologically and psychologically determined motives, Rogers' account seems rather threadbare. As Krause (1964) pointed out, the construct of the actualising tendency "appears to explain too much too vaguely for any differential predictions to derive from it" (p. 70).

There are some definite limitations of the personality theory developed by Rogers. He assumed that nearly everyone has a nature which is basically good and positive, with problems and disturbances occurring only because of particular experiences and the influence of others. These assumptions probably involve an unduly optimistic view of human nature. The notion that we all inherit somewhat similar personalities is also probably inaccurate. As we saw in Chapter 3, there is fairly convincing evidence (especially from twin studies) of considerable individual differences in inherited personality.

Bandura's social cognitive theory

Albert Bandura (1925–) has spent many years developing his approach to personality. Initially, he worked very much within the behaviourist tradition. That is to say, he argued that we need to study the environment very carefully in order to understand why people behave as they do. The rewards and punishments provided by the environment have a substantial impact on people's learning and on their behaviour. However, he has consistently argued that behaviour cannot be understood simply by considering *external* factors in the environment. We also need to investigate *internal* factors, such as precisely what it is that an individual learns from his or her interaction with the environment.

Some of the theoretical differences between Bandura and the behaviourists can be seen if we contrast their views on the role of reward or reinforcement in conditioning (e.g. a rat being rewarded with food for pressing a lever). According to behaviourists such as Skinner, reinforcement works in an automatic fashion by strengthening whatever response immediately preceded the reward (e.g. lever pressing)—in other words, it works backwards in time. In contrast, Bandura (1977) argued as follows: "Reinforcement serves principally as an informative and motivational operation rather than as a mechanical response strengthener." Thus, reward provides useful information about which responses (e.g. lever pressing) may be worth producing in the future. Crucially, conditioning in humans generally requires conscious awareness of the relationships among stimuli and responses (Brewin, 1988). In other words, what the subject thinks is happening is of more importance than what is actually happening. This is entirely consistent with Bandura's emphasis on the role of cognitive factors in conditioning.

As the years have gone by, Bandura has increasingly emphasised the importance of understanding the cognitive processes that are used to understand the environment, to predict the future, and so on. Behaviour depends on an interaction between the person (with his or her own cognitive processes and knowledge) and the environment; this two-way interaction has been termed *reciprocal determinism* by Bandura.

In a nutshell, Bandura's approach has become more and more cognitive. This is reflected in changes in what his theory is called. Early versions were called social learning theory, which ties in with the behaviourist emphasis on the importance of learning. More recent versions (e.g. Bandura, 1986) are described as social cognitive theory, which indicates the distance he has moved away from the traditional, anti-cognitive behaviourist approach.

Basic processes

The notion of self-efficacy is of central importance within Bandura's (1986) social cognitive theory. It refers to an individual's perception or assessment of his or her ability to cope satisfactorily with given situations; in the words of Bandura (1977), self-efficacy judgements are concerned "not with the skills one has but with judgements of what one can do with the skills one possesses" (p. 391).

Self-efficacy in this sense is regarded as being predictive of several aspects of behaviour. According to Bandura (1977), "Given appropriate skills and adequate incentives, ... efficacy expectations are a major determinant of people's choice of activities, how much effort they will expend, and how long they will sustain effort in dealing with stressful situations" (p. 194). In general, "People will approach, explore, and try to deal with situations within their self-perceived capabilities, but they will avoid transactions with stressful aspects of their environment they perceive as exceeding their ability" (p. 203).

It is important to note that Bandura does not think of self-efficacy as a general and stable individual difference resembling self-esteem. He has made it very clear that he regards self-efficacy judgements as being of relevance to specific situations. He claimed that a very general self-concept "does not do justice to the complexity of self-efficacy perceptions, which vary across different activities, different levels of the same activity, and different situational circumstances" (Bandura, 1986, p. 41).

An individual's sense of self-efficacy in any given situation is affected by four major factors:

1. That individual's *previous experiences* of success and/or failure in that situation.
2. Relevant *vicarious experiences* (i.e. experiences undergone as the substitute for another). For example, if you see someone else cope successfully with a situation, that may increase your self-efficacy beliefs.
3. *Verbal (or social) persuasion.* Your feelings of self-efficacy may increase if someone argues persuasively that you have the skills needed to succeed in that situation.
4. *Emotional arousal.* High levels of arousal are often associated with anxiety and failure, and can serve to reduce feelings of self-efficacy.

Of the various factors influencing self-efficacy, Bandura has probably devoted most attention to the role of vicarious experiences (e.g. *modelling*). In essence, an individual who watches someone else (known as the model) coping with a given situation can acquire complex behaviour patterns. In one study (Rosekrans & Hartup, 1967), some children watched a model who behaved in an aggressive fashion, and who was consistently rewarded for this aggressive behaviour. Subsequently, these children displayed a high level of imitative aggressive behaviour, indicating the power of observational learning. However, children who saw the model behave in an aggressive fashion, but being consistently punished for being aggressive, subsequently exhibited very little aggression. Other research suggests that these children had learned the aggressive behaviour, but that it did not appear in their behaviour because of the potential threat of punishment.

Apart from self-efficacy expectancies, there are two other basic cognitive processes that are important in determining the initiation and maintenance of behaviour. First, there are *outcome expectancies*. These are expectations concerning whether the desired reward will be received if the appropriate behaviour is produced (e.g. if someone works hard, will they gain promotion?). Second, there is *outcome value*. This refers to the perceived value of the reward to the individual.

Apart from self-efficacy, Bandura (1986) has emphasised the importance of *self-regulation*. It is assumed that people set themselves standards of performance. If they achieve these performance standards, then there is a process of self-reinforcement through which they reward themselves. On the other hand, if they fail to match up to their own internal performance standards, feelings of failure and guilt can be created.

Self-efficacy and clinical therapy

Not surprisingly, clinical patients tend to be much lower in self-efficacy than most other people. According to Bandura (1986), an individual's self-efficacy expectancies are important because of their influence on his or her feelings of distress and on the extent to which appropriate coping behaviour is initiated and maintained.

The evidence indicates that low self-efficacy expectancies feature prominently in both clinical anxiety and clinical depression (see Maddux, 1991). In cases of depression, low self-efficacy expectancies are generally combined with high outcome expectancy and high outcome value. As this is correlational evidence, it does not demonstrate that low self-efficacy expectancies cause depression. However, depressive symptoms have been reported after low self-efficacy expectancies have been created (see Maddux, 1991), and this suggests that such expectancies can have a causal role in the development of depression.

According to Bandura (1986), many (or most) of the beneficial effects of clinical therapy arise because of improvements in the patient's feelings of self-efficacy. Therefore, it should be possible to devise effective therapeutic techniques based on altering those factors (performance experiences; vicarious experiences; verbal persuasion; emotional arousal) that affect self-efficacy expectancies. There is substantial evidence that vicarious experience in the form of modelling can produce beneficial therapeutic change. For example, Bandura, Blanchard, and Ritter (1969) used modelling to treat snake phobia or fear. Sufferers from snake phobia were asked to look at people (models) moving towards snakes under either live or filmed conditions. This led to a substantial reduction in the phobics' fear of snakes. Subsequent research (see Maddux, 1991) has indicated that modelling also leads to increased feelings of self-efficacy with respect to coping with snakes. It also leads to behavioural change in that phobics are willing to move closer to snakes than they were before treatment.

It has proved rather difficult to establish precisely why modelling has such beneficial effects on clinical patients. However, it is probable that various cognitive factors are involved. For example, there is evidence (see Bandura, 1986) that using a *code* to summarise information facilitates the patient's task of remembering the actions performed by the model. In general terms, modelling provides useful information about coping strategies which can be stored in long-term memory, and it is access to this information that leads to increased feelings of self-efficacy.

Critical evaluation

Bandura's (1977; 1986) theoretical approach has been extremely influential among both personality researchers and clinical psychologists. As we will see in Chapter 7, the notion that many clinical patients can be treated by changing cognitive processes and structures is one that has become increasingly popular in recent years. Therapists such as Aaron Beck and Albert Ellis have developed forms of cognitive therapy which resemble in some ways those devised by Bandura. Cognitive therapy is generally at least as effective as most other forms of therapy (see Davison & Neale, 1990). Thus, it is clear that Bandura and other cognitive therapists have made an important contribution to clinical treatment (especially of patients suffering from anxiety disorders or depression).

Bandura has been particularly successful in developing more realistic views of conditioning than those proposed by Skinner and other behaviourists. There is little doubt that cognitive processes are of considerably more importance in determining the effects of reward or reinforcement than was proposed by the behaviourists (see Brewin, 1988). Bandura was one of the first theorists and researchers to identify some of the cognitive processes involved in conditioning.

On the negative side, there are some doubts about the extent to which Bandura has put forward a theory that allows us to understand individual differences in personality. His major focus has been on predicting and understanding people's behaviour in specific situations, rather than in broad areas of life. In that respect, he clearly differs considerably from the factor theorists considered in Chapter 3, who have tried to address very wide-ranging individual differences in behaviour. There is a dynamic tension between the general and the specific in personality theory and research: those (like the factor theorists) who strive for generality lose the ability to make accurate predictions in specific situations, whereas those (like Bandura) who strive for predictive accuracy in specific situations lose the ability to predict behaviour more generally. It is arguable that Bandura is so far towards the specific end of the specificity–generality continuum, or line, that no general understanding of individual differences emerges.

Another problem is that the crucial theoretical construct of "self-efficacy" is assessed by means of verbal report procedures which depend on the individual's conscious awareness of his or her own internal processes. It is entirely possible that many people are unaware of some of the processes that determine whether or not they behave in a confident way in a given situation. If that is indeed the case, then the current techniques available for measuring self-efficacy are deficient.

As Pervin (1989) pointed out, Bandura does not seem to consider motivational issues fully. According to Bandura, people are motivated when they perceive that there is a discrepancy between their actual performance and the standard of performance they had set themselves. Within this approach, the goals for which individuals strive seem to be regarded as merely performance standards. Such an approach is relatively uninformative with respect to issues such as how individuals resolve conflicts of goals or how biologically determined motives affect behaviour.

Summary: Cognitive approaches to personality

- The three theories discussed in this chapter can all be regarded as cognitive theories, although there are substantial differences among them. George Kelly and Carl Rogers both argued that it is important to focus on the individual's direct experience of the world, whereas Albert Bandura has added a cognitive dimension to an approach having its origins in behaviourism.
- Kelly's personal construct theory is based on the assumption that people resemble scientists, in that they devote much time and effort to the task of construing or making sense of the world. According to Kelly, an individual's personality is very much defined by his or her personal construct system. The Role Construct Repertory Test can be used to assess an individual's personal constructs. Clinical patients suffer from problems with their personal construct systems. For example, there may be either excessive tightening, in which the individual makes the same predictions across a wide range of different situations, or excessive loosening, in which the predictions become very inconsistent and erratic. Therapy is designed to enable the patient to make more accurate predictions about the world and thus to be in tune with the environment. This is achieved by having an easy-going and supportive therapist who facilitates the patient's task of developing more appropriate personal constructs.
- In spite of the general usefulness of the approach, personal construct theory has various limitations, including an undue reliance on the conscious experience of the individual, and a de-emphasis on the role of emotional and motivational factors in personality and in the development of mental disorder.
- Carl Rogers proposed a phenomenological theory in which the main focus is on the self-concept. More specifically, he claimed that an individual's happiness depends in large measure on having a small discrepancy between self-concept and ideal self. The self-concept and ideal self can be assessed by means of the Q-sort method or by the semantic differential. At the motivational level, people have various needs, including those for positive regard from others and for positive self-regard. Abnormality can occur when distortion or denial of experience leads to an incongruence between real experiences and self-perceptions. Rogers' client-centred therapy focuses on reducing incongruence, and this is fostered by the therapist having positive regard for the patient, and by being genuine and empathic. This therapy seems to work better with relatively mild problems than with serious ones.

- Rogers has been instrumental in the development of encounter groups and the humanistic approach to psychology. On the negative side, his views on motivation are limited, and he shares Kelly's failure to consider sufficiently those processes of which the individual is not consciously aware.
- Albert Bandura accepts many of the assumptions of behaviourism, but argues that cognitive processes also need to be considered. In particular, he claims that self-efficacy expectancies play a vital role in determining the initiation of, and persistence in, particular patterns of behaviour. These expectancies depend on previous experiences, vicarious experiences, verbal or social persuasion, and emotional arousal. Patients suffering from anxiety disorders or depression characteristically have low self-efficacy expectancies, and a major focus in treatment is on enhancing feelings of self-efficacy.
- Bandura has played a prominent part in the development of cognitive therapy, and this form of treatment has proved to be successful with both anxiety and depression. On the negative side, the assessment of self-efficacy is based only on processes of which the individual is consciously aware; motivational factors are not considered sufficiently and the specificity of Bandura's approach means that general personality characteristics are de-emphasised.

Further reading

Clear and critical accounts of the theories discussed in this chapter are available in L.A. Pervin (1989), *Personality: Theory and research* (Fifth Edition) (Chichester: Wiley). The therapies developed by Albert Bandura and by Carl Rogers are discussed by G.C. Davison and J.M. Neale (1990), *Abnormal psychology* (Fifth Edition) (Chichester: Wiley). The fullest account of George Kelly's approach is in his own book, published in 1955: *The psychology of personal constructs* (New York: Norton).

Approaches to abnormality 5

The remainder of this book is devoted to that part of psychology which is concerned with psychological disorders. This area of psychology is often called *abnormal psychology* or *psychopathology*. In order to set the scene for our subsequent coverage of specific forms of psychopathology, we will focus in this chapter on some of the key general issues that confront anyone interested in this area. More specifically, there are three questions that will occupy us in this chapter:

1. What do we mean by abnormality, and how can it be distinguished from normality?
2. What are the main categories of psychological disorder?
3. What are the factors responsible for the development of each mental disorder?

The first question is obviously important, because we need to know as precisely as possible which patterns of behaviour fall, and do not fall, within the bounds of abnormal psychology. As we will see, it is surprisingly difficult to produce any clear-cut answer to the question, but a partial answer is proposed. The second and third questions refer to the *description* and the *explanation* of mental disorders. As with the first question, there are no definitive answers available. What we will do is to present the major current views, and to identify the advantages and disadvantages of each.

What is abnormality?

There are several different ways in which one might attempt to define "abnormality". One way is based on the statistical approach, according to which the abnormal is that which is statistically rare in the population. Consider, for example, trait anxiety as assessed by Spielberger's State-Trait Anxiety Inventory. The mean score for trait anxiety is approximately 40, and only about one person in 50 obtains a score higher than 55. Thus, people who score 55 or more can be regarded as abnormal in the sense that their scores deviate from those of the great majority of the population.

While this statistical approach addresses part of what is usually meant by "abnormality" in the clinical context, it does not provide a satisfactory basis for defining the term. There are numerous people whose scores on trait anxiety (or other measures of individual differences) are unusually high, but who nevertheless are leading contented and fulfilled lives. It would make little or no sense to claim that such people are clinically abnormal. It is also worth noting that very low scorers on trait anxiety (scores of 25 or less) are also statistically abnormal, but practically no-one has ever identified a low susceptibility to anxiety as an indication of clinical abnormality!

The fact that there is often a wide gulf between statistical and clinical abnormality can be seen even more clearly if we consider individual differences in intelligence. An individual with an IQ of 148 is very abnormal from a statistical point of view. However, most people would regard the possession of such an IQ as a matter of pride rather than as a mark of clinical abnormality.

"Social deviance".   Part of what is missing from the statistical approach to abnormality is any consideration of the impact of a given individual's behaviour on other people. This has led some psychologists to emphasise the notion of social deviance. According to advocates of this approach, those who behave in a socially deviant and apparently incomprehensible way which makes other people very uncomfortable should be regarded as abnormal.

It is true that most people who are labelled as clinically abnormal behave in a socially deviant fashion. However, clinical abnormality should not be equated with social deviance. There are various different reasons why an individual is socially deviant. Some people are so simply because they have chosen to adopt a non-conformist life-style. Others are socially deviant because their behaviour is motivated by high principles (e.g. those in Nazi Germany who spoke out against the atrocities that were being committed). Thus, social deviance on its own is by no means a sufficient criterion for regarding someone as abnormal.

There are other problems with attaching too much significance to social deviance. What is regarded by society as deviant or abnormal behaviour varies considerably from one culture to another. For example, in some societies homosexuality is regarded as a perversion and a criminal offence, whereas in others (e.g. Ancient Greece) it has been tolerated or even encouraged. Another example is given by Gleitman (1986). Apparently, Kwakiutl Indians engage in a special ceremony in which they burn valuable blankets in order to cast shame on their rivals. If someone in our society deliberately set fire to his or her most valuable possessions, he or she would be regarded as decidedly odd or mentally ill.

Even if social deviance must be rejected as the sole criterion of abnormality, that does not mean that it is wholly irrelevant. After all, people are social animals, and derive much of their pleasure in life from their interactions with other people. As a consequence, most people find it important for a contented existence to avoid behaving in socially deviant ways which bemuse or upset other people.

We have seen so far that abnormality is too complex a notion to be defined in terms of a single criterion such as statistical rarity or social deviance. It is thus time to turn to a more adequate approach which addresses this complexity more directly.

The features of abnormality

"Abnormality" is a concept, and concepts differ considerably in terms of how precisely they can be defined. The concept of a "square" is very precise, because it can be defined as a rectangle in which all of the sides are of the same length. Armed with this definition, it is straightforward to decide whether or not any given figure is, or is not, a square. In contrast, it is much more difficult to provide a simple definition of the concept or category of "games", because of the enormous range of activities which fall within that category. Wittgenstein (1958) argued that many concepts are complex in the same fashion. He went on to point out that the similarities between the members of a category such as "games" can be characterised as "family resemblances". Members of a category are like the members of a family in that they do not have to possess exactly the same features. It is even possible for two members of the same category to have no common features at all. Members of a category will tend to possess various features that are also possessed by several other members of the category, but may not.

What is the relevance of all this to the definition of abnormality? In essence, "abnormality" is a relatively imprecise concept which is as difficult to define as "games". In other words, abnormal behaviour can take many different forms, and involve different features. Moreover, there is no single feature that reliably permits us to distinguish between abnormal and normal behaviour. What is needed is to identify the major features that are more likely to be found in abnormal than in normal individuals. Rosenhan and Seligman (1989) have proposed seven such features, and we will discuss them in a moment. The more of these features possessed by an individual, the greater the likelihood that he or she will be categorised as abnormal. This implies, of course, that there is an area of uncertainty where someone possesses, say, two or three of the features. However, this is inevitable with a concept such as "abnormality". The seven features which Rosenhan and Seligman (1989) argue are relevant to a decision as to whether someone is abnormal owe something to the statistical rarity and social deviance approaches discussed earlier. However, their overall approach is considerably more sophisticated. Their seven features are as follows:

- *Suffering:* Most abnormal individuals (e.g. those with anxiety disorders) report that they are suffering, and so the presence of suffering is a key feature of abnormality. However, completely normal people grieve and suffer when a loved one dies, and some abnormal individuals (e.g. those with anti-social personality disorders) treat other people very badly but do not appear to suffer themselves.
- *Maladaptiveness:* Maladaptive behaviour is behaviour that prevents an individual from achieving major life goals such as having good relationships with other people or working effectively. Most abnormal behaviour is maladaptive in this sense (e.g. the agoraphobic who stays at home all the time because of his or her fear of open spaces).
- *Vividness and unconventionality:* Vivid and unconventional behaviour is behaviour that is relatively unusual. If we decide that someone is abnormal, part of the reason for that decision is very likely to be because the way in which that person behaves in various situations differs substantially from the way in which we would expect people to behave in those situations. However, as we have already argued, there are many people whose behaviour is vivid and unconventional, but who cannot be regarded as abnormal.
- *Unpredictability and loss of control:* Most people behave in a reasonably predictable and controlled way most of the time. In contrast, the behaviour of abnormal individuals is often highly variable and uncontrolled, and does not seem appropriate to the situation (e.g. being depressed at a party). However, most people's behaviour is occasionally unpredictable and relatively uncontrolled. Indeed, we would regard someone who was totally predictable and controlled as rather boring and strait-laced.
- *Irrationality and incomprehensibility:* A frequent characteristic of abnormal behaviour is that there appears to be no good reason why anyone would choose to behave in that fashion; in other words, the behaviour is irrational and incomprehensible. Sometimes behaviour will seem to be incomprehensible not because it is abnormal, but

because we do not know the reasons for it. For example, a splitting headache may cause someone to behave in ways that are incomprehensible to those who are not aware that the person has a headache.

- *Observer discomfort*: Our social behaviour is governed by a number of unspoken rules of behaviour. These include maintaining reasonable eye contact with the person with whom one is talking, not standing too close to other people, and wearing clothes that are appropriate to the situation. Those who see these rules being transgressed are likely to experience a certain amount of discomfort, and may conclude that the transgressor is abnormal. Observer discomfort is not an infallible guide to abnormality, and may reflect cultural differences in behaviour and style. For example, Arabs like to stand very close to other people, and this can be quite disturbing to Europeans.
- *Violation of moral and ideal standards*: Behaviour is sometimes judged to be abnormal when it violates moral standards, even when many or most people fail to maintain those standards. For example, religious people have sometimes claimed that masturbation is wicked and abnormal in spite of the fact that it is a widespread practice.

An obvious problem with most of the seven features of abnormality is that they involve subjective judgements. For example, behaviour that causes severe discomfort in one observer may have no effect on another observer, and behaviour that violates one person's moral standards may be entirely consistent with someone else's moral standards. In other words, it can be quite difficult to decide which of the features of abnormality are actually present in a given individual's behaviour.

Another problem with some of these features of abnormality (e.g. irrationality and incomprehensibility; unpredictability and loss of control; vividness and unconventionality) is that they apply to people who are merely non-conformists or who have a very idiosyncratic style. This issue is addressed in the introduction to the revised version of the *Diagnostic and Statistical Manual of Mental Disorders* (DSM-III-R), which is used extensively by psychiatrists for purposes of diagnosis. An attempt is made to distinguish between social deviance or non-conformity and mental disorder or abnormality:

> Neither deviant behaviour, e.g. political, religious, or sexual, nor conflicts that are primarily between the individual and society are mental disorders unless the deviance or condition is a symptom of a dysfunction (i.e. impairment of function) in the person (p. xxii).

Before moving on from the issues of definition surrounding abnormality, it is worth considering the other side of the coin—normality. What exactly do we mean by normality? Rosenhan and Seligman (1989) provided a very concise definition: "Normality is simply the absence of abnormality" (p. 17). In other words, the fewer of the seven features of abnormality that an individual displays in his or her everyday behaviour, the more he or she can be regarded as being normal. It follows that we should not really think simply in terms of the two categories, normal and abnormal. It is more accurate to regard both normality and abnormality as being matters of degree—i.e. it is perfectly possible for someone's behaviour to be either somewhat abnormal or very abnormal.

Categorisation of mental disorders

Most psychiatrists and clinical psychologists accept that abnormality exists, and that those individuals who exhibit abnormal symptoms should receive a psychiatric diagnosis or label which specifies the nature of the abnormality. This psychiatric diagnosis helps to determine the appropriate form of treatment.

Although that view may appear entirely reasonable, there have been numerous critics of it over the past 30 years or so. Many of these critics claim that there is a danger that an individual who acquires the stigma (i.e. mark of social disgrace) of a psychiatric diagnosis or label will be perceived and treated as a mentally ill person. As a consequence, his or her behaviour may change in directions that make the label more appropriate than it was in the first place. In other words, rather than the symptoms leading to the psychiatric label, it may sometimes be the case that the label plays a part in creating the symptoms. This general viewpoint is sometimes referred to as *labelling theory*, and was originally proposed by Scheff (1966).

The notion that the psychiatric label attached to a patient signifies rather little was taken to its extremes by Thomas Szasz (1974). His argument was that mental illness is a myth. All that is really meant by it is that an individual's behaviour deviates from the norms of society, and cannot readily be placed into any other category of non-conformist behaviour (e.g. criminality; prostitution). In other words, categorising patients as suffering from mental illness provides society with a convenient but largely meaningless label.

A somewhat different attack on the appropriateness of attaching psychiatric labels to patients was mounted by the Scottish psychiatrist, R.D.

Laing. He accepted that a major reason why patients are given psychiatric diagnoses is because their behaviour is different from that of most other members of society. However, he argued that in many ways it is society rather than the patient that is to blame for that state of affairs. In his own words, "By the time the new human being is 15 or so, we are left with a being like ourselves, a half-crazed creature more or less adjusted to a mad world. This is normality in our present age" (Laing, 1967, p. 58).

Rosenhan's studies. The general notion that the use of psychiatric diagnoses or labels can be extremely misleading found celebrated (though controversial) support in the work of David Rosenhan (1973). In his study, eight normal people (five men and three women) attempted to gain admission to 12 different psychiatric hospitals. They all complained of hearing indistinct voices which seemed to be saying "empty", "hollow", and "thud". Even though this was the only symptom they claimed to have, seven of them were diagnosed as suffering from *schizophrenia* (i.e. a very severe condition involving substantial distortions of thought, emotion, and behaviour) and the other person was diagnosed as suffering from *manic-depressive psychosis* (a condition in which there are great mood swings). After they had been admitted to psychiatric wards, all of them said that they felt fine and no longer had any symptoms. In spite of that, it took an average of 19 days before they were discharged. Their psychiatric classification at the time of discharge was "schizophrenia in remission", meaning that it was felt entirely possible that they would become schizophrenic again in the future.

Having apparently demonstrated that the sane can sometimes be categorised as insane, Rosenhan (1973) decided to see whether the insane could be categorised as sane under the appropriate circumstances. He told the staff at a psychiatric hospital that one or more pseudo-patients (i.e. normal people pretending to have schizophrenic symptoms) would attempt to gain admittance to the hospital. In spite of the fact that no pseudo-patients actually appeared, there were a total of 41 genuine patients who were judged with great confidence to be pseudo-patients by at least one member of staff. Nineteen of those genuine patients were suspected of being frauds by one psychiatrist and another member of staff. These findings led Rosenhan (1973) to conclude: "It is clear that we cannot distinguish the sane from the insane in psychiatric hospitals."

If one were to accept Rosenhan's (1973) conclusion, then the entire process of attempting to distinguish between normality and abnormality is fatally flawed. However, there are limitations in Rosenhan's study, which mean that we do not need to accept his conclusion. Perhaps the most powerful argument against Rosenhan's findings was mounted by Seymour Kety (1974), who offered the following analogy:

> If I were to drink a quart of blood and, concealing what I had done, come to the emergency room of any hospital vomiting blood, the behaviour of the staff would be quite predictable. If they labelled and treated me as having a bleeding peptic ulcer, I doubt that I could argue convincingly that medical science does not know how to diagnose that condition.

In other words, psychiatrists can hardly be blamed for not expecting completely normal people to attempt to gain admittance to a psychiatric hospital. There were errors of diagnosis under the very unusual conditions of Rosenhan's (1973) study, but that does not mean that psychiatrists generally cannot distinguish between the normal and the abnormal.

Rosenhan (1973) was on stronger ground in his contention that the way in which someone is treated is in part a function of the label they have been given (cf. Scheff, 1966). There were numerous occasions on which the pseudo-patients in the psychiatric ward approached a staff member with polite requests for information. The requests were ignored 88% of the time by nurses and attendants, and 71% of the time by psychiatrists. This unresponsiveness suggests that those who are labelled as schizophrenic are regarded as having very low status within society.

In summary, it is clear that there are several potential problems associated with the use of psychiatric diagnoses. The existence of these problems has led many authorities to argue that psychiatric diagnoses are virtually useless. As we will see, even those who believe that psychiatric diagnoses are of value are forced to admit that there are real problems in devising a satisfactory system for the diagnosis of psychiatric conditions.

The medical model

Most attempts to provide a comprehensive classificatory system (technically known as a *taxonomy*) within abnormal psychology have been heavily influenced by the classificatory systems used within medicine to diagnose physical illnesses. Indeed, the entire approach is based on the so-called *medical model*, according to which there are close similarities between mental and physical illness. In this section we will consider some of the advantages and disadvantages of the medical model approach to mental illness.

Within medicine, each physical illness is generally characterised by a particular set of symptoms (i.e. physical ailments). A doctor attempting to help a sick patient will typically seek to reach a diagnosis (an opinion about the nature of the illness) by comparing the patient's particular symptoms to those characteristic of various illnesses. Much is often known of the *aetiology* (the cause of a disease) of physical illnesses, so that the doctor can check that his or her diagnosis is accurate. For example, cholera is caused by certain bacteria, and a diagnosis of cholera can be confirmed by discovering evidence that those bacteria are present in the patient's body.

Most experts agree that the position with respect to the diagnosis of mental illnesses is much less satisfactory than it is with physical illnesses. The symptoms in physical illness are generally objective (e.g. a temperature of 104°F or 40°C), whereas those in mental illness are more likely to be subjective (e.g. "I feel very depressed"). However, the differences are not always so extreme. The only symptom reported by a patient with backache may be a certain amount of pain, which is not really an objective measure. Another difference is that the aetiology of most physical illnesses is known, whereas that of mental illnesses is usually known in only a very general fashion. Thus, unlike doctors diagnosing patients with physical diseases, those diagnosing a mental illness cannot usually check the accuracy of their diagnosis by establishing its cause.

The subjective nature of the symptoms reported by clinical patients, coupled with problems of identifying the causes of mental illnesses, mean that psychiatric diagnoses are bound to be rather imprecise. It is also reasonable to argue that the medical model provides no more than a shaky foundation for abnormal psychology. That there are genuine reasons for concern will become clear in the next section, in which the most commonly used approach to diagnosis (the *Diagnostic and Statistical Manual of the Mental Disorders*) is discussed. The evidence to date suggests that its reliability and validity are both rather disappointing in many ways.

In spite of these considerations, there still appear to be at least two reasons for attempting to establish as good a classificatory system or taxonomy of mental illnesses as possible:

1. It facilitates the task of finding an appropriate treatment. Just as a plumber does not set to work until it is clear which part of the plumbing system is faulty, so a psychiatrist or clinical psychologist wants to have a clear idea of the nature of the problem before attempting to treat it.
2. It would be extremely difficult to develop an understanding of the causes of mental disorder or abnormality (and of the appropriate form of treatment) if every patient were regarded as unique. Grouping patients according to their diagnoses provides a good basis for an exploration of the factors responsible for any

given form of disorder, and for the development of effective forms of treatment.

Classificatory systems

The starting point for any attempt to classify mental disorders is to identify the patient's symptoms. However, one of the limitations of an undue reliance on individual symptoms is that the same (or very similar) symptoms are found in what are otherwise quite different mental disorders. For example, anxiety is a major symptom in generalised anxiety disorder, obsessive-compulsive disorder, and the phobias. As a consequence, the emphasis in most classificatory systems is not on individual symptoms but on *syndromes* (i.e. a set of symptoms that are generally found together).

The symptom–syndrome approach to abnormality owes much to the pioneering work of Emil Kraepelin (1856-1926). He was an early advocate of the medical model approach to mental illness. In medicine, it is usual to diagnose the nature of the physical disease on the basis of the physical symptoms, and Kraepelin felt that the same approach was suitable for mental illness. As a consequence, he emphasised the use of physical or behavioural symptoms (e.g. insomnia; disorganised speech) rather than vaguer symptoms such as poor social adjustment or misplaced drives. In spite of numerous deviations from Kraepelin's original classificatory system, it is noticeable that most taxonomies still retain the medical flavour and emphasis on physical symptoms which he advocated.

One of the greatest problems encountered by anyone devising or using a classificatory system or taxonomy is the fact that different patients rarely present the same symptoms. As a consequence, patients given the same psychiatric diagnosis (e.g. schizophrenia) differ somewhat from each other in their sets of symptoms. In addition, they typically possess some rather than all of the symptoms which define the diagnostic category. There is inevitably a grey area in which the fit between a patient's symptoms and those forming the syndrome of a diagnostic category is relatively poor, and it is difficult to know whether or not the diagnostic category is appropriate.

Until the middle of the twentieth century, there were various competing classificatory systems. Then, in 1952, the American Psychiatric Association endorsed the publication of the first *Diagnostic and Statistical Manual of Mental Disorders* (DSM), which introduced a standard classificatory system or taxonomy. This version of DSM was replaced by DSM-II in 1968. The most obvious problem with DSM-II was that it was extremely unreliable, in the sense that two psychiatrists would often produce very different diagnoses of the same patient. Studies on the reliability of DSM-II were reviewed by Spitzer and Fleiss (1974). They concluded that reliability reached acceptable levels only with the broad categories of mental retardation, alcoholism, and organic brain syndrome.

A central reason why DSM-II was so unreliable was because many of its definitions of symptoms were imprecise. This deficiency of DSM-II can be contrasted with its successors, DSM-III (1980) and DSM-III-R (1987), where an attempt has been made to offer more precise definitions. For example, whereas DSM-II is vague about the length of time involved in a "major depressive episode", DSM-III-R indicates that five symptoms (including either depressed mood or loss of interest or pleasure) should be present over a two-week period in order to qualify.

DSM-III and DSM-III-R also represent an improvement over earlier versions of DSM in another important way. The two versions of DSM-III both focus very much on diagnosing patients on the basis of their observable symptoms. This contrasts with DSM-I and DSM-II, in which there was much more emphasis on the supposed causes of mental disorders. In other words, there has been a shift from a theoretically based approach to one that is more descriptive. This is clearly desirable in view of the inaccuracies in the theories that were used in the construction of DSM-I and DSM-II.

The Diagnostic and Statistical Manual of Mental Disorders (III & III-R). Since DSM-III-R is currently the most widely used taxonomy of mental disorders, it is worth considering it in some detail. Its basic structure consists of five axes or dimensions which are intended to be used not only to provide diagnoses but also to assist in the planning of treatment and the prediction of outcomes (see the panel overleaf).

If a taxonomy is to be useful, it needs to be both reliable and valid. As was mentioned earlier, a taxonomy is reliable if different psychiatrists agree on patients' diagnoses. Validity is more complicated and encompasses three factors:

1. *Aetiological validity*, which is high when the aetiology or cause of a disease or disorder for those suffering from a given mental disorder is the same.
2. *Descriptive validity*, which refers to the extent to which patients in the various diagnostic categories differ from each other.
3. *Predictive validity*, concerning the extent to which the diagnostic categories in the taxonomy allow one to predict both the course and the eventual outcome of treatment.

It should be noted that reliability and validity are not entirely independent of each other, in that a taxonomy which is unreliable cannot be valid.

The Five DSM Axes

Axis I: Clinical syndromes

This axis contains a large number of clinical syndromes, such as mood disorders, anxiety disorders, sexual disorders, sleep disorders, psychoactive substance use disorders, and schizophrenia. It also includes various conditions that are not attributable to a mental disorder, but which are a focus of attention or treatment. These conditions include marital problems, occupational problems, parent–child problems, and other interpersonal problems.

Axis II: Developmental disorders and personality disorders

This axis contains various disorders that are not listed on Axis I, but which are often found in patients who are suffering from one of the Axis I disorders. The major distinguishing characteristic of the disorders listed on Axis II is that they typically start in childhood or adolescence, but continue through to adulthood. The Axis II disorders include mental retardation of varying degrees of severity, academic skills disorders, and various personality disorders (e.g. paranoid; anti-social; dependent).

Axis III: Physical disorders and conditions

Axis III consists of any medical problems that appear to be of relevance to the psychological ones which have been identified under Axis I and Axis II.

Axis IV: Psychosocial stressors

Axis IV consists of ratings of the severity of the psychosocial stressors confronting the patient. These stressors may be acute (i.e. coming sharply to a crisis) or they may reflect enduring circumstances. The ratings are carried out on a six-point scale ranging from 1 (an absence of any psychosocial stressors) to 6 (catastrophic stressors such as suicide of spouse or captivity as a hostage). There are separate scales for adults and for children and adolescents.

Axis V: Global assessment of functioning at present and during the past year

Axis V consists of an overall assessment in the areas of psychological, social, and occupational functioning. The scale runs from 1 to 90. At the low end, there may be a persistent danger of the patient severely hurting himself or others, or of a serious suicidal act with clear expectation of death. At the high end, there is a general satisfaction with life, the presence of no more than minimal symptoms (e.g. mild anxiety with good cause), involvement in a wide range of activities, and so on. One of the values of having these Axis V assessments is that patients typically return to their own previous highest level of functioning when they have recovered from their mental disorder.

Reliability. Reliability data are available for DSM-III but not for the more recent DSM-III-R. Most of the information on DSM-III is for classes of diagnosis rather than for specific diagnoses (e.g. for personality disorders as a broad category rather than for specific forms of personality disorder). It is clearly possible for two psychiatrists to agree on the broad diagnostic category for a patient, but to disagree on the specific diagnosis within that category. When reliability is assessed at the level of broad categories, then such a state of affairs would be recorded as one involving perfect reliability.

Although the reliabilities of DSM-III are higher than those of DSM-II, they are still disappointingly low. This is true of Axis I, Axis II, and Axis IV. Relatively little information is available about the reliability of Axis III, and the reliability of Axis V is reasonably good. In view of the effort that was put into making the reliability of DSM-III better than that of DSM-II, it may seem strange that diagnostic reliability is still so modest. As discussed earlier in the chapter, one general problem is that the patient's subjective reporting of his or her symptoms typically forms the basis for deciding on a diagnostic category. Such reports may be intrinsically unreliable.

Another, related, reason for the low reliability of diagnosis of mental disorders is the fact that the evidence provided to the psychiatrist or clinician by a patient is often somewhat ambiguous, and so diagnoses can be influenced by other sources of information. This was demonstrated in an interesting study by Temerlin (1970). Psychiatrists, psychologists, and clinical psychology graduate students listened to the taped interview of a man who claimed that he enjoyed his work, was happily married, and had good relationships with other people. After they had listened to the interview, they were told by a respected authority either that the man seemed neurotic but was actually "quite psychotic", or that he was quite healthy. The psychiatrists and psychologists were greatly influenced in their assessment and diagnosis by this additional information.

Validity. As we will see later in this chapter and in Chapter 6, it has proved extremely difficult to establish the aetiology or cause of most forms of mental disorder. As a consequence, it is difficult to assess the aetiological validity of DSM-III and DSM-III-R. However, the great majority of mental disorders can probably be produced by a wide range of different factors, with the precise factors involved and their relative importance varying considerably from patient to patient.

Although aetiological validity is probably rather low for most diagnostic categories, there are some partial exceptions. For example, there is reasonably convincing evidence that genetic factors play a major role in the aetiology of both schizophrenia and bipolar, or manic, depression. Even with these two disorders, however, it is not clear which environmental factors play a causal role, nor is it clear to what extent the relevant environmental factors vary from patient to patient.

There is relatively little information available on the descriptive validity of DSM-III and DSM-III-R. However, many clinicians have the distinct impression that the diagnostic categories used by these classificatory systems are not very informative. One problem is that there are symptoms that characterise patients in several different diagnostic categories. For example, anxiety is found not only in patients suffering from anxiety disorders, but also in patients with mood disorders, sexual disorders, personality disorders, and so on. Depression is another symptom that is commonly found in patients with a range of different diagnoses. This overlap of symptoms tends to blur the distinctions between diagnostic categories, and reduces descriptive validity.

So far as can be judged, the predictive validity of the diagnostic categories in DSM-III and DSM-III-R is relatively low. One way of assessing predictive validity is to investigate how effectively patients given a particular diagnosis can be treated by a single kind of therapy. In most cases, the patients who are within a given diagnostic category (e.g. schizophrenia) are rather heterogeneous or variegated, so that no single form of treatment is successful with all (or even most) of them. In addition, we know so little about the aetiology of most mental disorders that it is not entirely clear what approach to therapy should be preferred. However, the predictive validity appears to be reasonable for some diagnostic categories. For example, approximately 70% of patients with unipolar depression (distinguished from bipolar depression by the absence of mania) respond reasonably well when tricyclic anti-depressants are administered, and approximately 80% of patients with bipolar depression or manic-depressive illness benefit from the administration of the drug lithium.

Explaining mental disorders

There are two very general points that need to be emphasised in connection with the explanation of mental disorders. First, the aetiology can be explained at a number of different levels, and so it is incorrect to assume that there is a *single* explanation for each disorder. For example, the immediate cause of a mental disorder may involve altered physiological and/or psychological functioning, but there may well also be a number of additional factors which played a part in producing this altered functioning (e.g. unfavourable environmental circumstances). In other words,

a full explanation of a psychological disorder generally involves identifying a complex chain of causal events.

Second, it is often a matter of great difficulty to establish the role played
by any particular factor in the aetiology or causation of mental disorder.
For example, theorists have generally argued that environmental events
are of relevance in the development of most (or all) forms of psychopathology. However, as most adult patients have encountered hundreds or
even thousands of significant environmental events, it is an intrinsically
complex matter to decide which of these events have had an effect in
producing their psychiatric conditions.

Another reason why it is difficult to pinpoint the role of any given factor
is that it is usually impossible on practical and ethical grounds to conduct
experiments to investigate the issue. For example, Freud claimed that
adverse experiences in early childhood often play a part in the development of adult psychopathology. Perhaps the only way of providing strong
evidence in favour of this theory would be to assign children at random
to groups who were then given or not given adverse experiences! As it is,
what we have is only an *association* or *correlation* between adverse childhood experiences and adult mental disorder, and correlations do not
necessarily identify causes.

The diathesis–stress approach

In spite of the problems involved in working out the aetiology of mental
disorders, some progress has been made, as we will see in Chapter 6. Many
theorists have made use of a very general framework known as the
diathesis–stress approach. According to this approach, any given mental
disorder occurs as a joint function of a diathesis (i.e. a predisposition
towards that mental disorder) and stress (i.e. certain negative environmental events). The strict definition of diathesis limits it to a hereditary
predisposition, but in practice it is usually extended to include acquired
predisposition. Although it is assumed that both diathesis and stress must
be present for the disorder to manifest itself, the relative contributions of
diathesis and stress may vary from one individual to another. More
specifically, individuals who have a strong predisposition or diathesis
towards the disorder will need only relatively mild stress to produce the
disorder, whereas those with low vulnerability or diathesis will need
considerably more stress to produce the disorder.

The application of the diathesis–stress approach can be illustrated by
research carried out by McKeon, Roa, and Mann (1984). They investigated
patients suffering from obsessive-compulsive disorder (i.e. a condition
characterised by highly repetitive actions and negative thoughts).
McKeon et al. (1984) argued that an anxious personality was a diathesis

for this disorder, from which it follows that those patients with a highly anxious personality would require fewer stressful events than those with a non-anxious personality to succumb to the disorder. As predicted, the former group experienced only half as many stressful events as the latter group during the 12 months preceding the onset of the disorder.

Although most theorists in the field of abnormal psychology subscribe to the diathesis–stress approach, there are also considerable differences among them in their theoretical assumptions. There are at least three major models of abnormality, each with its own view of the causes of mental disorder. These are the behavioural, medical, and psychoanalytic models; they are considered in turn in the following sections of the chapter. As we will see, each model is somewhat narrow and blinkered in its approach because of the particular preconceptions and assumptions built into it. The focus here is on what the models have to say about the causes of mental disorder. Issues about the appropriateness and effectiveness of therapy based on each of these theoretical models are dealt with at some length in Chapter 7.

The behavioural model

The behaviourist school was started by Watson in 1912, and was the dominant approach to psychology for most of the next 50 years. Watson was determined to turn psychology into a scientific discipline, and he felt that psychology's previous emphasis on introspection (i.e. examination of one's own thoughts) was inappropriate. Watson favoured the study of behaviour because it was directly observable and objective in a way that introspections were not, which led him to declare that the goal of psychology should be "the prediction and control of behaviour" (Watson, 1913).

Of particular importance so far as abnormal psychology is concerned, is the behaviourists' claim that behaviour is very largely determined by the environment rather than by heredity. The reason why people behave in different ways is because they have been exposed to different environments, and so have had different learning experiences. It follows that mental disorder occurs because of maladaptive forms of behaviour which have been learned through experience. Some understanding of the environmental factors responsible for producing abnormal behaviour can be obtained by carrying out experiments in which the effects of various environmental manipulations are observed.

Behaviour therapy is the form of treatment that arose out of behaviourism. As we will see in Chapter 7, behaviour therapy is based on the assumption that appropriate manipulation of the environment can lead the clinical patient to learn to replace maladaptive behaviour with more useful kinds of behaviour. In other words, learning produces abnormal behaviour, and further learning can then eliminate that behaviour.

In terms of the diathesis–stress approach, the position of those who support the behavioural model is that mental disorder is far more a function of environmental stress than of some diathesis or predisposition. The notion that heredity might make some individuals vulnerable or predisposed to certain forms of mental disorder is inconsistent with the general environmentalist flavour of the behaviourists' approach. The evidence discussed in Chapter 6 makes it clear that heredity is of importance in the aetiology of a number of conditions, including schizophrenia and bipolar depression. Thus, the most obvious criticism of the behavioural model is that it has an extremely limited view of the factors causing mental disorder. More detailed criticisms of this approach are offered in Chapter 7.

The medical model

As we have already seen, the most important assumption of the medical or biomedical model is that mental disorders resemble physical diseases in that they are both illnesses of the body. In other words, we should approach mental disorders from the perspective of medicine.

According to the medical model, the aetiology or cause of a mental disorder should resemble that of a physical illness. One possible cause of abnormality is a germ (i.e. a micro-organism producing disease). Another possible cause lies in genetic factors, and can be investigated by considering patterns of mental disorder within families. A third possible cause of abnormality lies in the patient's biochemistry. For example, several theorists have proposed that one of the factors involved in schizophrenia is an excessive amount of dopamine in the brain. A fourth possible cause lies in *neuroanatomy* (i.e. the structure of the nervous system). For example, amnesia may occur because that part of the brain in which long-term memories are stored is easily damaged.

The medical model has obvious implications so far as treatment is concerned. If mental disorders are essentially illnesses of the body, then treatment should involve direct manipulation of bodily processes. For example, if a mental disorder is caused by biochemical abnormalities, then drugs can be used in an attempt to correct these abnormalities. As is discussed in Chapter 7, drugs have been used with some success to treat various mental disorders such as schizophrenia, anxiety disorders, and depression.

How useful is the medical model approach to abnormality? On the positive side, it has the merit of being based on well-established sciences such as medicine and biochemistry. It is clear that at least some forms of mental disorder (e.g. schizophrenia) can be understood reasonably well from the perspective of the medical model. On the negative side, it has been argued that there is only a rather loose analogy between physical and mental illnesses, and some of the relevant considerations were discussed earlier in the chapter. However, probably the greatest weakness of the medical model is that a majority of mental disorders do not appear to be caused by the germs, genetic factors, and so on, which it emphasises. Instead, the aetiology of many forms of mental disorder involves the psychological distress caused by major negative life events (e.g. divorce; loss of job).

The same weakness of the medical model is apparent in terms of treatment. Mental disorders are often treated successfully by forms of therapy that are designed to produce psychological rather than bodily changes. Advocates of the medical model point out that psychological changes almost certainly involve physiological changes as well. However, psychological rather than physiological factors seem to lie at the root of many forms of mental disorder, and it is not clear that focusing on the physiological changes at the expense of the psychological ones is a generally useful approach to therapy.

The psychoanalytic model

Sigmund Freud (1856–1939) was the founder of psychoanalysis, and is probably the most influential single individual in the entire area of abnormal psychology. The essence of his theoretical approach was that the root of mental disorder is to be found in unresolved conflicts and traumata (i.e. powerful shocks) from childhood which are locked away in the unconscious mind and so are not accessible to the conscious mind. Many adult problems can be regarded as pale reflections of these childhood conflicts. Psychoanalytic treatment involves the use of various techniques to expose these conflicts, and to provide the patient with "insight" into the ways in which these childhood conflicts are continuing to affect his or her life in an adverse fashion.

A neat encapsulation of the psychoanalytic model was provided by Wachtel (1977; cited by Davison & Neale, 1986):

> The patient's neurosis is seen as deriving most essentially from his continuing and unsuccessful efforts to deal with internalized residues of his past which, by virtue of being isolated from his adaptive and integrated ego (i.e. conscious self), continue to make primitive demands wholly unresponsive to reality. It is therefore maintained that a fully successful treatment must create conditions whereby these anachronistic

DESPITE THE DOCTOR'S ENCOURAGEMENT, WALLY FELT THAT THERE HAD TO BE A BETTER WAY TO RESTORE HIS SELF-CONFIDENCE.

(i.e. belonging to a different time) inclinations can be experienced consciously and integrated into the ego, so that they can be controlled and modified (p. 36).

What is the relationship between the psychoanalytic model and the diathesis–stress approach? Basically, Freud claimed that an acquired diathesis or predisposition resulting from childhood experiences was of central importance in the aetiology of mental disorder, and he minimised the role of the other factors (i.e. inherited diathesis or predisposition and stress).

A great weakness of the psychoanalytic model as put forward by Freud was his relative lack of interest in the current problems that his patients were facing. Even if childhood experiences stored in the unconscious play a part in the development of mental disorders, that does not mean that adult experiences can safely be ignored. However, it should be pointed out that many psychoanalytically oriented clinicians who followed in Freud's footsteps did recognise that the current situation needs to be considered fully in treatment.

The psychoanalytic approach has been criticised repeatedly because of the lack of scientific evidence concerning its major theoretical assumptions. Freud's theories tend to be very complicated and extremely difficult to test scientifically. As a consequence, many psychologists have argued that the psychoanalytic model should not be taken seriously.

Evaluation of the three models

The behavioural, medical, and psychoanalytic models have all been of major significance in the development of ideas about the description, explanation, and treatment of mental disorders. Each approach presents a reasonably coherent account of the factors responsible for causing mental disorders, and each is associated with its own distinctive form of treatment. The behavioural model led to the development of behaviour therapy; the medical model led to drug and other somatic (i.e. of the body) therapies; and the psychoanalytic model led to classical psychoanalysis and to more contemporary psychoanalytically oriented therapies. A detailed evaluation of the relative merits of the three models must await the discussion of these forms of therapy in Chapter 7. However, it is possible here to consider them at a rather general level.

These three models can be understood in terms of the diathesis–stress approach. That approach can be regarded as allowing for three major causal influences on mental disorder:

- a genetically determined diathesis or predisposition;
- an environmentally determined diathesis or predisposition; and
- environmentally determined stress or negative life events.

At the risk of over-simplification, the medical model emphasises the causal influence of a genetically determined diathesis; the psychoanalytic model focuses on an environmentally determined diathesis; and the behavioural model emphasises environmentally determined stress. As it is highly probable that all three factors actually play a role in the development of mental disorder, it is clear that all of the models are unduly limited in terms of the factors which they identify as important.

The therapies associated with the three models are also limited, in that their primary focus is on only some of the factors involved in mental disorder. For example, behaviour therapists and psychoanalysts typically do not consider the possibility that part of a patient's problems may stem from biochemical abnormalities; and behaviour therapists and somatic therapists do not investigate the possible role of childhood events in causing and maintaining mental disorder. An implication is that therapists should not be too constrained by the assumptions underlying the form of therapy that they are practising. Fortunately, it appears that therapists themselves have the same idea. Far more therapists than one might imagine describe themselves as "eclectics", meaning that they are perfectly willing to incorporate elements of different kinds of therapy in order to produce improvement in the patient.

Summary: Approaches to abnormality

- The concept of "abnormality" is imprecise and consequently difficult to define. One approach is to argue that there are several features of behaviour that can suggest abnormality. The more of these features that are present, the more confident we can be that the behaviour is, indeed, abnormal.
- Among the features that can be used to identify abnormality are: suffering; maladaptiveness; vividness and unconventionality; unpredictability and loss of control; irrationality and incomprehensibility; and observer discomfort. Drawbacks of some of these features are that they depend on subjective judgements and people who are simply non-conformist can be mistaken for abnormal.
- Some theorists have argued that calling patients abnormal and attaching psychiatric labels to them may be an unwise thing to do. Other people may treat the labelled individuals as if they were mad, and this can have the effect of creating new symptoms in those individuals. Still others claim that mental illness is so different from physical illness that adopting the medical model and introducing diagnostic systems is inappropriate.
- Most theorists, however, argue that it is extremely important to develop a reliable and valid classificatory system or taxonomy for mental illnesses. Most taxonomies are based on syndromes, which are sets of symptoms generally found together. The most recent systematic attempt to provide such a taxonomy is the revised version of the third *Diagnostic and Statistical Manual of Mental Disorders*. It represents a significant improvement over previous classificatory systems, but still suffers from relatively low reliability, aetiological validity, descriptive validity, and outcome validity.
- It has proved difficult to establish the causes or aetiology of most mental disorders. There are various reasons for this. Most disorders have multiple causes, and environmental events are so numerous that it is hard to isolate those that influence the development of mental disorders. Many theorists subscribe to the diathesis–stress approach, according to which mental disorders arise due to the combined influence of some predisposition or diathesis and stress in the form of negative environmental events.

- There are three major models or approaches to abnormal psychology, and they differ in terms of which aspect of the diathesis–stress approach they emphasise. The behavioural model is based on the assumption that stressful environmental events can lead to maladaptive learning, and so treatment involves new learning designed to promote adaptive habits. The medical model assumes that genetic factors producing a predisposition or diathesis exert a causal influence in the development of many kinds of mental disorder, and that these genetic influences often produce biochemical abnormalities. The psychoanalytic model also assumes that predispositions play an important role in the aetiology of mental disorder, but the main predispositions are claimed to stem from conflicts and traumatic events of childhood. The available evidence suggests that the factors identified by the three major models are all important in the aetiology of mental disorder. However, each model is somewhat narrow in its outlook, and this leads advocates of each model to ignore important aetiological factors.

Further reading

There are several textbooks of abnormal psychology which give more detailed coverage of the various approaches to abnormality than can be provided here. A readable book of this type is G.C. Davison and J.M. Neale (1990), *Abnormal psychology: An experimental clinical approach* (Fifth Edition) (Chichester: Wiley). Comprehensive coverage of the topics discussed in this chapter is also available in D.L. Rosenhan and M.E.P. Seligman (1989), *Abnormal psychology* (Second Edition) (London: Norton).

Forms of psychopathology 6

As we saw in Chapter 5, the most commonly used classificatory system or taxonomy for psychiatric diagnosis is the *Diagnostic and Statistical Manual of Mental Disorders* (DSM-III-R). It describes a substantial number of different forms of mental disorder or psychopathology, and it would clearly be impossible to do justice to them all in a single chapter. Accordingly, our coverage will be selective, and will focus on discussing a range of different mental disorders.

Although it is not officially recognised within DSM-III-R, the distinction between psychoses and neuroses is of relevance to our coverage in this chapter. Those suffering from *psychosis* have such severe disturbances of emotion and thinking that they are out of touch with reality, whereas sufferers from *neurosis* experience very high levels of anxiety but are in reasonable contact with reality. Schizophrenia and bipolar depression (or manic-depression) are two of the major forms of psychosis, and the anxiety disorders are prevalent forms of neurosis.

In addition to neuroses and psychoses, this chapter also deals with some of the major personality disorders. Children resemble adults in that they can suffer from mental disorder, and some of the more common forms of childhood disorder are discussed. In general, those disorders that are the focus of discussion are those about which most is known.

Schizophrenia

Schizophrenia is an extremely serious psychopathological condition, and it has proved difficult to treat. The term *schizophrenia* comes from two Greek words: *schizo* meaning "split" and *phrene* meaning "mind". This has led to the popular (but mistaken) view that schizophrenics are suffering from split or multiple personalities.

Symptoms

Approximately 1% of the population becomes schizophrenic at some point in their lives. The symptoms they exhibit vary somewhat, but typically include problems with attention, thinking, social relationships, motivation, and emotion. According to DSM-III-R, the criteria for schizophrenia include:

- onset before the age of 45;
- symptoms that last for at least six months;
- gross impairment of reality testing; and
- marked deterioration in several different psychological processes.

Schizophrenics generally have confused thinking, and often suffer from *delusions*. Many of these delusions involve what are known as "ideas of reference", in which the schizophrenic patient attaches great personal significance to external objects or events. Thus, for example, a schizophrenic seeing his neighbours talking may be convinced that they are hatching a plot to kill him. This is an example of a delusion of persecution. Sometimes schizophrenics imagine that they are someone important or famous, such as Napoleon or Alexander the Great; such beliefs are known as delusions of grandeur.

At the social level, schizophrenics generally have very poor relationships with other people. There is a progressive withdrawal from interaction with others. This plays a part in the more general loss of contact with reality that characterises schizophrenia.

" DO WE <u>HAVE</u> TO GO THROUGH THIS EVERY TIME WE COME HERE?…"

Schizophrenics also often suffer from *hallucinations*. Whereas delusions arise from mistaken interpretations of actual objects and events, hallucinations occur in the absence of any external stimulus. Most of the hallucinations experienced by schizophrenic patients consist of voices, usually saying something of personal relevance to the patient. An interesting study by McGuigan (1966) suggested that these auditory hallucinations occur because patients mistake their own inner speech for someone else's voice. The evidence for this was that the patient's larynx was often active during the time that the auditory hallucination was being experienced.

In severe cases of schizophrenia there are often great disorders at the motivational and emotional levels. Many patients appear to be almost totally lacking both motivation and emotion, sitting around listlessly with expressionless faces and talking in a bored and monotonous way. Some schizophrenic patients are highly sensitive emotionally during the early stages of the disorder, but this is generally replaced by apathy later on.

Finally, there are some schizophrenic patients whose behaviour is even more different from that of normal individuals. Perhaps the most common behavioural abnormality is the tendency to remain almost entirely motionless for hours at a time. Some patients make strange grimaces or repeat an odd gesture over and over again.

You may be somewhat bewildered by the disparate set of symptoms that characterise schizophrenia. If schizophrenia is genuinely a single psychiatric disorder, then it might be possible to find an underlying psychological condition of which these symptoms are all visible effects. Possibilities include the following:

1. Schizophrenic symptoms may revolve around subjects' inability to focus their attention and the over-stimulation that results. Unfocused attention could certainly explain the schizophrenic's incoherent patterns of thought, and over-stimulation may play a part in the schizophrenic's withdrawal from social contact.
2. More speculatively, the immobility of some schizophrenics may represent a desperate attempt to prevent the level of stimulation from becoming excessive.
3. The hallucinations experienced by schizophrenic patients may occur when their attention shifts rapidly from their internal thoughts to the external environment without them registering the shift.

It is very important to note that there are various types of schizophrenia, which are characterised by different patterns of symptoms. DSM-III-R identifies five types as follows: paranoid; catatonic; disorganised; residual; and undifferentiated (see panel below).

It is also possible to categorise patients into Type I and Type II schizophrenia:

- Type I schizophrenia is characterised by the presence of positive symptoms such as delusions and hallucinations.
- Type II schizophrenia, in contrast, is characterised by negative symptoms involving a marked reduction in emotional and motivational responsiveness, and by very limited speech.

One reason why the distinction appears to be important is because it is generally much easier to treat the positive symptoms of Type I schizophrenia than the negative symptoms of Type II schizophrenia.

Causes of schizophrenia

As with most other forms of psychopathology, there are several different factors that play a part in the aetiology or causation of schizophrenia. These will be considered in turn.

Genetic factors.   There is reasonably strong evidence that schizophrenia has an hereditary basis. Much of the relevant evidence comes from the study of twins, one of whom is known to be schizophrenic. What is the

Five types of schizophrenia identified in DSM-III-R.

Type of schizophrenia	Typical symptoms
Paranoid	Delusions of persecution and/or grandeur
Catatonic	Shifts between wildly agitated behaviour and almost complete immobility for hours at a time
Disorganised	Bizarre and silly behaviour. Sufferers will often express totally inappropriate emotions (e.g. laughing loudly for no apparent reason)
Residual	Extremely poor personal hygiene, apathy, inappropriate emotions, and social isolation
Undifferentiated	Undifferentiated schizophrenics do not seem to belong to any of the other categories

probability that the other twin is also schizophrenic—a state of affairs known as *concordance*? The concordance rate averaged over several studies was found to be 44% when the twins were monozygotic or identical, but was only 9% when the twins were dizygotic or fraternal and of the same sex (Rosenthal, 1970). As monozygotic twins are essentially the same genetically, whereas dizygotic twins are no more alike than any two siblings, the implication of these findings is that there is a substantial genetic basis to schizophrenia.

This conclusion is supported by a number of adoption studies. The children of schizophrenic mothers who were taken for adoption very soon after birth were much more likely to become schizophrenic in adult life than were adopted children who were born to normal mothers (Heston, 1966).

If there is a genetic basis to schizophrenia, then it must manifest itself in some way (e.g. via biochemical abnormalities). One possibility is that the brain neurons of schizophrenic patients are unduly sensitive to a chemical neurotransmitter known as *dopamine*. The evidence is discussed at greater length in Chapter 7, but it is appropriate here to refer to one of the main successes of the dopamine hypothesis. There are drugs known as *phenothiazines* which block dopamine, and so should theoretically have a beneficial effect on schizophrenic symptoms. This effect has been obtained numerous times. However, recent evidence indicates that the phenothiazines have much more effect on Type I than on Type II schizophrenia, which suggests that the dopamine hypothesis is only a partial explanation.

Many Type II schizophrenics suffer from abnormalities in brain structure rather than biochemical disturbances. For example, the brain ventricles or cavities of some schizophrenics are much larger than those of normal individuals. This increased ventricle size is more noticeable in the left hemisphere of the brain than in the right hemisphere (Losonczy et al., 1986). The precise effects of ventricular enlargement are not known as yet.

Environmental factors.   The finding that schizophrenia sometimes has a genetic basis does not mean that environmental factors are irrelevant. If schizophrenia were entirely determined by genetic factors, and if different psychiatrists adopted the same criteria for a diagnosis of schizophrenia, then the concordance rate for identical twins would be 100%. As it is actually only approximately 44%, there are probably several environmental factors which contribute to the development of schizophrenia.

Some theorists who believe that environmental factors are important have argued that abnormal and inadequate patterns of communication exist within the families of schizophrenic patients. For example, Bateson,

Jackson, Haley, and Weakland (1956) proposed a double-bind theory, according to which the members of families of schizophrenics tend to communicate in a destructively ambiguous fashion (e.g. the mother will tell her child that she loves him, but in a tone of voice that is not indicative of love). The double-bind theory represents an interesting attempt to account for the confused thinking of schizophrenic patients, but it suffers from the serious problem that little or none of the relevant evidence supports it.

In spite of the failure of the double-bind theory, it is nevertheless the case that the families of schizophrenics do tend to be characterised by deficient interpersonal communication. Mischler and Waxler (1968) discovered that mothers talking to their schizophrenic daughters were rather aloof and unresponsive. This might suggest that each mother's aloofness was at least partially responsible for her daughter's schizophrenia. However, the same mothers behaved in a much more normal, responsive fashion when talking to their normal daughters. Thus, it may be the presence of a schizophrenic patient in a family that causes poor communication patterns rather than the other way around.

Rather different environmental factors were identified by Laing (1967). He argued that schizophrenia occurs largely because of society's failure to tolerate non-conformity and independence of spirit among its members. In other words, schizophrenia is caused by the schizophrenic's attempts to struggle with a mad society. Laing contrasted the self-deceptions and blinkered thinking of those regarded as normal members of society with the greater awareness of schizophrenics. He suggested that many schizophrenics are engaged on an exciting "voyage of discovery", in which they attempt to come to a fuller understanding of their inner beings.

Some of Laing's views seem to be of more value than others. It may well be the case that a lack of sympathetic understanding from society often exacerbates the symptoms of schizophrenia. However, those who have recovered from schizophrenia generally claim that they felt entirely miserable and unhappy while suffering from schizophrenia, and vehemently deny that it was anything like an exciting voyage of discovery.

Depression

Depression is the most common form of mental disorder. It is characterised by:

- great sadness;
- reduced involvement in (and enjoyment of) social activities, etc.;

- feelings of helplessness; and
- listlessness.

There is a distinction in DSM-III-R between major depression (sometimes called unipolar depression) and bipolar depression (or manic-depression). Patients with bipolar depression experience both depression and mania (a mood state involving elation, talkativeness, and unwarranted high self-esteem). In contrast, patients with major or unipolar depression experience depression but not mania. Approximately 10% of men and 20% of women become clinically depressed at some time in their lives, with over 90% of them suffering from unipolar rather than bipolar depression.

Unipolar depression

The main distinction among depressive disorders is between major or unipolar depression and bipolar depression. However, it is not the only important distinction. For example, DSM-III-R draws a distinction between long-lasting or chronic depression (termed *dysthymia*) and the much more prevalent episodic depression, which lasts for under two years.

What are the factors responsible for clinical depression? According to Beck (e.g. Beck & Clark, 1988), cognitive structures and processes play an important role. As a result of severe problems and losses, an individual may develop negative schemata or cognitive structures concerning himself or herself, the world, and the future. These schemata lead to distorted and unduly pessimistic thought-processes, and make that individual vulnerable to depression. This theory probably possesses some validity, but the key problem is to establish causality: does negative thinking cause depression, or does depression cause negative thinking? Some evidence suggesting that negative thinking is *not* a cause of depression was obtained by Lewinsohn, Steinmetz, Larsen, and Franklin (1981). They discovered that those who were soon to become depressed, "did not subscribe to irrational beliefs, they did not have lower expectancies for positive outcomes or higher expectancies for negative outcomes...nor did they perceive themselves as having less control over the events in their lives" (p. 218).

There is plenty of evidence to suggest that depressed people have experienced more stressful life events than non-depressed people in the period preceding the onset of depression. For example, Brown and Harris (1978) carried out an interview study on women in London. They discovered that 61% of the depressed women had experienced a very stressful life event in the nine months before the interview, compared with only

25% of non-depressed women. However, many women manage to cope with major stresses without becoming clinically depressed. Of those women who experienced a serious life event, 37% of those without an intimate friend became depressed against only 10% of those who did have a very close friend.

In addition to environmental factors, there are clear suggestions that genetic factors play a role in the causation or aetiology of unipolar depression. Allen (1976) reviewed the relevant twin studies, and reported that the concordance rate was approximately 40% for identical twins compared with only 11% for fraternal twins. Although these findings indicate that genetic factors are involved, the fact that the concordance rate for identical twins is considerably lower than 100% means that environmental factors are of great importance. It has also been found (Wender et al., 1986) that the natural or biological relatives of adopted sufferers from unipolar depression are approximately eight times more likely than adoptive relatives to have had unipolar depression themselves.

If genetic factors are important, it then becomes necessary to try to identify the physiological processes involved. Some headway was made when it was discovered approximately 40 years ago that two groups of drugs known as the "monoamine oxidase (MAO) inhibitors" and the "tricylics" were effective in alleviating the symptoms of depression (see Chapter 7 for more details). Because both groups of drugs seem to increase the levels of *serotonin* and *noradrenaline*—both of which are *neurotransmitters*—it was proposed that low levels of these neurotransmitters might play a role in the development of depression. However, there is a great problem with this simple theory. Although MAO inhibitors and the tricylics do initially raise the levels of serotonin and noradrenaline, the raised levels gradually disappear with continued administration of these drugs. An alternative view which appears to be in better accord with the evidence is that the drugs allow serotonin and noradrenaline to be used more effectively in the brains of depressed patients.

Bipolar depression

We saw earlier that bipolar depression is a clinical condition in which there are mood swings between mania and depression. It is tempting, but probably wrong, to assume that the bipolar depressive in a manic state is at the opposite extreme to depression. In fact, patients in a manic state often experience great irritability, and can be reduced to tears if thwarted. Thus, negative mood states can form part of a manic episode. A depressed or manic episode typically lasts for somewhere between a few days and several months. These episodes often become worse during the first few years of the disorder, but tend to reduce gradually thereafter. However, bipolar depression is such a severe condition that a significant proportion of sufferers from it commit suicide.

What are the factors responsible for bipolar depression? There is reasonably strong evidence to indicate that genetic factors are important. Twin studies were reviewed by Allen (1976). The concordance rate for bipolar depression was considerably higher in identical twins than in fraternal twins (72% and 14%, respectively). The view that genetic factors are involved in bipolar depression is supported by adoption studies as well. For example, it has been found with adopted children who subsequently developed bipolar depression that their natural parents were more likely than their adoptive parents to have suffered from clinical depression (e.g. Mendlewicz & Rainer, 1977).

The fact that the concordance rate for bipolar depression is well below 100% suggests that environmental factors are also important. The presence of major life changes can certainly increase the mood swings observed in bipolar depression, and it may also play a part in its aetiology (see Davison & Neale, 1990).

Anxiety disorders

According to DSM-III-R, there are a number of different anxiety disorders in adults. They include panic disorder, various forms of phobia, obsessive-compulsive disorder, post-traumatic stress disorder, and generalised anxiety disorder. This section of the chapter will be devoted to a consideration of some of these.

Phobias

Phobias involve a high level of fear of some object or situation, with the fear being sufficiently strong that the object or situation is avoided whenever possible. The most common form of phobia so far as seeking treatment is concerned is agoraphobia (a fear of open spaces). Approximately half of all phobics seen clinically are agoraphobics. The great majority of agoraphobics report fear of enclosed spaces and of heights as well as of open spaces. An interesting aspect of agoraphobia is that at least three-quarters of those suffering from it are women.

Other relatively common forms of phobia are claustrophobia (a fear of enclosed spaces) and social phobia (a fear of social situations and of being evaluated by others). Approximately 6 or 7% of the population suffers from phobias, but it is important to note that some phobias are much more disruptive of everyday life than are others. The three phobias mentioned already are usually very disabling, whereas snake or spider phobias may have a negligible impact on the phobic's enjoyment of life.

Conditioning explanation.   Where do phobias come from? It is probable that they can occur for various different reasons. According to some behaviourists, phobias develop through two kinds of conditioning. First, a neutral or conditioned stimulus can come to produce fear if, on several occasions, it is presented at the same time as an unpleasant or unconditioned stimulus. For example, John Watson and Rosalie Rayner (1920) found that a little boy became frightened of a rat when the sight of the rat was paired with a loud noise. The fear that was then produced by the previously neutral stimulus (i.e. a rat) could be reduced by avoiding it. Such avoidance involves *operant conditioning*, because the reduction in fear that occurs is rewarding.

There are various problems with this conditioning account of the origins of phobias. First, it has been found (e.g. Keuthen, 1980) that only half of all phobics can remember any highly unpleasant experiences in the feared situation. Second, although the study by Watson and Rayner (1920) is often cited as providing strong evidence that phobias can develop through classical conditioning, it has actually proved rather difficult to repeat their findings. Most laboratory studies have obtained little or no evidence that people can be conditioned to fear neutral stimuli by pairing them with unpleasant ones (see Davison & Neale, 1990, for details).

Third, if phobias develop because of accidental pairings of a neutral and a fearful stimulus, then people could become phobic about almost anything. In fact, however, many more people have phobias about spiders and snakes than about cars, in spite of the fact that most people have seen considerably more cars than either spiders or snakes. Seligman (1971) argued that the objects and situations forming the basis of most phobias were genuine sources of danger hundreds or thousands of years ago, and only those individuals who were sensitive to such objects and situations were favoured by evolution. In other words, there is a "preparedness" (a physiological predisposition) to be sensitive to, and become phobic about, certain stimuli rather than others.

In spite of the limitations of the behaviourist approach to phobias, it is still probably the dominant account of the way in which phobias develop. Part of the reason for this concerns the effectiveness of forms of treatment for phobias based on behaviourist principles. As we will see in Chapter 7, systematic desensitisation and flooding are two forms of behaviour therapy which have been used to cure thousands of phobic patients.

Genetic involvement.   Many people are exposed at one time or another to situations that would appear to be conducive to the development of a phobia, but most of them do not subsequently become phobic. The fact that some people seem resistant to becoming phobic whereas others do not suggests that there are individual differences in the susceptibility to phobia, and these individual differences may have a genetic basis. This approach is very different to the behaviourist approach, with its emphasis on environmental events rather than on characteristics of the individual.

There is some limited evidence to support the view that genetic factors play a part in the development of phobias. Harris, Noyes, Crowe, and Chaudhry (1983) discovered that the close relatives of agoraphobic patients were more likely to be suffering from agoraphobia than were the close relatives of non-anxious normal individuals. Torgersen (1983) considered pairs of identical and fraternal twins, at least one of whom was agoraphobic. The other twin was more likely also to be agoraphobic in identical twins than in fraternal twins. As identical twins are essentially the same genetically but fraternal twins are no more similar genetically than any two siblings, these findings are consistent with the view that genetic factors play a part in the aetiology of phobias.

Unfortunately, there are problems with interpreting these findings, especially those of Harris et al. (1983). The close relative of an agoraphobic patient may tend to become agoraphobic simply because he or she imitates the behaviour displayed by the patient, rather than because of genetic inheritance. In view of these considerations, it is entirely possible that the great majority of phobias develop as a result of environmental experiences with the phobic stimuli, and that genetic factors play only a marginal aetiological role.

Panic disorder

Panic disorder is a condition in which the patient experiences extremely frightening panic attacks. These attacks are characterised by:

- extreme fear;
- thoughts that there may be a loss of control; and
- several physical symptoms (e.g. pains in the chest, shortness of breath, dizziness).

According to DSM-III-R, a patient must have at least four panic attacks within a one-month period in order to be regarded as suffering from panic disorder. Each attack typically lasts for several minutes. Panic attacks differ from the anxiety experienced by phobic patients in that there is no obvious stimulus that triggers off panic attacks. However, there are clear links with agoraphobia, because many patients who suffer from panic disorder also suffer from agoraphobia.

There is evidence indicating that genetic factors play a part in the development of panic disorder. Torgersen (1983) investigated identical and fraternal twins in which at least one member of each pair was suffering from panic disorder or from agoraphobia with panic disorder. The concordance rate was 31% for identical twins against 0% for fraternal twins. Further support for the notion that panic disorder can be accounted for by the medical model was obtained by Liebowitz et al. (1985). They discovered that sodium lactate infusions produced panic attacks in approximately 75% of panic disorder patients, but in not more than 20% of patients with other anxiety disorders.

Further evidence that panic disorder can be regarded as a disease of the body was obtained by Nesse et al. (1984). They found evidence that patients with panic disorder have relatively inefficient *adrenergic functioning*. It may be that this inefficiency is one of the factors involved in producing panic attacks.

Although genetic factors clearly play a part in the aetiology of panic disorder, the fact that the concordance rate for identical twins is markedly less than 100% means that environmental factors are probably more important than genetic ones. There is reasonably strong evidence of the involvement of environmental factors. For example, patients have often experienced more life events than usual in the months preceding the onset of panic disorder (see Davison & Neale, 1990).

It has been suggested (e.g. by Beck & Emery, 1985) that panic disorder can be viewed as a cognitive malfunctioning. One suggestive piece of evidence is that panic attacks are frequently accompanied by catastrophic thoughts about death or severe disease (Hibbert, 1984). According to Beck and Emery (1985), panic disorder patients suffer from panic attacks because they *misinterpret* the symptoms of anxiety (e.g. dizziness) as the warning signs of disaster (e.g. a heart attack). On this line of argument, the reason why sodium lactate infusions lead to panic attacks is because they produce some of the bodily symptoms of anxiety, which are then misinterpreted by panic disorder patients.

The cognitive view of panic disorder has gained support from the results of cognitive therapy, in which the patient is trained not to misinterpret his or her bodily symptoms. In the initial stages of therapy the patient is required to over-breathe into a bag; this produces a shortness of breath and often induces a panic attack. The patient learns that the symptoms associated with over-breathing are typically caused by stress rather than by the presence of imminent disaster. This form of therapy has proved extremely successful.

At present, it is not clear whether panic disorder is better regarded from the medical or from the cognitive perspective. Perhaps in the long run it will turn out that a theory combining elements of the two perspectives will prove more fruitful than either perspective on its own.

Obsessive-compulsive disorder

Obsessive-compulsive disorder often starts in early adulthood. It consists of a mixture of *obsessions* (i.e. intrusive, irrational thoughts which keep recurring) and *compulsions* (i.e. repetitive, stereotyped rituals). For example, someone with obsessive-compulsive disorder may have repeated obsessional thoughts about personal cleanliness, and these thoughts lead the individual to spend several hours a day washing himself or herself. Rachman and Hodgson (1980) carried out a questionnaire survey, and discovered that most of the compulsions of patients with obsessive-compulsive disorder revolve around either cleaning or checking. Their compulsions differ from those of compulsive drinkers, gamblers, and so on, in that they provide no pleasure at all.

Relatively little is known about the aetiology or causation of obsessive-compulsive disorder. However, Carey and Gottesman (1981) found that the concordance rate for the disorder was greater among identical than fraternal twins, which suggests that genetic factors play a role. The fact that many of the identical twins were not concordant means that environmental factors must be important, but it has not proved possible to identify them. Rachman and Hodgson (1980) have argued that obsessions occur because they cause anxiety, and the anxiety makes it more difficult to eliminate the obsessional thought. They also argued that compulsions occur because they serve to reduce the anxiety created by the obsessional thought.

It is possible that technological advances will increase our understanding of obsessive-compulsive neurosis. A brain-imaging technique known as the PET scan has revealed differences between obsessive-compulsive disorder patients and normal *controls* (Baxter et al., 1987). The patients show greater activity in the orbital gyrus, which may be involved in ignoring unwanted stimuli. They also show enhanced activity in the caudate nuclei, which may be involved in repetitive behaviour.

It has proved difficult to find suitable forms of treatment for the disorder. Perhaps the most promising approach comes from behaviour therapy and involves a combination of *flooding* and *response prevention* (see Rachman & Hodgson, 1980; see also Chapter 7). Consider a patient who is obsessed with personal cleanliness. Flooding might involve covering the patient all over with dirt, and response prevention would involve preventing the patient from taking steps to remove the dirt. The intention is that the patient should learn that ignoring personal cleanliness does not produce any disastrous consequences. This form of treatment is very unpleasant for the patient, but the success rate is encouraging.

Personality disorders

Many forms of mental disorder occur, at least in part, because of specific highly stressful life events. As a consequence, there are reasonable prospects of recovery provided that the patient can adjust to the adverse effects of those life events on his or her life. In contrast, the personality disorders are (as the term implies) primarily due to the patient concerned having the kind of personality that makes satisfactory adjustment difficult.

DSM-III-R lists a total of 12 categories of personality disorders. Some of these personality disorders (e.g. schizoid; schizotypal; paranoid) are similar to a mild form of schizophrenia, whereas others reflect different kinds of exaggerated and maladaptive modes of behaviour (e.g. avoidant; dependent; passive–aggressive; histrionic). The status of most of these personality disorders is a matter of some controversy. There are various reasons for this:

1. The reliability of diagnosis is generally rather low, and sometimes unacceptable.
2. Related to the first point, several of the personality disorders obviously resemble other diagnostic categories. For example, there is a clear overlap between obsessional-compulsive personality and obsessive-compulsive disorder.
3. It is assumed that individuals suffering from personality disorders show consistently abnormal personality characteristics over long periods of time. However, as we saw in Chapter 3, there are doubts as to whether personality really is consistent over time and across situations. Moreover, we often have insufficient evidence to be confident that a patient allegedly suffering from a personality disorder has actually been behaving in his or her current fashion for several years.

The personality disorder that has been studied in most detail is what used to be known as psychopathy or sociopathy, but which is referred to by DSM-III-R as "anti-social personality disorder". In view of the greater available knowledge of anti-social personality than of the other personality disorders, we will focus on it here.

Anti-social personality disorder

Patients suffering from anti-social personality disorder not only behave in a callous and insensitive way towards other people, but they also exhibit strikingly little remorse or concern at the effects that their anti-social behaviour has on other people. In a nutshell, those with anti-social personality disorder inflict much suffering on others, but do not appear to suffer themselves.

It is difficult to capture some of these aspects of anti-social personality disorder in objective terms, and so DSM-III-R makes use of relatively straightforward behavioural measures as criteria for the diagnosis. First, the anti-social behaviour should have gone on for several years, and should have started before the age of 15. Second, there must be at least four different categories of anti-social behaviour in the recent actions of the patient being diagnosed. These categories include irresponsible parenting, repeated aggressiveness, recklessness that endangers others, and repeated lying.

One of the peculiar features of patients with anti-social personality disorder is that much of their criminal and other anti-social behaviour does not seem to make any real sense, even to them. Consider, for example, the case of Gary Gilmore. He was the first person since 1966 to be executed in the United States of America. This is how he described one of the murders he committed: "I told the service station guy to give me all his money. I then took him to the bathroom and told him to kneel down and then I shot him in the head twice. The guy didn't give me any trouble but I just felt like I had to do it."

Causal factors.   Where does anti-social personality disorder come from? One possibility which has attracted much interest is that it has a genetic basis. Most of the studies we will discuss have investigated criminality rather than anti-social personality disorder. Although many patients with anti-social personality disorder are also criminals, it needs to be borne in mind that criminality is not synonymous with anti-social personality disorder.

Christiansen (1977) reviewed twin studies on criminality. He noted that when one identical twin was a criminal, there was a 69% probability that the other twin was as well (this is known as the concordance rate). The corresponding concordance rate for same-sex dizygotic or fraternal twins was only 33%. As identical twins share the same heredity, whereas fraternal twins have no more genetic similarity than ordinary siblings, these data are consistent with the view that there are genetic influences on criminality (and presumably on anti-social personality disorder). However, there are two reasons for caution in interpreting these data. First, the environments experienced by identical twins may be more similar than those experienced by fraternal twins. Second, the fact that the concordance rate for identical twins is substantially below 100% suggests that environmental factors are also important.

"...THAT'S BETTER...FIRST DAY ON THE JOB, SON...GOTTA LOOK SMART..."

Further evidence that genetic factors play a part in producing criminality comes from Danish research on boys who had been adopted at an early age. Mednick, Gabrielli, and Hutchings (1984) discovered that boys whose adoptive father had committed a crime were no more likely to become criminal offenders than were those whose adoptive father had not. However, there was a greatly increased probability that the boy would go on to commit a crime if the biological father had a criminal record, even if the adoptive father did not. Finally, there was an even greater probability that a boy would become a criminal if both his biological and adoptive father were criminals. This last finding strongly indicates that heredity and environment both play a role in criminality.

If there are genetic factors involved in criminality and anti-social personality, then it is probably worthwhile to look for physiological differences between them and normal individuals. Although it is not easy to interpret the findings, a number of such physiological differences have been found. For example, it appears from electroencephalograms (EEG) that almost half of those with anti-social personality disorder have short bursts of brain-wave activity known as "positive spiking", compared with a much lower figure of approximately 1 or 2% of normals (Kurland, Yeager, & Arthur, 1963). This positive spiking may well indicate unusual functioning in the limbic system, which plays an important role in emotion and motivation.

There is evidence that the childhood environment of those who subsequently develop anti-social personality disorder is often rather different from that of other children. Parental deprivation through separation or divorce is a common childhood feature of those who later exhibit anti-social behaviour (e.g. Oltman & Friedman, 1967). However, parental deprivation through physical illness or death of a parent does not seem to be associated with the development of anti-social behaviour. These findings suggest that it is not really parental deprivation as such that is responsible, but rather the emotional insecurity produced by the rows and other disturbing events preceding divorce or separation.

The fact that most people with anti-social personality disorder are constantly getting into trouble suggests that they are very poor at learning from experience. However, they are often reasonably intelligent and good at many kinds of learning (e.g. school work). What appears to be the case is that they are generally rather unaffected by punishment, and this prevents them from learning to avoid those forms of behaviour (e.g. criminal acts) that are punished. This unresponsiveness to punishment was shown by Hare (1965). The numbers 1 to 12 were presented in sequence, with the subjects having been told beforehand that an electric shock would be given when the number 8 was reached. The galvanic skin response (GSR), which is an indirect measure of sweating on the palm of the hand, was recorded to provide an indication of the level of anxiety. Not surprisingly, normal individuals and criminals not having an anti-social personality showed mounting anxiety as the numbers increased up to 8. In contrast, criminals with an anti-social personality disorder showed very little increase in anxiety, and were even relatively unaffected by the electric shock itself.

In summary, there are several factors involved in the development of anti-social personality disorder. There is clearly a genetic component, and this may operate by influencing the functioning of those parts of the brain involved in emotion and motivation. On the environmental side, the stress caused by the disintegration of their parents' marriage appears to be a major influence on the development of anti-social behaviour. Perhaps these genetic and environmental influences together produce the lack of responsiveness to punishment which makes it very difficult to stop the anti-social behaviour from occurring.

Childhood disorders

According to DSM-III-R, there are several types of childhood disorder. One major category is that of developmental disorders, which include mental retardation of varying degrees of severity, more specific learning disorders (e.g. developmental arithmetic disorder), and autism (a condition characterised by extreme lack of social responsiveness). Another major category is that of disruptive behaviour disorders. This category includes sub-categories referring to hyperactivity, solitary aggressive behaviour, and defiant behaviour. Among the other major categories are anxiety disorders, eating disorders (e.g. anorexia nervosa), gender identity disorders, in which a child wants to be a member of the opposite sex, and elimination disorders (e.g. bed-wetting).

There are a number of complexities associated with the diagnosis of childhood disorders which make it even more difficult to arrive at an accurate diagnosis with children than with adults. First, children (and especially younger children) often lack the language skills to express their problems in a clear fashion. That means that the decision to seek treatment and the subsequent diagnosis are heavily dependent on adults' interpretations of the meaning of a child's behaviour. Second, even children who are entirely normal sometimes behave in a very disruptive and aggressive fashion. As a consequence, it can be difficult to decide whether the frequency of, say, tantrums is sufficiently high to qualify as a childhood disorder. Third, there are substantial differences from one child to another in the rate of development, and this complicates the issue of deciding whether or not there is a serious problem. This is certainly the case with many developmental disorders. For example, consider a child whose academic performance is much lower than that of most children of the same age. It may simply be that the teaching has been poor or that the child has inherited a low level of intelligence. On the other hand, the poor school performance may reflect some more deep-rooted problem, and so qualify as a developmental disorder.

Developmental disorders

According to DSM-III-R, there are three major categories of developmental disorder. These are pervasive developmental disorders, mental retardation, and specific developmental disorders. As relatively little is known about specific developmental disorders, they will not be discussed in detail.

Pervasive developmental disorders. The major form of pervasive developmental disorder is known as *autism*. It is a very disturbing condition in which the young child almost totally fails to form the normal relationships with other people. In the words of Leo Kanner, the child psychiatrist who first identified it, autism is characterised by "an inability to relate...in the ordinary way to people and situations...an extreme autistic aloneness that, whenever possible, disregards, ignores, shuts out anything that comes to the child from outside" (Kanner, 1943). There is also very poor language acquisition, with approximately half of all autistic children never learning to speak. Even those who do speak, exhibit peculiarities of speech, such as *echolalia* (meaningless repetition of what someone else has said). In addition, the autistic child often engages in repetitive, compulsive activities, and becomes extremely agitated if there are any sudden changes in his or her environment. The onset of autism is before the age of 30 months, and is often clearly present even in the first few weeks of life. It is a rather rare condition affecting only one child in 2000; approximately 80% of autistic children are boys.

The social unresponsiveness of autistic children means that it is rather difficult to obtain an accurate assessment of their intellectual ability. However, the available evidence suggests that most autistic children have IQs below 70, indicating the presence of mental retardation. Their poor language skills mean that they generally perform very poorly on all intelligence-test items that are dependent on the use of language, but some autistic children do rather better on tests which require visuo-spatial skills.

Origins and treatment of autism.   Several theorists have attempted to explain the origins of autism. Initially, the emphasis was on the allegedly inadequate parental treatment which autistic children received. For example, Bruno Bettelheim (1967) claimed that autistic children have rejecting parents whose failure to respond warmly leads to the apathy and hopelessness characteristic of autism. Bettelheim went so far as to compare the mental state of autistic children to that of the inmates of concentration camps. The problem for this theory, and other similar ones, is that there is no good evidence that the parents of autistic children differ significantly from other parents. There may possibly be subtle differences, but it is highly improbable that any such differences could explain the onset of a serious condition such as autism.

The rarity of autism means that it is difficult or impossible to look for a genetic basis of autism in a large-scale study. However, revealing evidence in a small study was obtained by Folstein and Rutter (1978). They studied 11 pairs of identical twins in which one member of each pair was autistic; in 36% of the pairs, the other twin was also autistic. In contrast, the other twin was not autistic in any of 10 pairs of fraternal twins in which one was autistic. The evidence for genetic factors was even greater when cognitive impairments such as delayed speech were considered. The concordance rate was 82% in the identical twins, compared with only 10% in the fraternal twins.

There is also evidence that brain damage is involved in autism. Assessment by means of the EEG, which measures brain-wave activity, has revealed that many autistic children have abnormal brain functioning. Moreover, the extent of these abnormalities tends to be greater in more severe cases of autism. In addition, autistic children are 10 times more likely than non-autistic children to have mothers who had rubella (German measles) during the pre-natal period. Rubella may cause brain damage in at least some unborn children, and this brain damage can lead to autism.

How can autism be treated? Because autism is a condition involving very severe abnormalities, it has proved difficult to treat successfully. Some improvement can be produced by the use of operant conditioning techniques (see Chapter 7). A problem with these techniques is that they require the use of rewards or reinforcers, and autistic children generally fail to respond to most social rewards such as praise or smiling. However, food can be used as the reward for desired behaviour, with punishment being administered for undesired behaviour. Lovaas (1987) carried out a study using such techniques on an intensive basis, and found that 47% of the autistic children so treated reached the normal level of intellectual functioning by the time they were six or seven. This figure should be compared with the approximately 2% of autistic children in institutions who reach that level.

Autism has also been treated by means of drug therapy. Some autistic children have elevated levels of serotonin, which is a neurotransmitter involved in transferring impulses from one nerve cell to another. This suggests that it might be helpful to administer to autistic children a drug which would lower their serotonin level. Fenfluramine is such a drug, and it was used in a study on 14 autistic children (Geller, Yokota, Schroth, & Novak, 1984). The drug led to increased social responsiveness, improved behaviour, and increased IQ, and it shows real promise for the treatment of at least some autistic children.

Mental retardation. Children suffering from mental retardation exhibit a level of intellectual functioning which is consistently well below that of most children of their age. Two-thirds of mentally retarded children are boys. DSM-III-R identifies four different levels of mental retardation differing in the degree of retardation:

- the mild level covers IQs between 55 and 69;
- the moderate level 40 to 54;
- the severe level 25 to 39; and
- the profound level below 25.

Approximately 75% of retarded children fall into the mild category, and 20% into the moderate category.

There are various causes of mental retardation. Approximately 70% of mentally retarded children have had no known injury or disease that could account for their condition. As genetic factors seem to play an important role in the determination of intelligence (see Chapter 2), it is reasonable to assume that mental retardation in these children depends at least in part on heredity. This view is supported by the fact that mental retardation tends to run in families (see Quay, Routh, & Shapiro, 1987).

Environmental factors are also of importance in producing mental retardation in these children. As Quay and colleagues (1987) point out, the incidence of mental retardation is considerably greater in families of low socio-economic class. Part of this relationship between retardation and socio-economic class reflects genetic factors, but most of it is probably due to the limited stimulation and educational facilities available to many children from poor families.

The remaining 30% of mentally retarded children have suffered some identifiable organic aetiology. Approximately 5% of mentally retarded children suffer from Down's syndrome or mongolism. Down's syndrome children have 47 chromosomes rather than the usual 46 in their cells. This causes them to have moderate or severe mental retardation, plus physical weaknesses (especially heart lesions). Many children with Down's syndrome die at an early age.

Some cases of mental retardation are caused by disrupted metabolic processes. For example, phenylketonuria is a disease in which the infant is unable to metabolise the amino acid phenylalanine. As a consequence, the concentration of phenylalanine increases, and there is irreversible brain damage. There are numerous other metabolic diseases causing retardation: these include Tay-Sachs disease and Nieman-Pick disease. Still further causes of mental retardation are accidents causing head injury, and various infectious diseases suffered by the mother (e.g. rubella; syphilis) which can damage the foetus.

The more severe the mental retardation from which a child is suffering, the more difficult it tends to be to provide adequate treatment. Children at the severe and profound levels of retardation often benefit from treatment based on operant conditioning. In such treatment, they are rewarded for making responses that are approximately correct. As training proceeds, so the response must become increasingly accurate in order for a reward to be given. Children at the mild level of mental retardation frequently develop reasonably good social skills at an early age, and often derive much benefit from attending ordinary schools.

Disruptive behaviour disorders

There are three types of disruptive behaviour disorder:

1. Attention-deficit hyperactivity disorder. A child suffering from this disorder typically behaves in an impulsive fashion with a very high level of activity and an inability to concentrate.
2. Conduct disorders. These involve aggressive and other kinds of anti-social behaviour. Many children with conduct disorders become criminals in adolescence or adulthood.
3. Oppositional defiant disorder. This disorder is characterised by hostile, negative, and defiant behaviour.

There is some overlap between this last type and conduct disorders, but the behaviour of children with conduct disorders is generally more disruptive than that of children with oppositional defiant disorder. Because oppositional defiant disorder resembles conduct disorders, it will not be discussed separately.

Attention-deficit hyperactivity disorder. Most children tend to be rather active and to have a much shorter attention span than adults. However, there are some children whose high level of activity and low level of attention in all situations is such that they are classified as suffering from attention-deficit hyperactivity disorder. It is important to note the phrase "in all situations", because there are many normal children who are highly active only in some situations. For example, it was reported in one study (Klein & Gittelman-Klein, 1975) that approximately three-quarters of children who appeared to be over-active at school were not so either at home or in the clinic.

Attention-deficit hyperactivity disorder is considerably more common in boys than in girls. According to Anderson, Williams, McGee, and Silva (1987), there are over five times as many boys as girls suffering from the disorder. Children with attention-deficit hyperactivity disorder tend to show continuing symptoms into adolescence. They also tend to have conduct disorders and are more likely than other children to become involved in drug abuse.

Several theorists have proposed that there is malfunctioning of the physiological systems controlling the level of arousal in children with attention-deficit hyperactivity disorder. However, opinions differ as to the specific nature of the physiological problem. It has been argued that children with the disorder are chronically over-aroused, and certainly their behaviour suggests an excited internal state. Other theorists (e.g. Zentall & Zentall, 1983) have put forward the alternative view that hyperactive children are chronically under-aroused, and seek to increase their level of arousal by a high level of activity. This theory is supported by the fact that stimulant drugs (which increase the level of arousal) generally have a calming effect on hyperactive children.

It is possible that there is an hereditary predisposition to attention-deficit hyperactivity disorder, and that this predisposition may play a part in producing abnormalities of physiological arousal. It has been found, for example, that 20% of hyperactive children have at least one parent with a history of hyperactivity, compared with a figure of only 5% of non-hyperactive children (Morrison & Stewart, 1971). A limitation of this study is that the hyperactive children may simply have learned how to behave in a hyperactive fashion from observing their hyperactive parent. However, it is also found that hyperactive children who have been adopted are also more likely to have a natural parent who is hyperactive (see Cantwell, 1975, for a review), which strengthens the argument that there may be a genetic predisposition involved. In addition, of course, there are undoubtedly important environmental factors, but these have not been identified clearly as yet.

Treatment. One common form of therapy involves the administration of stimulant drugs such as an amphetamine called methylphenidate. Although such drugs in fairly high doses are effective in reducing hyperactive children's level of activity, the same high doses impair their rate of learning at school (see Sprague & Berger, 1980). If lower doses are given, then there is generally an improvement in attention span. However, low doses have little or no effect on the child's hyperactivity. Another important problem with drug therapy for attention-deficit hyperactivity disorder is that it merely controls some of the symptoms without producing any real cure. When the drugs are no longer administered, the attentional problems and the hyperactivity tend to re-occur. A final problem with the use of stimulant drugs is that they sometimes produce unfortunate side-effects such as high blood pressure or insomnia.

The other major form of treatment for attention-deficit hyperactivity disorder involves the use of operant conditioning. In essence, the child is reinforced or rewarded for behaving in the desired fashion (e.g. sitting still; attending in class). This approach is often very successful in producing an almost immediate improvement in the behaviour of hyperactive children. However, very little is known of the long-term effectiveness of the operant conditioning approach in treating hyperactivity, and it is obviously the long-term effects that are of greatest practical relevance.

Conduct disorders.   An overwhelming majority of children commit minor offences such as stealing small sums of money, telling lies, or fighting with their fists. However, there are some children (mostly boys) who persistently behave in an under-controlled way which causes offence to other people, and whose behaviour leads to the diagnosis of conduct disorders. As Davison and Neale (1986) pointed out, the term "conduct disorders" covers a great variety of behaviour patterns, including "aggression, defiance, and disobedience, verbal hostility, lying, destructiveness, vandalism, theft, promiscuity, and early drug and alcohol use" (p. 380).

Approximately 8% of adolescents appear to have conduct disorders. This makes it one of the most common psychological childhood disorders, if not the most common. It is difficult to be precise on this issue for two reasons. First, because most children sometimes behave in the same way as children with conduct disorders, it is not possible to draw a sharp distinction between children with and without conduct disorders. Second, there is evidence to suggest that only relatively few children whose behaviour is severely disruptive are referred for counselling.

What factors are responsible for the development of conduct disorders? As with attention-deficit hyperactivity disorder, it seems that heredity and environment both play a part. An influence of heredity is suggested by adoption studies. The criminal behaviour of adopted children resembles that of their real fathers more than their adoptive fathers, presumably due to genetic influences. In addition, identical twins have been found to show a higher concordance rate than fraternal twins for conduct disorders.

So far as environmental factors are concerned, there is much evidence that the incidence of conduct disorders is far higher in one-parent than two-parent families. Such evidence is subject to more than one interpretation: it might be the fact of *separation* from one parent which is responsible, or it might be the presence of *conflicts* in unhappy families leading to separation and divorce. The fact that the death of a parent does not lead to an increased incidence of conduct disorders (e.g. Rutter, 1979) suggests that it is the existence of conflicts rather than just the fact of separation which produces disorders in children.

The background of children with conduct disorders also tends to be more deprived than that of other children in other ways. They often come from large families lacking in affection and proper discipline. In addition, children with conduct disorders often live in areas characterised by poor housing and schooling.

Treating conduct disorders. Unfortunately, it has proved rather difficult to develop forms of therapy that eliminate conduct disorders and prevent the children concerned from turning to a life of crime. However, there are indications that rather expensive and time-consuming therapy based on the principles of operant conditioning can be successful. One of the best examples is known as "Achievement Place" (e.g. Kirigin, Braukmann, Atwater, & Wolf, 1982). In essence, two highly trained "teaching parents" live with between six and eight children with conduct disorders. These teaching parents award points to the children for desirable forms of behaviour (e.g. keeping themselves neat and clean; doing housework), and take points away for undesirable behaviour (e.g. speaking aggressively; disobeying). The teaching parents also provide role models for the children, and encourage them to take responsibility for their own behaviour.

Kirigin et al. (1982) produced evidence that Achievement Place is more effective than traditional institutions. Over a one-year period, 86% of the boys and 80% of the girls in traditional institutions committed criminal offences, compared with the lower figures of 56% of the boys and 47% of the girls in Achievement Place. Of course, the rates of criminality even for Achievement Place children are still rather high. Presumably the main reason is that the children return to their deprived family environments, and these environments can undo much of what has been achieved.

Problems with aetiology

Some of the general problems associated with establishing the aetiology or causal factors involved in different forms of mental disorder were mentioned in Chapter 5. Now that we have discussed several mental disorders in some detail, it is appropriate to re-consider the issue of aetiology by examining both genetic and environmental factors.

Genetic determinants

One of the most striking features of the mental disorders discussed in this chapter is the fact that there is evidence for the influence of genetic factors with respect to many of them.

Of course, the impact of heredity appears to be much stronger with some disorders than with others. Bipolar depression and anti-social personality disorder appear to be at one extreme, with concordance rates for identical twins of 72% and 69%, respectively. In addition, the concordance rates for identical twins exceed 30% for schizophrenia, unipolar depression, panic disorder, and autism. Generalised anxiety disorder, obsessive-compulsive disorder, phobias, attention-deficit hyperactivity disorder, and conduct disorders appear to be at the other extreme, in that the evidence suggests that heredity plays no more than a modest role in their aetiology.

Although it appears that genetic factors are involved in many different mental disorders, it has proved extremely difficult in most cases to establish the mechanisms by which these genetic factors operate. Some progress has been made. For example, we know that:

- sensitivity to dopamine is involved in many cases of schizophrenia;
- serotonin and noradrenaline probably play a role in unipolar depression;
- adrenergic functioning is affected in panic disorder;
- there are brain abnormalities in anti-social personality disorder;
- brain damage and/or high serotonin levels are found in autistic children; and
- various metabolic disturbances and infectious diseases can produce mental retardation.

However, it has not so far been possible to discover in detail how these mechanisms work. Moreover, the mechanisms involved in bipolar depression, phobias, generalised anxiety disorder, obsessive-compulsive disorder, attention-deficit hyperactivity disorder, and conduct disorders remain extremely unclear.

Environmental factors

The picture with respect to environmental determinants is somewhat similar. There is strong evidence that certain features of the environment are involved in the aetiology of various disorders, but precisely how they have their effects is usually unclear. For example:

- low socio-economic class appears to play some part in schizophrenia and mental retardation;
- life events and lack of social support are involved in unipolar depression;
- conflicts within the family are relevant to anti-social personality disorder and conduct disorders;
- specific encounters with phobic stimuli sometimes underlie phobias; and
- cognitive vulnerability may play a role in generalised anxiety disorder.

However, very little is known of the environmental factors contributing to most phobias, to bipolar depression, to panic disorder, to obsessive-compulsive disorder, to autism, or to attention-deficit hyperactivity disorder.

Most research on environmental determinants of mental disorders has focused on long-lasting factors such as socio-economic class or family conflicts. However, some researchers have argued that the presence of major negative life events (e.g. death of a spouse; loss of job) in the year or so before the onset of a mental disorder is significant. It will be remembered that Brown and Harris (1978) found that depressed women were more than twice as likely as other people to have experienced a very stressful life event in the nine months preceding the onset of the depression. In addition, there is an increased incidence of negative life events in the few weeks before a schizophrenic episode, and an above-average level of life events is often found in the months preceding the onset of anxiety disorders (Finlay-Jones & Brown, 1981). However, the fact that most people encounter major life events without suffering from mental disorder indicates that life events generally only provide the trigger for mental disorder in those who are already vulnerable.

To sum up, it is now clear that genetic factors play some role in the aetiology of several different mental disorders, and some of the major environmental factors have also been identified. When we move from this descriptive level to the more explanatory level, and attempt to provide a detailed account of *how* the genetic and environmental factors produce disorders, matters become decidedly less clear. Complications arise because the factors responsible for any given disorder vary from one person to another. For example, some sufferers from clinical depression experienced several life events in the months before the onset of their depression, whereas others experienced no life events at all. As we saw in Chapter 5, some cases of obsessive-compulsive disorder are due primarily to anxious personality, whereas others are due much more to negative life events (McKeon et al., 1984). In other words, *the aetiology of any given disorder differs across individuals.*

Summary: Forms of psychopathology

- The most widely used approach to diagnosis of psychopathology is DSM-III-R. Among several major categories of mental disorder included in it are schizophrenia; depression; anxiety disorders; personality disorders; and childhood disorders.
- Schizophrenia is a very serious disorder which is difficult to treat. It involves a loss of contact with reality, and the symptoms can include disturbed thinking, hallucinations, emotional disturbances, poor motivation, and immobility for hours at a time. Genetic factors are involved in its aetiology, but environmental factors are suggested by the fact that the incidence of schizophrenia is several times greater at the bottom of the social scale than at the top.
- Depression is the most common form of mental disorder. Over 90% of sufferers have unipolar depression. However, a small minority have bipolar depression, which includes manic as well as depressed episodes. Both forms of depression have a genetic basis. In the case of unipolar depression, there is evidence that the neurotransmitters serotonin and noradrenaline are involved in the disorder. Environmental factors in the aetiology of unipolar depression include recent stressful life events and lack of social support.
- The category of anxiety disorders includes panic disorder, phobia, obsessive-compulsive disorder, post-traumatic stress disorder, and generalised anxiety disorder. Genetic factors seem to play a modest role in most anxiety disorders; the strongest evidence is with respect to panic disorder, where there appears to be disturbed adrenergic functioning. With the obvious exception of post-traumatic stress disorder, it has proved difficult to establish environmental determinants of anxiety disorders.
- There are several different personality disorders. Most is known about anti-social personality disorder, and there is some controversy about the existence of other personality disorders. There appears to be a genetic basis to anti-social personality disorder, and there are accompanying brain abnormalities. On the environmental side, the conflicts and other stressful events preceding divorce are contributory factors.

- Two of the main categories of childhood disorders are developmental disorders and disruptive behaviour disorders. There are three major categories of developmental disorder: pervasive developmental disorders, mental retardation, and specific developmental disorders. Autism is the most common form of pervasive developmental disorder. Autistic children are almost completely unable to establish normal relationships with other people, and often never learn to speak. Genetic factors are involved, and in some cases rubella in the mother causes brain damage to the foetus. High levels of serotonin are also involved. Mental retardation involves poor intellectual functioning which can be at varying levels of severity. There are several different causes of mental retardation, ranging from Down's syndrome, through diseases involving disrupted metabolism and head injury, to the negative effects of low socio-economic class.
- Disruptive behaviour disorders fall into three categories: attention-deficit hyperactivity disorder, conduct disorders, and oppositional defiant disorder. Genetic factors are involved in attention-deficit hyperactivity disorder. There is some controversy as to whether children suffering from this disorder are basically over- or under-aroused. Environmental factors are also involved, but have not been identified with precision. Conduct disorders have some genetic basis. However, family conflicts, living in poor areas, and a lack of affection within the family all contribute to the development of conduct disorders.
- It has proved possible with many disorders to establish their aetiology in a very general sense (e.g. that genetic factors or low socio-economic class are involved). However, it is considerably more difficult to identify the mechanisms determining how these factors have their effects. Part of the problem is that the aetiology of any given disorder varies across individuals.

Further reading

Most textbooks on abnormal psychology discuss in some detail the major forms of mental disorder or psychopathology. Two textbooks that can be recommended are as follows: G.C. Davison and J.M. Neale (1990), *Abnormal psychology: An experimental clinical approach* (Fifth Edition) (Chichester: Wiley); and D.L. Rosenhan and M.E.P. Seligman (1989), *Abnormal psychology* (Second Edition) (London: Norton).

7 Therapeutic approaches

As we saw in Chapter 6, patients suffering from mental disorders can exhibit a wide range of symptoms. More specifically, there can be problems associated with thinking and the mind (e.g. hallucinations), with behaviour (e.g. the avoidance behaviour of the phobic patient), or with physiology and the body (e.g. the highly activated physiological system of the anxious patient). However, it is important to remember that all thinking and behaviour ultimately depend on physiological processes within the body, and thus thinking, behaviour, and the body are highly inter-dependent most of the time.

It follows from what has been said so far that therapeutic approaches to mental disorder could reasonably focus on producing changes in behaviour, in thinking, or in physiological functioning within the body. At the risk of over-simplification, this is precisely what has happened. Three of the major approaches to the treatment of mental disorder are behaviour therapy, psychoanalysis and related forms of psychotherapy, and somatic therapy. Behaviour therapy, as its name suggests, emphasises the importance of changing behaviour. Psychoanalysis was developed by Sigmund Freud as a method of changing the functioning of the mind. Somatic therapy focuses on manipulations of the body by various means including drugs and surgery. A fourth major approach to treatment—cognitive therapy—falls somewhere between behaviour therapy and psychotherapy. Cognitive therapists endeavour to alter their patients' thought processes and their behaviour.

This chapter is devoted to a description and evaluation of these four major therapeutic approaches. To anticipate a little, we will see that each therapeutic approach has proved effective in curing mental illness. Not surprisingly, some forms of mental illness are better treated by one approach, whereas other forms respond better to another.

Behaviour therapy

One of the major approaches to the treatment of mental illness is known as *behaviour therapy*. The underlying notions are that most forms of mental illness occur as a result of maladaptive learning, and that the best treatment consists of appropriate new learning or re-education. More specifically, behaviour therapists believe that abnormal behaviour develops through conditioning, and that it is through the use of the principles of conditioning that cures can be produced. In other words, behaviour therapy is based on the assumption that classical and operant conditioning can change unwanted behaviour into a more desirable pattern of behaviour. In order to make sense of the specific forms of treatment advocated by behaviour therapists, it is necessary first of all to describe some of the elements of conditioning, and then to discuss the relevant form of therapy. We will do this for *classical conditioning* and then for *operant conditioning*.

Classical conditioning

Easily the best-known example of classical conditioning comes from the work of Ivan Pavlov (1849–1936) on dogs. Dogs (and other animals) usually salivate when food is put in their mouths. In technical terms, what we have here is an unlearned or *unconditioned reflex*, in which there is a connection between the *unconditioned stimulus* of the food in the mouth and the *unconditioned response* of salivation. Pavlov discovered that it was possible to train a dog to salivate to an entirely neutral stimulus such as a tone. What he did was to present a tone (the training stimulus) just before food on several occasions, so that the tone effectively signalled the imminent arrival of food. Finally, he presented the same tone (the test stimulus) on its own without any food, and found that the tone led to the dog salivating. In technical terms, the dog had acquired a *conditioned reflex*, in which the conditioned stimulus was the tone and the *conditioned response* was salivation.

Pavlov discovered many other important characteristics of classical conditioning. For example, there is the phenomenon of *stimulus generalisation*. The conditioned response of salivation was greatest when the tone presented on its own (i.e. the test stimulus) was exactly the same as the tone which had been presented just prior to food. However, a smaller conditioned response was still obtained when a somewhat different tone was presented. The phenomenon of stimulus generalisation refers to the fact that the strength of the conditioned response is determined by the similarity between the test stimulus and the previous training stimulus.

Another key feature of classical conditioning is the phenomenon of *experimental extinction*. If Pavlov presented the tone on its own several times, he discovered that the conditioned response of salivation gradually disappeared. In general terms, the repeated presentation of the conditioned stimulus in the absence of the unconditioned stimulus removes the conditioned response, and this is known as experimental extinction.

What is going on in the classical conditioning situation? In essence, the conditioned stimulus (e.g. a tone) allows the dog to *predict* that the unconditioned stimulus (e.g. food) is about to be presented (Rescorla, 1967). In other words, the tone provides a clear indication that food is due to arrive, and so it produces an effect (i.e. salivation) which is similar to the effect produced by the food itself. Experimental extinction or the disappearance of the conditioned response occurs when the conditioned stimulus no longer predicts the imminent presentation of the unconditioned stimulus.

Why is classical conditioning of potential relevance to an understanding of psychopathology? According to behaviour therapists, classical conditioning plays a major role in the development of many cases of mental illness. For example, consider patients suffering from a phobia (i.e. a relatively specific irrational fear). The experience of falling down a flight of stairs and hurting himself badly led a patient described by Marks (1969) to develop a phobia of heights. By the process of stimulus generalisation, to this patient all high places became conditioned stimuli that evoked a conditioned fear response.

Behaviour therapists have focused largely on patients (such as phobics) who have acquired unrealistic fears or anxieties. It is assumed that these fears are acquired by means of classical conditioning in which a neutral stimulus is associated with a painful or unpleasant stimulus. For example, consider a famous study by Watson and Rayner (1920). A little boy who liked rabbits learned to fear them when a rabbit was repeatedly presented just before a loud noise was heard. The rabbit here acted as the conditioned stimulus and the loud noise as the unconditioned stimulus, and the conditioned stimulus came to evoke the fear produced by the loud noise.

Flooding. According to behaviour therapists, one way of breaking the link between the conditioned stimulus and fear is by means of experimental extinction. This can be achieved by a technique known as *flooding*, which involves presenting the patient with an extremely fear-provoking situation. In the case of a spider phobic, for example, the patient could either be put in a room full of spiders or be asked to imagine being surrounded by dozens of spiders. Of course, the patient is initially flooded or overwhelmed by fear and anxiety. However, this fear typically begins to subside after some time. If the patient can be persuaded to remain in the situation for a sufficient length of time, then there is often a marked reduction in fear. In a sense, flooding teaches the patient that there is no objective basis to his or her fears (e.g. the spiders do not actually cause any bodily harm). In everyday life, the phobic patient would avoid those stimuli relevant to the phobia, and so he or she has no opportunity to learn this.

".. IT'S FOR YOUR OWN GOOD MR. LIDFLIP... YOU'LL THANK ME FOR THIS..."

The main problem with the flooding technique is fairly obvious. It is deliberately designed to produce very high levels of fear. It can, therefore, have a very disturbing effect on the patient. Furthermore, if the patient feels compelled to bring the session to a premature end, this may teach him or her that avoidance of the phobic stimulus is rewarding in the sense of reducing fear. This may make the subsequent treatment of the phobia more difficult.

Systematic desensitisation. An alternative approach to the treatment of phobias was developed by Joseph Wolpe (1958), and is known as *systematic desensitisation*. It is based on *counterconditioning*, and involves the attempt to replace the fear response to phobic stimuli with a new response that is incompatible with fear. This new response is generally muscle relaxation. Patients are initially given special training in deep relaxation until they reach the stage at which they can rapidly achieve muscle relaxation when instructed to do so.

When the patient has mastered muscle relaxation, the treatment by systematic desensitisation can begin. The patient and the therapist together construct what is known as an "anxiety hierarchy", in which the patient's feared situations are ordered from the least to the most anxiety-provoking. Thus, for example, a spider phobic might regard one small, stationary spider five metres away as only modestly threatening, but a large, rapidly moving spider one metre away as highly threatening. The patient attains a state of deep relaxation, and is then asked to imagine the least threatening situation in the anxiety hierarchy. The patient repeatedly imagines this situation until it fails to evoke any anxiety at all, indicating that the counterconditioning has been successful. The treatment continues by repeating this process while working through all the situations in the anxiety hierarchy, culminating in the most anxiety-provoking situation of all.

Why does systematic desensitisation start with the least threatening situation? The argument is that it is difficult for the phobic patient to imagine any phobia-related situation without producing a fear response that eliminates muscle relaxation. The best hope is to start with a relatively unthreatening situation, where the muscle relaxation response will probably compete successfully with the fear response. As the level of fear declines, it then becomes possible to work up through the anxiety hierarchy to more threatening situations.

It should be clear from this account of systematic desensitisation that it can only be used when the stimuli producing a patient's clinical anxiety can be identified. Thus, it would not be appropriate to use systematic desensitisation with a patient suffering from generalised anxiety disorder, where the stimuli evoking anxiety are very numerous and ill-defined.

One of the controversial aspects of systematic desensitisation therapy is whether or not the fear reduction observed in the therapeutic situation generalises to the patient's everyday life. It is likely that Wolpe was unduly optimistic in assuming that there is automatic generalisation from one situation to another. Many therapists acknowledge this limitation of the treatment, and instruct their patients to put themselves in progressively more anxiety-provoking situations in their everyday lives.

Aversion therapy.   Aversion therapy is used when there are stimulus situations and associated behaviour patterns that are attractive to the patient but which the therapist and the patient regard as undesirable. For example, alcoholics enjoy going to pubs and consuming large quantities of alcohol. In essence, aversion therapy involves associating such stimuli and behaviour with an extremely unpleasant unconditioned stimulus. In the case of alcoholism, what is often done is to require the patient to take a sip of alcohol while under the effect of a nausea-inducing drug. Sipping the drink is followed almost immediately by vomiting.

Aversion therapy is controversial in a number of ways:

1. Many people are concerned at the pain and discomfort caused to patients by the administration of strong electric shocks or nausea-inducing drugs.
2. It is not altogether clear precisely how the shocks or drugs have their effects. It may be that they make the previously attractive *stimulus* (e.g. sight of alcohol) aversive, or it may be that they inhibit the *behaviour* of drinking.
3. There are considerable doubts about the long-term effectiveness of aversion therapy. It has dramatic effects in the therapist's office, but is probably very much less effective in the outside world when no nausea-inducing drug has been ingested and it is obvious that no electric shocks will be administered.

Operant conditioning

The best-known example of operant conditioning is provided by the work of B.F. Skinner (1904–1990). He placed a hungry rat in a small box (often referred to as a Skinner box) containing a lever. When the rat pressed the lever, this resulted in the presentation of a food pellet. The rat gradually learned that food could be obtained by lever pressing, and so engaged in more and more lever pressing. Lever pressing is an example of what Skinner called "operants"—responses that operate on the environment to produce a change leading to reward. According to Skinner, a crucial principle of learning is the law of *reinforcement*: the probability of a response occurring increases if that response is followed by a positive reinforcer or reward (e.g. food). In contrast, the probability of a response will decrease if it is not followed by a positive reinforcer; this phenomenon is known as experimental extinction.

Skinner and others have discovered numerous additional characteristics of operant conditioning. For example, instead of providing reinforcement after each response, it is possible to reward only some of the responses; this is known as partial reinforcement. There are several different varieties or schedules of partial reinforcement. They include fixed-ratio schedules, in which a certain fixed number of responses must be made for each reward (e.g. every tenth response is followed by reinforcement) and variable-ratio schedules, in which reward occurs on average after a certain number of responses, but the actual number varies unsystematically around that average figure (e.g. on average every tenth response is rewarded, but reward may follow anything between one and 19 responses).

One of the features of operant conditioning is that the required response must be made before it can be reinforced. How then can we condition an animal to produce a complex response that it would not do naturally? The answer is by means of *shaping* or the method of successive approximations. For example, suppose that we wanted to teach pigeons to play table tennis. Initially, they would be rewarded for making any contact with the table-tennis ball. Subsequently, their actions would need to correspond more and more closely to those involved in playing table tennis in order for them to be rewarded. By this means, Skinner did actually manage to persuade two pigeons to play a rudimentary game of table tennis.

Therapy based on operant conditioning. Operant conditioning as a form of therapy is based on a careful analysis of the individual patient's behaviour. In particular, the focus is on the maladaptive behaviour of the patient, and on the reinforcers or rewards which serve to maintain that behaviour. When the therapist has a clear idea of the current patterns of behaviour and their causes, he or she will endeavour to create environmental changes which will increase the rewards for adaptive behaviour and decrease the rewards for maladaptive behaviour.

There are various techniques open to the behaviour therapist using operant conditioning:

- Selective positive reinforcement: a specific adaptive behaviour (or "target behaviour") is selected, and positive reinforcement is provided whenever this target behaviour is produced by the patient.
- Selective punishment: a specific maladaptive behaviour is punished by means of an aversive stimulus (e.g. electric shock) whenever it occurs.
- Extinction: if a maladaptive behaviour is perfomed by a patient because it is followed by positive reinforcement, then the incidence of that behaviour can be reduced or extinguished by ensuring that the behaviour is no longer followed by reward.

One important form of therapy based on selective positive reinforcement is called the *token economy*. Token economies are used with institutionalised patients who are given tokens (e.g. poker chips) for behaving in appropriate ways; these tokens can subsequently be used to obtain various privileges (e.g. cigarettes). One of the classic studies of token economies was carried out by Ayllon and Azrin (1968). They studied female patients who had been hospitalised for an average of 16 years, rewarding them with plastic tokens for actions such as making their beds or combing their hair. The tokens were exchanged for pleasant activities such as seeing a film or having an additional visit to the canteen. The token economy was very successful, in the sense that the number of chores the patients performed each day increased from a very low baseline of approximately five to over 40 when performance of chores was rewarded or reinforced with tokens.

The main problem with token economies is that the beneficial effects they produce often disappear or are greatly reduced as soon as good behaviour is no longer followed by the rewards that the patients have become used to receiving. In other words, there is a danger that token economies produce only token (i.e. minimal) learning. There is no easy answer to this problem. Token economies work because the environment is carefully structured so that good behaviour is consistently rewarded and bad behaviour is not. The outside world is quite different, and patients find it difficult to transfer what they have learned in a token economy to the considerably less structured environment outside the hospital or other institution.

As we saw in Chapter 6, operant techniques have been used in the treatment of several kinds of childhood disorders. These include autism, attention-deficit hyperactivity disorder, and conduct disorders. Part of the reason why operant conditioning techniques have been used extensively with children is because in general it is easier to control the environment of children than of adults. As Davison and Neale (1986) pointed out, "The range of childhood problems dealt with through operant conditioning is very broad indeed, including bed-wetting, thumb-sucking, aggression, tantrums, hyperactivity, self-mutilation, disruptive classroom behaviour, poor school performance, extreme social withdrawal, and asthmatic attacks" (p. 505).

When reinforcers are under the control of the therapist, operant conditioning techniques are typically rather successful in changing behaviour. However, as we have seen, there is a problem in generalising these gains to everyday life. Therapists have tackled this problem in various ways. One possibility is to try to make use of reinforcers (e.g. praise or encouragement) that are likely to be present in the outside world. Another possibility is to persuade influential people in the patient's everyday environment to act as therapists by providing reinforcers at appropriate times. For example, Lovaas, Koegel, Simmons, and Long (1973) found that the desirable changes in the behaviour of autistic children that had been produced by operant conditioning were maintained only when parents continued to reinforce their children's good behaviour.

Biofeedback is a therapeutic procedure that is based in part on operant conditioning principles. In essence, biofeedback involves using complex apparatus to provide an individual with immediate feedback on some aspect or aspects of his or her physiological functioning (e.g. heart rate; blood pressure). The relevance of operant conditioning is that it is presumably rewarding for, say, an anxious person to reduce his or her blood pressure, and the apparatus used in biofeedback indicates when blood pressure has gone down. Biofeedback has been used in the treatment of various conditions, including essential hypertension (high blood pressure with no obvious bodily cause) and migraine.

Most clinical studies have suggested that biofeedback can be effective in allowing individuals to obtain greater control over their physiological functioning. However, there has been much controversy over the reasons for its success. For example, although biofeedback often alleviates essential hypertension, it appears that the relaxation training that often accompanies biofeedback is more effective than the biofeedback itself (see O'Leary & Wilson, 1987, for a review). Holroyd et al. (1984) discovered that tension headaches were reduced in patients who believed that biofeedback was reducing muscle tension, even when there was no actual reduction. This suggests that cognitive factors (e.g. beliefs) may play an important role in the success of biofeedback.

Evaluation

Behaviour therapy is based on the assumption that there are close links between animal and human behaviour. More specifically, it is assumed that light can be shed on the development and elimination of neurotic symptoms in human patients by studying conditioning in animals. There are reasons for querying this assumption. Human beings possess considerable powers of language and cognition, and these powers can greatly affect performance in conditioning studies. For example, although extinction usually takes several trials in animal experiments, it can occur very rapidly in humans if they are simply told that the conditioned stimulus (e.g. a tone) will no longer be followed by the unconditioned stimulus (e.g. electric shock) (see Brewin, 1988, for a review). Such findings suggest that human conditioning may differ substantially from animal conditioning.

As Brewin (1988) has pointed out, such findings (and others) have led many theorists to believe that conditioning and extinction in human adults depend importantly on *conscious awareness* of the relationship between the conditioned and unconditioned stimuli. As other species presumably do not have such conscious awareness, it can be very misleading to assume that what is true of animal conditioning is also true of human conditioning. The important role played by conscious awareness is embarrassing to behaviour therapists because they typically assume that conditioning and extinction occur in rather mechanical ways which depend solely on the objective relationships among stimuli and responses.

We have just seen that human performance in laboratory studies of conditioning probably depends considerably more on conscious awareness than is admitted by behaviour therapists. The same is probably true of the various forms of clinical treatment advocated by behaviour therapists. For example, behaviour therapists claim that systematic desensitisation works because patients learn to link to phobia-related stimuli a response that is incompatible with the fear response (this is counterconditioning). Evidence that this is not the whole story was obtained by Lick (1975). He persuaded his patients that he was presenting them with subliminal phobic stimuli (i.e. stimuli below the threshold of conscious awareness), and that repetition of these stimuli reduced their physiological fear reactions. In fact, he did not present any stimuli, and the feedback about physiological responses was faked! In view of Lick's (1975) complete failure to follow the correct procedures of systematic desensitisation, it would be predicted by behaviour therapists that he would observe no beneficial changes. In fact, he discovered that his "make believe" procedure was as effective as conventional systematic desensitisation in reducing the patients' fear responses to phobic stimuli. Presumably the "make believe" procedure had the merit of producing cognitive change (e.g. making the patients believe they could control their fear of phobic stimuli) even though the counterconditioning emphasised by behaviour therapists did not occur.

It is clear at the very least that the animal conditioning model used by behaviour therapists provides a substantially over-simplified account of the processes involved in human conditioning and of the processes underlying improvement during behaviour therapy. In addition, the notion that most mental illness occurs as a consequence of a maladaptive conditioning history is highly dubious for various reasons, including:

1. As was discussed in Chapter 6, the fact that genetic factors predispose to many forms of mental illness invalidates a purely environmental approach to the development of mental illness.
2. Detailed examination of the previous life history of patients very often fails to uncover the predicted conditioning experiences. For example, phobias allegedly develop because of very unpleasant, fear-arousing experiences in the presence of stimuli relating to the phobia. However, only approximately 50% of phobic patients claim to have had any such experiences (Keuthen, 1980).

A final point which should be made is that the distinctions among the different major categories of therapy are becoming increasingly blurred. Consider, for example, the theoretical approach of Albert Bandura, which was discussed in Chapter 4. Although many of his beliefs correspond to those of the behaviourists, he regards cognitive processes as being of considerably more importance than do most behaviourists. As a consequence, he can be viewed either as a behaviour therapist with interests in cognition, or as a cognitive therapist with interests in behaviourism.

Psychotherapy

Psychotherapy is the term used to refer to methods of treatment for psychopathology that attempt to produce changes within the patient's mind (e.g. his or her thought patterns). The first (and most important) form of psychotherapy is psychoanalysis, which was introduced by Sigmund Freud at the beginning of the twentieth century. Since that time, several other forms of psychotherapy have been proposed. However, most of them are based to a greater or lesser extent on psychoanalysis, and so we will devote most of our coverage to psychoanalysis in its original and subsequent forms. George Kelly and Carl Rogers both proposed idiosyncratic versions of psychotherapy, and their approaches were considered in detail in Chapter 4.

Psychoanalysis

According to Freud, the central problem in neurosis revolves around the phenomenon of *repression*. Repression involves forcing painful, threatening, or unacceptable thoughts and memories out of consciousness into the unconscious mind. The forces of repression then prevent these thoughts and memories from re-appearing in consciousness. Almost invariably, the repressed ideas concern impulses or memories which the patient could not contemplate without experiencing intense anxiety. In other words, repression serves the function of reducing the level of anxiety experienced by the patient.

Repressed memories mostly refer to childhood, and to the conflicts between the instinctive (e.g. sexual) motives of the child and the restraints on his or her behaviour imposed by his or her parents. According to Freud, children pass through a series of stages of psychosexual development. The young child initially derives pleasure from activities involving its mouth (the oral stage), but during toilet training there is a shift to the anus (the anal stage). After that, there is the phallic stage, in which pleasure is obtained from stimulation of the genitals. Finally, there is the genital stage, in which pleasure is obtained from providing bodily satisfaction to another person as well as to oneself. Conflicts at any of these stages can mean that the child spends an unusually long time at that stage before proceeding to the next stage (this process is known as fixation). If an adult subsequently experiences great personal problems, he or she will tend to show regression (i.e. going backwards through the stages of psychosexual development) to the stage at which he or she had previously been fixated.

Freud argued that the way to cure neurosis was to allow the patient to gain access to his or her repressed ideas and conflicts from the fixated stage, and to encourage him or her to face up to whatever emerges from the unconscious. He was insistent that the patient should focus on the feelings associated with the repressed ideas, and should not simply regard them in an intellectual fashion. Freud used the term "insight" to refer to these processes, and so the ultimate goal of psychoanalysis is to provide the patient with insight. However, there are great obstacles in the way, because the emergence of extremely painful ideas and memories into consciousness produces a very high level of anxiety. As a consequence, the attempt to uncover repressed ideas generally encounters much resistance from the patient. In the words of Freud (1917):

> The patient attempts to escape by every possible means. First he says nothing comes into his head, then that so much comes into his head that he can't grasp any of it...At last he admits that he really cannot say something, he is ashamed to...So it goes on, with untold variations, to which one continually replies that telling everything really means telling everything (p. 289).

Freud and other psychoanalysts have used various different methods to uncover repressed ideas and to permit the patient to gain insight into his or her unresolved problems. The three main methods are as follows: hypnosis; free association; and dream analysis.

Hypnosis.   Historically, the use of hypnosis came first. Freud and Breuer (1895) treated a 21-year-old girl called Anna O., who suffered from several neurotic symptoms such as paralyses and nervous coughs. Hypnosis uncovered a repressed memory of Anna hearing the sound of dance music coming from a nearby house as she was nursing her dying father, and her guilty feeling that she would rather be dancing than looking after her father. Her nervous coughing disappeared after that repressed memory re-appeared.

Hypnosis is still used today by police forces in the attempt to uncover additional information from eyewitnesses to accidents or crimes. However, Freud himself became disenchanted with hypnosis. One limitation is that many patients are difficult or impossible to hypnotise. Another problem is that people under hypnosis become very suggestible. For example, hypnotised subjects will confidently "recall" events which lie in the future! What appears to happen under hypnosis is that people become less cautious in what they claim to remember. As a consequence, some previously forgotten memories are brought to light as well as many manufactured ones. Thus, little reliance can be placed on the accuracy of what is "remembered" by the hypnotised individual.

Free association.   The method of free association is very straight-forward. The patient is simply asked to say the first thing that comes into his or her mind. The hope is that fragments of repressed memories will emerge in the course of free association. However, as we have already seen, free association may not prove fruitful if the patient shows resis-tance, and is reluctant to say what he or she is thinking. On the other hand, the presence of resistance (e.g. an excessively long pause) often provides a powerful clue that the patient is getting close to some important re-pressed idea in his or her thinking, and that further probing by the therapist is called for.

Dream analysis.   The third method used by psychoanalysts is that of dream analysis. According to Freud, the analysis of dreams provides "the *via regia* (royal road) to the unconscious". He argued that there is a censor inside the mind which keeps repressed material outside conscious aware-ness, but this censor is often less vigilant during sleep. As a consequence, repressed ideas from the unconscious are more likely to appear in dreams than in waking thought. However, these ideas usually emerge in dis-guised form because of their unacceptable nature. For example, the ideas are sometimes transformed by the process of condensation—i.e. combin-ing different ideas into a smaller number—or by the process of displace-ment (shifting emotion or meaning from the appropriate object to another one). The best-known examples of displacement involve sexual symbol-ism, such as someone dreaming about riding a horse rather than engaging in sexual intercourse.

How plausible is Freud's theory of dreams? It is probably correct that a dreamer's major concerns are often expressed in a symbolic fashion

We have seen that Freud distinguished between the actual dream (which he called the *manifest dream*) and the underlying repressed ideas forming the raw material of the dream (which he called the *latent dream*). The unacceptable content of the latent dream is transformed into the more acceptable content of the manifest dream. Why do people dream? Accord-ing to Freud, the main purpose of dreams is wish fulfilment—i.e. we dream about things that we would like to see happen. Thus, dream analysis can prove useful in making sense of the neurotic patient's basic motives.

How plausible is Freud's theory of dreams? It is probably correct that a dreamer's major concerns are often expressed in a symbolic fashion rather than directly. It has been found, for example, that patients who are due to have major surgery typically dream about standing on an unsteady bridge or falling from a tall ladder rather than about having an operation (Breger, Hunter, & Lane, 1971). The notion that dream symbols are used as a means of disguising unacceptable ideas has been challenged. It has been suggested (Hall, 1953) that thinking is simpler and more concrete when we are asleep than when we are awake. From this perspective, dream symbols are simply a convenient shorthand way of expressing underlying ideas.

Interpretation.   All the methods of psychoanalysis depend heavily on the therapist's interpretation of what the patient says. How, for example, does the therapist know that a girl dreaming about riding a horse is actually thinking about having sex rather than simply about horse-riding? Freud argued that the acid test was the patient's reaction to the therapist's proposed interpretation. If the patient accepts the accuracy of the interpretation, then it is probably correct. However, matters are often more complicated than that. If a patient vehemently rejects the therapist's interpretation of a dream, that may simply be resistance by the patient's conscious mind to an unpalatable but entirely accurate interpretation.

There is obviously a difficulty here, because the therapist can use either the patient's acceptance or his or her denial of the reasonableness of a dream interpretation as supporting evidence that the interpretation is correct! Freud proposed a way of getting around this problem. We can regard psychoanalysis as similar to solving a jigsaw puzzle. It may, indeed, be difficult to decide whether a particular interpretation is correct. However, the interpretations of dozens of patients' free associations and dreams should form a coherent picture if the therapist has done his job properly, just as the pieces of a jigsaw puzzle can only really be arranged in one way.

Transference.   We have focused so far on the methods by which psychoanalysts attempt to bring repressed ideas and memories to the surface. However, Freud also emphasised the notion that the patient should gain access not only to repressed information but also to the feelings that accompanied it. A major factor in ensuring adequate emotional involvement on the patient's part is provided by *transference*, which involves the patient transferring onto the therapist powerful emotional reactions that were previously directed at his or her own parents (or other highly significant individuals). As Gleitman (1986) pointed out, transference provides "a kind of emotional reliving of the unresolved problems of the patient's childhood" (p. 696).

A crucial aspect of transference is that the therapist responds in a relatively neutral way to the emotional outpourings of the patient. The fact that the therapist will not retaliate in any way may allow the patient freedom to express long-repressed anger or hostility to his or her parents in an uninhibited fashion. Furthermore, the neutrality of the therapist helps to make it clear to the patient that his or her emotional outbursts stem from repressed memories rather than from the therapeutic situation itself.

Neo-Freudian psychoanalysis

Many of Freud's followers were willing to accept much of his theoretical approach, but were unwilling to go along with all of his views. In particular, therapists such as Alfred Adler (1870–1937), Erich Fromm (1900–1980), Karen Horney (1885–1952), and Harry Stack Sullivan (1892–1949) were all unhappy about Freud's emphasis on biological (especially sexual) factors as being at the root of mental illness. According to them, social factors are generally much more important than sexual ones. In other words, failures and conflicts relating to interpersonal relationships form the main reasons for psychopathology. Even when a neurotic patient has severe sexual problems, it may be that those problems are a consequence of poor and neurotic interpersonal relationships and not a cause.

One of the differences between Freud and the neo-Freudians concerns the extent to which the conflicts causing neurosis are the same all over the world. According to Freud, men and women both have their own biologically determined sexual natures, and neurosis can develop when the natural course of their sexual development is thwarted. This viewpoint implies that the roles of men and women are relatively constant in different cultures. In contrast, the neo-Freudians emphasised the importance of the specific cultural conditions in which individuals are reared, and this allows for the possibility that there are considerable variations between cultures.

The neo-Freudian position received a boost from the work of anthropologists on different cultures. Margaret Mead (1935) studied three New Guinea tribes: the Arapesh; the Mundugomor; and the Tchambuli. Both men and women in the Arapesh tribe were gentle and co-operative in their personal dealings, whereas both sexes in the Mundugomor tribe were very aggressive. Of greatest interest was the Tchambuli tribe, in which the women were the breadwinners who went fishing while the men gossiped and stayed at home. Although this work suggested that it was culture rather than biology that was of vital importance, it should be noted that it was the Tchambuli men rather than the women who participated in warfare.

Psychoanalysis as practised by the neo-Freudians resembles traditional psychoanalysis in that the goals of therapy remain those of uncovering unconscious conflicts and enabling the patient to gain emotional insight into the nature of his or her personal problems. However, as we have already seen, the neo-Freudians are much less concerned than Freud about the patient's psychosexual development and much more concerned about his or her cultural background and interpersonal relationships. Another difference is that Freud's emphasis on the conflicts and problems of early childhood is replaced in neo-Freudian psychotherapy by a focus on the patient's current problems and difficulties.

A couch, or face-to-face?   A further way in which contemporary psychoanalysis differs from the traditional version is perhaps more important than might initially appear. Freud required his patients to lie on a couch while he sat behind them out of sight, but it is now more common for the psychoanalyst and the patient to spend therapeutic sessions in a more natural face-to-face situation. There are advantages and disadvantages associated with each approach. Freud's approach may make the patient less inhibited, and it prevents the patient from being influenced by the therapist's non-verbal behaviour (e.g. facial expressions). On the

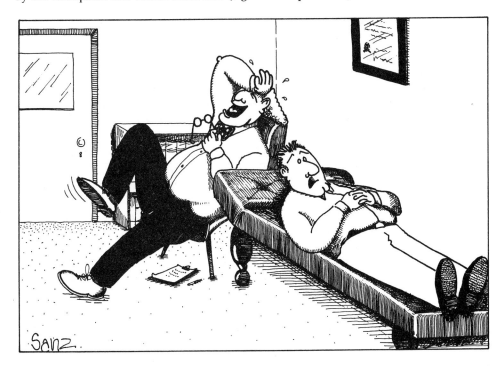

other hand, the fact that the patient is lying down may increase his or her dependency on the therapist, and this could slow down the rate of recovery. The contemporary approach reduces any tendency towards dependency, but may mean that what the patient says is distorted by the therapist's reaction.

Finally, there are differences of opinion about the relevance of the therapeutic sessions to the patient's everyday life. Freud seems to have assumed that the emotional insights obtained from psychoanalysis would readily generalise to the patient's everyday life. In contrast, contemporary psychoanalysts are generally less optimistic about the likelihood of such generalisation occurring automatically. They provide activities for the patient to perform outside the therapeutic setting in the hope that the process of generalisation will be facilitated.

Evaluation

One of the great weaknesses of the psychoanalytic approach to therapy is that it is not based on a solid foundation of scientific research. There have been some attempts to study aspects of psychoanalytic theory (e.g. repression) under laboratory conditions, but most of these attempts seem largely irrelevant. Freud's emphasis on the complexities of cognitive functioning means that it is almost worthless to study other species in order to test his theoretical views. So far as human research is concerned, it would be totally unethical to try to produce neurotic symptoms in the laboratory; the trivial fears that have actually been studied probably bear very little relationship to the traumata suffered by clinical patients.

In fact, the theoretical views of Freud and his followers were based very largely on information obtained from interactions with their patients in the therapeutic situation. However, even good agreement between the information provided by the patients and the theories proposed by psychoanalysts does not provide strong support for the psychoanalytic approach. The reason is that there are grave dangers of "contamination" in the data obtained from patients in at least two different ways:

1. What the patient says may be much influenced by what the therapist has said on previous occasions, and thus be contaminated by the therapist's theoretical views.
2. The therapist may use his or her theoretical preconceptions to interpret what the patient says in ways that distort what has been said and contaminate it.

Another general problem with psychoanalysis and most other forms of psychotherapy is the notion that patient–therapist interaction and the provision of "insight" into the patient's problems can produce substantial changes in the patient's behaviour. In fact, there is a considerable amount of evidence to suggest that it can be extremely difficult to alter established ways of behaving. For example, patients with chronic heart disease very often disregard recommendations on smoking, diet, alcohol intake, and so on, even though this may very well shorten their lives (see Roskies et al., 1989). Thus, the failure of psychoanalysis to focus directly on behaviour change probably weakens its ability to produce long-term desirable changes in behaviour.

There has been a considerable amount of controversy concerning the effectiveness (or otherwise) of psychotherapy. According to Eysenck (1952), psychotherapy is totally ineffective, because the rate of recovery with psychotherapy is no higher (or even lower) than the rate of spontaneous remission in essentially untreated patients. This implies that psychotherapy is actually bad for you! In fact, subsequent investigation of psychotherapy indicates that it is at least moderately effective (e.g. Bergin, 1971).

More precise information was provided by Luborsky and Spence (1978) in a review of studies on the effectiveness of psychotherapy. They argued that psychoanalysis generally works better with more educated patients, presumably because such patients are better able to provide detailed and coherent accounts of their thought processes. They also pointed out that psychoanalysis appears to be much more successful for the treatment of various neuroses (such as anxiety disorders) than for the treatment of psychoses (such as schizophrenia). This is not altogether surprising, as most of Freud's theoretical contributions were concerned with anxiety rather than with psychotic disorders.

Cognitive therapy

Recent years have witnessed a substantial increase in the use of what is generally known as cognitive therapy. This form of therapy was introduced primarily by two clinicians, Albert Ellis and Aaron Beck. However, the views of Albert Bandura (see Chapter 4) have also been extremely influential in the development of cognitive therapy.

In essence, it is assumed by cognitive therapists that cognitive processes and structures—for example, expectations, beliefs, long-term memories—have a significant influence on behaviour. It is also assumed that the existence of negative or self-defeating cognitive processes and structures is an important ingredient in many forms of mental disorder (e.g. anxiety; depression). Changing these processes and structures so as to make them resemble those of normal individuals is a primary goal of cognitive therapy, and is expected to produce recovery from mental disorder.

Although cognitive therapy is a relatively recent development, and has become popular only in the past 10 or 15 years, it is clearly similar in some respects to older forms of therapy. The view that cognitive change can lead to behavioural change and to recovery resembles the psychoanalytic approach. However, there are major differences:

1. Cognitive therapists are mainly concerned with the patient's current concerns and beliefs, whereas psychoanalysts attach great significance to the events of childhood.
2. Cognitive therapists are much less interested than psychoanalysts in exploring the notion that crucial information is buried deep within the unconscious mind.

Cognitive therapy also resembles behaviour therapy in some ways. For example, Albert Bandura has made substantial contributions to cognitive therapy even though he emerged from the behaviourist tradition. Cognitive and behaviour therapists agree that therapy should focus on changing what the patient is thinking and doing currently, rather than on his or her past history. They also agree on the importance of altering the patient's behaviour if a cure is to be produced. In the words of Beck, Rush, Shaw, and Emery (1979), "Acting against an assumption is the most powerful way to change it" (p. 644). In spite of these points of agreement, there are some key differences. Cognitive therapists are much more concerned than behaviour therapists about the patient's thought processes. They also differ from behaviour therapists at a theoretical level, in that they do not believe that conditioning principles provide a suitable basis for treatment.

Depression

There are various different forms of cognitive therapy that have been used in the treatment of depression. However, the best-known approach is the one adopted by Aaron Beck (1976). He argues that therapy should involve uncovering and challenging the negative and unrealistic beliefs of the depressed patient. Of particular significance is the *cognitive triad*, which consists of negative thoughts about the self, about the world, and about the future. The depressed patient typically regards himself or herself as helpless, worthless, and inadequate. He or she interprets events in the world in an unjustifiably negative and defeatist fashion, and sees the world as posing insurmountable obstacles. The final part of the cognitive

triad involves the depressed person seeing the future as totally hopeless, because his or her worthlessness will prevent any improvement from occurring.

A depressed patient will often have repetitive negative thoughts which occur so fleetingly that the patient may be scarcely aware of their existence. According to Beck, these "automatic thoughts" play an important part in the maintenance of the depressed state.

In addition to the cognitive triad, depressed people make a number of errors in logic in their thinking. The errors in logic identified by Beck are as follows:

- arbitrary inference: drawing a conclusion that is not really supported by the evidence;
- selective abstraction: emphasising one small aspect of a situation while ignoring all the other aspects;
- personalisation: taking responsibility for negative events that are not actually the individual's fault;
- magnification and minimisation: minor negative events are magnified and major positive events are minimised; and
- over-generalisation: drawing general conclusions about one's worth on the basis of very limited evidence.

There is considerable experimental and clinical evidence to indicate that the distortions of thinking identified by Beck do typically characterise depressed individuals (Beck & Clark, 1988). According to Beck, one of the major objectives of cognitive therapy is to change the depressed patient's distorted and self-defeating thought patterns (and automatic thoughts) in a more positive and realistic direction. This is done in part by having the therapist challenge the assumptions of the patient, and put forward arguments as to why he or she should adopt more positive assumptions about himself or herself, the world, and the future. This can involve reattribution training, in which the therapist points out the various factors other than the patient's worthlessness which have contributed to the patient's negative experiences.

Cognitive therapists use a range of additional techniques in order to change negative ways of thinking. One example is "activity raising", in which the patient is rewarded for becoming involved in more activities. Another example is "graded task assignment", in which the patient is rewarded for behaving in a progressively more positive fashion.

How successful is cognitive therapy in the treatment of depression? Evidence for the effectiveness of cognitive therapy was obtained in a large-scale study by Elkin et al. (1986). There were four groups of patients with unipolar depression: one group received cognitive therapy; one group received tricyclic drugs; one group received a placebo; and the fourth group received interpersonal therapy, which provided training in resolving interpersonal conflicts. More than 50% of the patients in the cognitive therapy, interpersonal therapy, and drug therapy groups recovered, compared with only 29% in the placebo control group.

In spite of the success of the cognitive approach to depression, it does not provide a complete account. For example, drug therapy is reasonably effective in treating depressed patients in spite of the fact that no attempt is made to change cognitive functioning. This suggests that depression (and its treatment) involves bodily processes that have no direct relevance to the cognitive system.

Anxiety

Beck and Emery (1985) argued that there were important similarities between depression and anxiety. Depressed and anxious patients both engage in irrational and self-defeating thoughts, and, with both kinds of patients, changing patterns of thought by means of cognitive therapy can produce a cure. However, there are differences in the nature of these irrational thoughts. The thinking of depressed patients is characterised by negativity, whereas that of anxious patients is preoccupied by psychological or physical dangers and threats and by an exaggerated sense of vulnerability. Different groups of patients with anxiety disorders differ somewhat in the perceived source of threat. Patients with generalised anxiety disorder regard many life situations as threatening, whereas phobic patients regard only certain specific situations as posing a threat. In contrast, patients with panic disorder interpret certain bodily experiences as being highly threatening.

The approach of Albert Ellis is similar to that of Beck. He argues that patients suffering from anxiety disorders have a great tendency to hold irrational beliefs that most normal people would reject. Good evidence that this is, indeed, the case was obtained by Newmark, Frerking, Cook, and Newmark (1973). They found that 65% of anxious patients (but only 2% of normals) agreed with the statement "It is essential that one be loved or approved of by virtually everyone in his community." The statement "One must be perfectly competent, adequate, and achieving to consider oneself worthwhile", was endorsed by 80% of anxious patients compared with 25% of normals.

The version of cognitive therapy that is advocated by Ellis is known as rational-emotive therapy. The basis of this therapeutic approach was summed up by Ellis (1978) in the following way:

> The client is calmly, logically, forcefully, taught that he'd better stop telling himself nonsense, accept reality, desist from condemning himself and others, and actively persist at making himself as happy as he can be in a world that is far from ideal ... If he wants to be minimally disturbable and maximally sane, he'd better substitute for all his absolutistic "It's terrible's" two other words which he does not parrot or give lip-service to but which he incisively thinks through and accepts — namely, "Too bad!" or "Tough shit!"

So far there have been relatively few attempts to assess the effectiveness of cognitive therapy in the treatment of anxiety disorders. However, Marks (1987) reviewed 33 studies that compared behavioural and cognitive treatments for phobias and obsessional-compulsive disorders. In general, the behavioural treatments involved exposure to the phobic stimuli (e.g. flooding). The cognitive treatments sometimes involved exposure, but tended to focus on disputing the patients' irrational beliefs. Cognitive therapy was often reasonably effective, but was rarely more effective than behaviour therapy.

Evaluation

As we have seen, cognitive therapy has been demonstrated to be an effective form of treatment (e.g. Elkin et al., 1986). It is a relative newcomer as a therapeutic approach, and so cognitive therapists have been able to incorporate elements of behaviour therapy and of psychotherapy into their methods of treatment. In addition, cognitive therapy follows in the tradition of theorists such as Rogers and Kelly (see Chapter 4) in paying serious attention to the patient's own views of the world, no matter how distorted those views might be. If one is attempting to produce beneficial change, it is obviously of value to have clear evidence of the patient's current state.

In spite of these advantages of cognitive therapy, there are various limitations and unresolved problems. First, cognitive therapy focuses almost exclusively on cognitive processes of which the patient is consciously aware. There is considerable evidence that there are important processes within the cognitive system that occur below the level of conscious awareness (see Eysenck, 1992), and it is a real limitation of cognitive therapy that such processes are ignored. Most importantly, most of the conscious cognitive processes studied by cognitive therapists probably depend on earlier pre-conscious processes.

Second, although it is true that predictable changes in patients' cognitions take place during the course of cognitive therapy, it is generally not clear how these changes have occurred. Cognitive therapists claim that their form of treatment produces direct changes to the information stored in the cognitive system. However, it is clear that cognitive changes can occur in several different ways (e.g. drugs can reduce a patient's anxious and depressed cognitions). In other words, the cognitive changes produced during cognitive therapy may be the *consequence* of change produced in some other way.

Third, and related to the second point, many forms of cognitive therapy involve a mixture of numerous different cognitive and behavioural ingredients. If any given form of cognitive therapy proves effective, it is no easy matter to decide which of the various ingredients have played a significant part in producing that effectiveness. If cognitive therapy is to develop further, it will be very important to clarify this issue.

Somatic therapy

Medical practitioners have often claimed that mental illness should be regarded as resembling physical illness. According to this *medical model* (see Chapter 5), so-called mental illness depends on some underlying organic problem, and the appropriate form of treatment involves manipulations of the body. *Somatic therapy* is the term used to refer to this method of treatment.

It is perhaps natural to assume that somatic therapy, if it is successful, provides support for the view that mental disorders have a physiological basis. However, matters are actually more complicated than that. Somatic therapy obviously affects the physiological system, but so little is known of the reasons why some forms of somatic therapy (e.g. electroconvulsive shock treatment for depression) are successful that it sheds practically no light on the factors causing mental disorder.

The early history of somatic therapy was not very encouraging. For example, as far back as the Stone Age those suffering from mental illness had holes cut in their skulls in order to allow the devils allegedly causing the illness to escape. This practice, which is known as trephining, cannot be recommended. It did not produce any cures, and many of those subjected to trephining did not survive the operation.

The first real indication that somatic therapy might be of use in treating patients came in the early years of this century. There is a psychosis known as "general paresis", which involves a progressive deterioration of physical and psychological functioning. The condition produces substantial changes in personality, and patients suffering from general paresis often have wildly irrational thoughts (e.g. completely unjustified concern about their health). It was suspected that general paresis was caused by syphilis, and this was shown to be the case in 1897. Patients suffering from general paresis were inoculated with matter from syphilitic sores. None of them went on to develop the symptoms of syphilis, which suggested that they had previously contracted syphilis. Penicillin is an effective way of treating syphilis, and it also forms a successful treatment for general paresis. Indeed, the number of patients suffering from general paresis is dramatically lower nowadays than it was 100 years ago.

Electroconvulsive shock treatment

Electroconvulsive shock treatment (ECT) is sometimes used in cases of depression. In essence, what happens in ECT is that a fairly strong electric current is passed for approximately half a second between two electrodes attached to each side of the depressed patient's forehead. The application of this current causes almost immediate loss of consciousness and a convulsive seizure. In order to prevent the patient from injuring himself or herself during these convulsive seizures, muscle relaxants are generally administered before the treatment itself. To obtain the optimal results, ECT is generally administered on several different occasions.

Why is ECT sometimes used rather than drugs in the treatment of depression? The most important reason is that some severely depressed patients fail to respond to drugs, but do respond to ECT. A useful feature of ECT is that it generally reduces depression more rapidly than do anti-depressant drugs. This is of particular value when there are concerns that a depressed patient is at risk of committing suicide.

On the negative side, it is discouraging that we have very little idea of precisely why ECT is so effective. However, it is likely that at least part of its effectiveness is due to the fact that it increases available *noradrenaline*. As ECT is such a blunderbuss procedure, it is not surprising that it produces several side-effects. For example, it can cause a general memory impairment that may last for several months and a more specific loss of memory for the events preceding the onset of treatment. It can also produce impaired speech, but this side-effect is much less common if ECT is administered only to the right side of the brain (the speech centre is usually in the left side of the brain).

Drug therapy

Schizophrenia. As we saw in Chapter 6, there is reasonable evidence that biochemical abnormalities typically play an important role in the development of schizophrenia. More specifically, it has been claimed that numerous neurons in the brains of schizophrenics are over-sensitive to the transmitter *dopamine*. If that is correct, then drugs that block dopamine should presumably alleviate the symptoms of schizophrenia. There is a group of drugs called *phenothiazines*, which have been found to block dopamine at the synapse (i.e. the juncture between the axon of one neuron and the dendrite of another neuron). As expected, the phenothiazines (and phenothiazine derivatives such as chlorpromazine) have been found to reduce many of the symptoms of schizophrenia, including hallucinations and thought disorders. In addition, those phenothiazine drugs producing the greatest dopamine blockade tend to have the most beneficial effects (Snyder, 1976).

Do the phenothiazines really alleviate schizophrenic symptoms specifically by producing a dopamine blockade? An alternative possibility is that they simply act as sedatives which calm schizophrenic patients down. This is improbable, because powerful sedatives such as phenobarbital are much less effective than the phenothiazines in reducing the symptoms of schizophrenia. If the phenothiazines do act primarily on the symptoms of schizophrenia by means of a dopamine blockade, then the drugs should have little or no effect on any symptoms that do not depend on dopamine activity. It has been found that the phenothiazines have very little effect on non-schizophrenic symptoms such as guilt, anxiety, and depression (Klein & Davis, 1969).

In spite of the widespread use of the phenothiazines with schizophrenic patients, there are some problems associated with these drugs. They produce a range of side-effects such as blurred vision, grogginess, muscular rigidity, drooling, and a shuffling gait. These symptoms are sufficiently unpleasant that most schizophrenic patients dislike taking the drugs, in spite of the good effects that are generated. Some of these symptoms can be reduced by other drugs, but many cannot.

Depression and mania. Drug therapy has also proved useful in treating patients suffering from unipolar and bipolar depression (also known as manic-depression). As was mentioned in Chapter 6, some theorists argue that mania is caused by an excess supply of the *neurotransmitter* noradrenaline, and depression by a shortage of the same neurotransmitter, whereas others believe that the crucial neurotransmitter that may be present in an inappropriate amount is *serotonin*.

One implication of these views is that an effective drug therapy for depression would involve the administration of a drug that increased the supply of noradrenaline and serotonin. Two groups of such drugs are the monoamine oxidase (MAO) inhibitors and the tricyclics. Both groups of drugs decrease the symptoms of depression in most (but not all) depressed patients. However, the tricyclics are generally more effective than the MAO inhibitors, and they also have the advantage of producing fewer unwanted side-effects. However, even the tricyclics can produce dizziness, blurred vision, and dryness of the mouth. It is not entirely clear why the drugs are ineffective with some patients, but it is worth noting that the tricyclics are more effective with the more severe forms of depression (Stern, Rush, & Mendels, 1980).

It could be argued that the tricyclics and the MAO inhibitors are simply stimulants producing physiological activation rather than drugs that correct depressed patients' biochemical deficits. However, there is a range of evidence which is inconsistent with the view that these drugs act as stimulants. For example, neither the tricyclics nor the MAO inhibitors have much effect on the mood of normal individuals without biochemical deficits (Cole & Davis, 1975).

Drug treatment for mania has lagged behind that for unipolar depression. However, lithium salts such as lithium carbonate produce a rapid improvement in most manic patients, and can delay the onset of depression in patients suffering from bipolar depression. Lithium carbonate has proved to be of greatest value in reducing the occurrence of manic and depressed episodes in bipolar depressives (Gerbino, Oleshansky, & Gershon, 1978), but it can have rather serious side-effects on the central nervous system, on the cardiovascular system, and on the digestive system, and an overdose can be fatal.

Anxiety disorders. Patients suffering from anxiety (e.g. those with generalised anxiety disorder) are often given minor tranquillisers to reduce the level of anxiety and permit normal functioning. Until about 15 or 20 years ago, *barbiturates* were the most common form of anti-anxiety drug. Barbiturates are depressants of the activity of the central nervous system, and long-acting barbiturates are certainly effective in reducing anxiety. However, they do have unfortunate side-effects. These include problems of concentration, lack of co-ordination, and slurred speech. Even more disturbingly, the barbiturates tend to be addictive. Anxious patients who cease taking barbiturates report numerous symptoms such as delirium, irritability, and increased sweating.

The problems with the barbiturates led to their rapid replacement by the *benzodiazepines* (e.g. Valium; Librium) in the 1960s. The benzodiazepines are more specific than the barbiturates in their functioning, and so typically produce fewer side-effects. However, the benzodiazepines often have sedative effects, with patients who take them reporting symptoms of drowsiness and lethargy. They can also impair long-term memory. If they are taken over long periods of time, then there are problems of addiction.

Although it is clear that the benzodiazepines are much safer than the barbiturates, the search has been on for other anti-anxiety drugs that will reduce anxiety without producing the unfortunate side-effects of previous drugs. One such drug is buspirone, which does not appear to have the potentially dangerous sedative effects of the benzodiazepines. However, more research is needed to establish whether or not it has any unwanted side-effects.

Attention-deficit hyperactivity disorder. As was discussed in Chapter 6, children suffering from attention-deficit hyperactivity disorder are sometimes given stimulant drugs such as methylphenidate. These drugs are often successful in reducing impulsive behaviour and improving the children's attention, but can have an adverse effect on school learning. Overall, however, the stimulant drugs generally improve matters for approximately 75% of children with attention-deficit hyperactivity disorder. The side-effects of these drugs include insomnia and loss of appetite, but these problems tend to become less severe over time.

Attention-deficit hyperactivity disorder is sometimes treated by means of behaviour therapy based on operant conditioning, in which hyperactive children are rewarded or reinforced for behaving in an appropriate fashion. As this form of treatment can be quite successful in improving the school performance of hyperactive children, there are grounds for arguing that a combination of stimulant drugs and operant techniques would be especially valuable. Some support for this viewpoint was obtained by Gittelman-Klein et al. (1976). They discovered that hyperactive children who received stimulant plus operant conditioning showed greater improvement over an eight-week period than did those who received operant conditioning plus a placebo, or operant conditioning on its own.

Evaluation

Although there are several different forms of somatic therapy, most of them involve the administration of drugs. Many drugs have proved to be valuable in therapy, but they are typically limited in at least three important ways. First, as we have seen, most drugs have a number of effects over and above those that are desired—i.e. side-effects. Second, drugs usually suppress the symptoms of mental illness but do not actually produce a cure. As a consequence, patients often have to remain on what is known as a maintenance dose for long periods of time, in order to prevent them from relapsing into their original condition with all its associated symptoms.

Third, some drugs have caused concern because they are alleged to cause addiction. This appears in particular to be the case with some of the anti-anxiety drugs such as the barbiturates and the benzodiazepines, but the extent to which it may be true of other drugs is not entirely clear. When some drugs are withheld, there are various withdrawal symptoms, the most important of which are generally the opposite of the effects produced by the drug. Thus, in the case of the benzodiazepines, the withdrawal symptoms can include panic and extreme anxiety.

There is another important issue relating to the use of drugs. Because powerful drugs can be addictive and can cause unpleasant side-effects, it is obviously extremely important to ensure that drugs are administered only under the most stringent ethical guidelines. Among other things, that means that patients should give their informed consent—i.e. they should agree to be given drugs after being fully informed about the possible effects of the drugs. However, there are doubts as to whether this system actually works properly. Irwin et al. (1985) questioned patients who were receiving medication. Although most of the patients claimed that they were fully informed about the drugs they were taking, only approximately 25% could actually describe accurately the possible side-effects of the drugs they were taking.

Evaluating the success of therapy

On the face of it, it may appear relatively straightforward to evaluate the success of therapy. All that needs to be done is to compare the percentage of patients who recover after treatment with the percentage who recover in the absence of treatment. In practice, however, there are several reasons why it has proved extremely difficult to assess the effectiveness of therapy with precision, and some of the more important ones are discussed in this section.

One of the complicating factors is that therapy is more of an art than a science. That means that two therapists who are allegedly making use of the same form of therapy (e.g. behaviour; cognitive) may differ substantially in the treatment that they actually provide, and so recovery rates may show considerable variation from one therapist to another. A good description of what therapy is like was provided by two behaviour therapists, Lazarus and Davison (1971):

> The clinician in fact approaches his work with a given set, a framework for ordering the complex data that are his domain. But frameworks are insufficient. The clinician, like any other applied scientist, must fill out the theoretical skeleton. Individual cases present problems that always call for knowledge beyond basic psychological principles (p. 203).

Definition of recovery

Although the goal of therapy is recovery, there is no agreement on the appropriate criteria for deciding that recovery has occurred. Therapists and patients may both have a vested interest in arguing that therapy has been effective—therapists because producing improvement is what they are paid to do, and patients because they have often devoted considerable time and money to therapy. As a consequence, their opinions may be somewhat biased. However, it is often possible to make use of information about a patient's behaviour. If a patient goes for therapy because he or she has a specific behavioural problem, then one can determine the extent to which therapy is successful in altering that behaviour.

Because there is no single measure of recovery that can be relied on, the best approach is to make use of a variety of different measures. This was done by Paul (1966) in a study on the effects of desensitisation and insight therapy on students suffering from a phobia about public speaking. These students were required to speak in front of a class before and after treatment. Three different kinds of measures were taken:

1. objective behaviour (e.g. quivering voice; hand trembling);
2. physiological responses (e.g. pulse rate; sweating); and
3. self-reports of anxiety from the students.

Both forms of therapy produced more improvement on all three measures than was found in control students who received no treatment at all.

You may be wondering about the ethics of denying treatment to some of the students in studies like the one described. It is possible to accept the notion of controls not receiving treatment when we are dealing with a relatively minor problem such as a phobia about public speaking, but obviously there is no way in which patients suffering from a serious disorder should be denied (even for a short period of time) the treatment they need. It thus follows that it will often be difficult to have an appropriate baseline against which to assess the effectiveness of therapy.

There is a further issue with respect to recovery. Patients who appear to have recovered on some criterion shortly after a series of therapeutic sessions sometimes no longer seem to have recovered when looked at again several months later. The fact that recovery may not be permanent means that it is extremely important to carry out a follow-up at least once or twice after recovery has allegedly occurred, in order to make sure that there has been no relapse.

Control groups

Suppose we discover that patients receiving a particular form of therapy are much more likely to recover than those receiving no therapy at all. Does that prove that the therapy itself is effective? Not really, because there are various possible reasons why the two groups differ in their recovery rates. First, the patients in one group may have suffered from more severe disorders than the patients in the other group, and this would obviously make it more difficult for them to recover.

Second, there is what is generally known as the "placebo effect". This effect has been found numerous times in drug research, where it refers to the finding that patients given a neutral substance (e.g. a salt tablet) but told that they have been given a powerful drug will often show signs of medical improvement. In other words, the mistaken belief that one has received an effective form of treatment (e.g. a powerful drug) can produce surprisingly strong beneficial effects. In more general terms, the placebo effect in treatment refers to improvements that occur as a result of the patient's *expectations of help* rather than because of the treatment itself.

Many clinicians would agree that much of the benefit of therapy is nothing more than a placebo effect. Indeed, Davison and Neale (1986) went so far as to argue: "All therapies derive at least some of their power from the faith that people have in the healer" (p. 475). In order to decide whether the improvements found with a particular form of treatment are due to the "special ingredient" of that treatment (e.g. provision of insight in the case of psychoanalysis), it is necessary to compare that treatment against a control group which is led to believe that recovery will occur. If the patients in the control group are given believable reasons for *expecting* their condition to improve, then the superiority of the treatment group often diminishes or even disappears.

Why are there such strong expectancy effects in treatment? Lick and Bootzin (1975) reviewed the effects of expectancy on fear reduction, and argued that there were various reasons why expectations of help might produce genuine benefit. One possibility is that raised expectancies lead patients to engage in reassuring self-talk (e.g. "I can handle social situations"), and this reduces the level of anxiety. Another possibility is that phobic patients who have been led to believe that they have been given a powerful form of treatment will be less likely than before to avoid their phobic stimuli, and the discovery that the phobic stimuli are actually harmless will facilitate the curing process.

Therapist–patient relationship

It is generally accepted that much of the success of any given form of therapy depends on the nature of the relationship that exists between the therapist and the patient. Such evidence as is available suggests that therapy tends to be more effective when the therapist possesses personal warmth and empathy (i.e. an understanding of the feelings of others). It also appears to be the case that more experienced therapists tend on average to be more successful than less experienced ones.

One aspect of the therapist–patient relationship that may be of great significance is the extent to which the therapist and the patient have shared expectations about the treatment. For example, Nash et al. (1965) tried to facilitate the development of shared expectations by using a role induction interview at the outset of therapy. Lower-class patients were told what would be involved in psychotherapy, and it was made clear to them why the therapist would be focusing on their dreams and emotional states. There was a control group of lower-class patients who were not given any initial information about the form of treatment they would receive. There was a much lower drop-out rate among the patients given the role induction interview. They also showed greater improvement than the control group as assessed by both therapists and the patients themselves.

There are some therapists who believe that it is important to go a step beyond simply putting their patients in the picture about the treatment they are to receive. They argue that there should be a "therapeutic alliance", in which the therapist and the client co-operate in determining the goals of therapy and how those goals may best be achieved. There is evidence that this approach leads to more effective treatment (Alexander & Luborsky, 1984).

In summary, it appears that anything which increases the trust that therapist and patient have in each other is beneficial in terms of increasing the likelihood that the treatment will be successful. The establishment of trust seems to be important regardless of the particular kind of therapy involved. It is probably true to say that trust is not sufficient in order for the patient to recover, but it may well be a necessary precondition.

Comparing different therapies

We have seen that it is rather difficult to gauge exactly the degree of success of any given form of treatment. It is, if anything, even more difficult to compare the relative effectiveness of two forms of treatment. Differences in the recovery rates associated with the two treatments may be due to differences in the specific treatment provided. However, they may also be due to differences in the ages, social class, motivation for treatment, and so on, in the two groups, or to differences in the severity of mental illness. They could also be due to differences in the criteria for recovery, differences in the warmth and empathy of the therapists, or differences in the strength of the therapeutic alliance.

In spite of these difficulties, there have been some studies which have compared different kinds of therapy. However, most of these studies were relatively small-scale and inconclusive. Probably the most common finding is that different forms of therapy are roughly equivalent in their effects. For example, Teasdale (1986) reviewed five studies which had compared drug therapy and cognitive therapy in the treatment of depression. Both forms of therapy were effective, with the cognitive therapy being, if anything, more effective. In addition, there was evidence to suggest that cognitive therapy reduced the likelihood of relapse.

As we saw earlier in the chapter, Eysenck (1952) claimed that psychoanalysis and other forms of psychotherapy were totally ineffective in the treatment of neurotic patients. According to his review of the evidence, approximately 60% of those treated by psychotherapy recovered, compared with 70% of those who received no treatment. However, a subsequent review by Smith and Glass (1977) indicated that the spontaneous recovery rate is actually more like 40%, so that psychotherapy is of demonstrable value.

Although the different kinds of therapy are in general of approximately equal effectiveness, that doesn't mean that all forms of therapy are comparable in their ability to treat each and every mental disorder. One might anticipate that each form of therapy would be particularly successful in the treatment of certain disorders rather than others:

- Behaviour therapy emphasises changes in maladaptive behaviour, and thus seems well-equipped to treat disorders (e.g. many phobias) in which the maladaptive behaviour is readily identified. In fact, some of the greatest successes of behaviour therapy have occurred in the treatment of phobias.
- Somatic therapy emphasises changes in the physiological and biochemical systems, and so seems especially relevant to the treatment of disorders (usually having a genetic basis) involving physiological and/or biochemical abnormalities. The best example here is schizophrenia, which often used to be regarded as essentially untreatable. Drug therapy based on the phenothiazines has proved extremely effective in reducing the symptoms of schizophrenia.
- Psychotherapy and cognitive therapy in their different ways both emphasise the notion that patients need to change their thought processes. Because many of the anxiety disorders and at least some kinds of depression appear to involve distorted and unrealistic thought processes, one might suppose that psychotherapy and cognitive therapy would be of great usefulness in their treatment. In general terms, that appears to be the case.

Summary: Therapeutic approaches

- There are four major forms of therapy for mental disorders: behaviour therapy; psychotherapy; cognitive therapy; and somatic therapy.

- According to behaviour therapists, mental disorders arise from maladaptive learning, and can be cured by new learning. This learning involves the use of conditioning techniques. Phobias are generally treated by methods based on classical conditioning such as flooding and systematic desensitisation. Flooding involves presenting a fear-provoking situation relevant to the phobia for prolonged periods of time, and systematic desensitisation involves patients relaxing while imagining progressively more threatening situations. Operant conditioning based on rewarding or reinforcing desired behaviour has been used with several different disorders including autism, conduct disorders, and attention-deficit hyperactivity disorder.

- Most forms of psychotherapy stem from the psychoanalytic approach pioneered by Sigmund Freud. Freud argued that most mental disorders arise out of repressed childhood conflicts and traumata. Treatment is designed to provide the patient with insight into this repressed information, and makes use of a variety of techniques such as hypnosis, free association, and dream analysis. An important ingredient in psychoanalysis is transference, in which strong repressed emotions are directed towards the therapist. Neo-Freudians and other psychotherapists who followed Freud argued that he exaggerated the importance of childhood and of sexual conflicts as causes of mental disorder. They emphasise the role of current problems of a social and interpersonal kind as factors in the development of mental disorder, and their approach to treatment reflects that emphasis.

- Cognitive therapy is based on the assumption that cognitive processes and structure influence behaviour. Cognitive therapists such as Beck and Ellis argue that anxious and depressed patients have numerous unrealistic and self-defeating thoughts. One of the major techniques in cognitive therapy is to force patients to admit that much of their thinking is unrealistic. In addition, cognitive therapists often give their patients graded task assignments to ensure that any changes in thinking are reflected in behaviour.

- Somatic therapy consists largely of drug therapy. It has been found that drugs can improve several conditions such as schizophrenia, depression, mania, anxiety disorders, and attention-deficit hyperactivity disorder. However, drugs generally reduce the symptoms of these conditions rather than produce a cure. As a consequence, it is often necessary for patients to take what is known as a maintenance dose over long periods of time. Another problem with drug therapy is that nearly all drugs have unwanted side-effects, some of which can be severe. The most common form of somatic therapy apart from drug therapy is electroconvulsive shock treatment (ECT). This is effective in reducing very severe forms of depression, but it is not at all clear why it should have this effect.
- Evaluating the success of any form of therapy is more difficult than one might imagine. There are two main reasons for this. First, there are no good criteria for determining when recovery has occurred. Second, it is not easy to think of an appropriate control group against which to compare the effects of any given form of therapy. The success of any form of therapy also depends on the level of trust that is established between the therapist and the patient. All four major therapies are of approximately equal effectiveness, but there is some tendency for each therapy to be more effective in treating some disorders rather than others.

Further reading

There is a good account of the cognitive approach to treatment in C.R. Brewin (1988), *Cognitive foundations of clinical psychology* (London: Lawrence Erlbaum Associates Ltd). More general coverage of the major forms of therapy is to be found in the following two books: G.C. Davison and J.M. Neale (1990), *Abnormal psychology: An experimental clinical approach* (Fifth Edition) (Chichester: Wiley); D.L. Rosenhan and M.E.P. Seligman (1989), *Abnormal psychology* (Second Edition) (London: Norton).

References

Alexander, L., & Luborsky, L. (1984). Research on the helping alliance. In L. Greenberg & S. Pinsof (Eds.), *The psychotherapeutic process: A research handbook*. New York: Guilford Press.

Allen, M.G. (1976). Twin studies of affective illness. *Archives of General Psychiatry, 33*, 1476–1478.

Allport, G.W., & Odbert, H.S. (1936). Trait-names: A psycho-lexical study. *Psychological Monographs, 47*, No. 211.

Anderson, J.C., Williams, S., McGee, R., & Silva, P.A. (1987). DSM-III: Disorders in preadolescent children. *Archives of General Psychiatry, 44*, 69–76.

Ayllon, T., & Azrin, N.H. (1968). *The token economy: A motivational system for therapy and rehabilitation*. New York: Appleton-Century-Crofts.

Bandura, A. (1962). Social learning through imitation. In M.R. Jones (Ed.), *Nebraska symposium on motivation*. Nebraska: University of Nebraska Press.

Bandura, A. (1977). Self-efficacy: Toward a unifying theory of behavioural change. *Psychological Review, 84*, 191–215.

Bandura, A. (1986). *Social foundations of thought and action: A social cognitive theory*. Englewood Cliffs, NJ: Prentice-Hall.

Bandura, A., Blanchard, E.B., & Ritter, B. (1969). Relative efficacy of desensitization and modelling approaches for inducing behavioural, affective, and attitudinal changes. *Journal of Personality and Social Psychology, 13*, 173–199.

Bannister, D., & Fransella, F. (1966). A grid test of schizophrenic thought disorder. *British Journal of Social and Clinical Psychology, 5*, 95–102.

Bateson, G., Jackson, D.D., Haley, J., & Weakland, J. (1956). Toward a theory of schizophrenia. *Behavioral Science, 1*, 251–264.

Baxter, L.R., Phelps, M.E., Mazziotta, J.C., Guze, B.H., Schwartz, J.M., & Selin, C.E. (1987). Local cerebral glucose metabolic rates in obsessive-compulsive disorder: A comparison with rates in unipolar depression and normal controls. *Archives of General Psychiatry, 44*, 211–218.

Beck, A.T. (1976). *Cognitive therapy of the emotional disorders*. New York: New American Library.

Beck, A.T., & Clark, D.A. (1988). Anxiety and depression: An information processing perspective. *Anxiety Research, 1*, 23–36.

Beck, A.T., & Emery, G. (1985). *Anxiety disorders and phobias: A cognitive perspective*. New York: Basic Books.

Beck, A.T., Rush, A.J., Shaw, B.F., & Emery, G. (1979). *Cognitive therapy of depression*. New York: Guilford Press.

Bergin, A.E. (1971). The evaluation of therapeutic outcomes. In A.E. Bergin & S.L. Garfield (Eds.), *Handbook of psychotherapy and behavior change*. New York: Wiley.

Bettelheim, B. (1967). *The empty fortress*. New York: The Free Press.

Beutler, L.E., Cargo, M., & Arizmendi, T.G. (1986). Therapist variables in psychotherapy process and outcome. In S.L. Garfield & A.E. Bergin (Eds.), *Handbook of psychotherapy and behaviour change* (3rd Ed.). Chichester: Wiley.

Bieri, J. (1955). Cognitive complexity-simplicity and predictive behaviour. *Journal of Abnormal and Social Psychology, 51*, 263–268.

Binet, A., & Simon, T. (1905). Methodes nouvelles pour le diagnostic du niveau intellectual des anormaux. *L'Annee Psychologique, 11*, 191–244.

Binet, A., & Simon, T. (1916). *The development of intelligence in children.* Baltimore: Williams & Wilkins.

Blum, J.E., Jarvik, L.F., & Clark, E.T. (1970). Rate of change on selective tests of intelligence: A twenty-year longitudinal study. *Journal of Gerontology, 25*, 171–176.

Bowers, K. (1973). Situationism in psychology: An analysis and a critique. *Psychological Review, 80*, 307–336.

Breger, L., Hunter, I., & Lane, R.W. (1971). The effect of stress on dreams. *Psychological Issues, 7*, 1–213.

Brewin, C.R. (1988). *Cognitive foundations of clinical psychology.* London: Lawrence Erlbaum Associates Ltd.

Brody, N. (1988). *Personality: In search of individuality.* London: Academic Press.

Brown, G.W., & Harris, T. (1978). *Social origins of depression.* London: Tavistock.

Burt, C. (1955). The evidence for the concept of intelligence. *British Journal of Educational Psychology, 25*, 158–177.

Cantwell, D.P. (1975). Genetic studies of hyperactive children. In R. Fieve, D. Rosenthal, & H. Brill (Eds.), *Genetic research in psychiatry.* Baltimore: John Hopkins University Press.

Carey, G., & Gottesman, I.I. (1981). Twin and family studies of anxiety, phobic, and obsessive disorders. In D.F. Klein & J. Rabkin (Eds.), *Anxiety: New research and changing concepts.* New York: Raven Press.

Carroll, J.B. (1986). Factor analytic investigations of cognitive abilities. In S.E. Newstead, S.H. Irvine, & P.L. Dan (Eds.), *Human assessment: Cognition and motivation.* Nyhoff: Dordrecht.

Cartwright, D.S. (1956). Self-consistency as a factor affecting immediate recall. *Journal of Abnormal and Social Psychology, 52*, 212–218.

Cartwright, D.S. (1979). *Theories and models of personality.* Dubuque, Iowa: Brown Company Publishers.

Cattell, R.B. (1946). *Description and measurement of personality.* London: Harrap.

Cattell, R.B. (1963). Theory of fluid and crystallized intelligence: A critical experiment. *Journal of Educational Psychology, 54*, 1–22.

Cattell, R.B., & Child, D. (1975). *Motivation and dynamic structure.* London: Holt, Rinehart, & Winston.

Cattell, R.B., Eber, H.W., & Tatsouka, M.M. (1970). *Handbook for the Sixteen Personality Factor Questionnaire (16PF).* Champaign, Ill.: Institute for Personality and Ability Testing.

Cattell, R.B., & Kline, P. (1977). *The scientific analysis of personality and motivation.* New York: Academic Press.

Child, I.L. (1968). Personality in culture. In E.F. Borgatta & W.W. Lambert (Eds.), *Handbook of personality theory and research.* Chicago: Rand McNally.

Christiansen, K.O. (1977). A review of studies of criminality among twins. In S.A. Mednick & K.O. Christiansen (Eds.), *Biosocial bases of criminal behavior.* New York: Gardner Press.

Cole, J.O., & Davis, J.M. (1975). Antidepressant drugs. In A.M. Freedman, H.I. Kaplan, & B.J. Saddock (Eds.), *Comprehensive textbook of psychiatry — II*, Vol. 2. Baltimore: Williams & Williams.

Coopersmith, S. (1967). *The antecedents of self-esteem.* San Francisco: Freeman.

Darwin, C. (1859). *The origin of species.* London: Macmillan.

Davison, G.C., & Neale, J.M. (1986). *Abnormal psychology: An experimental clinical approach* (4th Ed.). Chichester: Wiley.

Davison, G.C., & Neale, J.M. (1990). *Abnormal psychology: An experimental clinical approach* (5th Ed.). Chichester: Wiley.

Diagnostic and Statistical Manual of Mental Disorders (3rd Ed., Revised). (1987). Washington, DC: American Psychiatric Association.

Digman, J.M. (1990). Personality structure: Emergence of the five-factor model. *Annual Review of Psychology, 41,* 417–440.

Elkin, I., Shea, T., Imber, S., Pilkonis, P., Sotsky, S., Glass, D., Watkins, J., Leber, W., & Collins, J. (1986). *NIMH treatment of depression collaborative research program: Initial outcome findings.* Paper presented at meetings of the American Association for the Advancement of Science, May.

Ellis, A. (1978). The basic clinical theory of rational emotive therapy. In A. Ellis & R. Grieger (Eds.), *Handbook of rational emotive therapy.* New York: Springer.

Endler, N.S., & Edwards, J. (1978). Person by treatment interactions in personality research. In L.A. Pervin & M. Lewis (Eds.), *Perspectives in interactional psychology.* New York: Plenum.

Erlenmeyer-Kimling, L., & Jarvik, L.F. (1963). Genetics and intelligence: A review. *Science, 142,* 1477–1479.

Eysenck, H.J. (1944). Types of personality—a factorial study of 700 neurotic soldiers. *Journal of Mental Science, 90,* 851–861.

Eysenck, H.J. (1952). The effects of psychotherapy: An evaluation. *Journal of Consulting Psychology, 16,* 319–324.

Eysenck, H.J. (1967). *The biological basis of personality.* Springfield, Ill.: C.C. Thomas.

Eysenck, H.J. (1977). *Crime and personality* (3rd Ed.). London: Routledge & Kegan Paul.

Eysenck, H.J., & Eysenck, M.W. (1985). *Personality and individual differences.* New York: Plenum.

Eysenck, M.W. (1992). *Anxiety: The cognitive perspective.* Hove: Lawrence Erlbaum Associates Ltd.

Eysenck, S.B.G., & Eysenck, H.J. (1967). Salivary response to lemon juice as a measure of introversion. *Perceptual and Motor Skills, 24,* 1047–1053.

Fahrenberg, J. (1987). The psychophysiology of neuroticism. In H.J. Eysenck & J. Strelau (Eds.), *Personality dimensions and arousal.* New York: Plenum.

Finlay-Jones, R.A., & Brown, G.W. (1981). Types of stressful life events and the onset of anxiety and depressive disorders. *Psychological Medicine, 11,* 803–815.

Fiske, D.W., Cartwright, D.S., & Kirtner, W.L. (1964). Are psychotherapeutic changes predictable? *Journal of Abnormal and Social Psychology, 69,* 418–426.

Folstein, S., & Rutter, M. (1978). A twin study of individuals with infantile autism. In M. Rutter & E. Schopler (Eds.), *Autism: A reappraisal of concepts and treatment.* New York: Plenum.

Freud, S. (1917). Introductory lectures on psychoanalysis, Part III. In J. Strachey (Ed.), *The complete psychological works,* Vol. 16. New York: Norton.

Freud, S., & Breuer, J. (1895). Studies on hysteria. In J. Strachey (Ed.), *The complete psychological works,* Vol. 2. New York: Norton.

Gale, A. (1983). Electroencephalographic studies of extraversion-introversion: A case study in the psychophysiology of individual differences. *Personality and Individual Differences, 4,* 371–380.

Galton, F. (1883). *Inquiry into human faculty and its development.* London: Macmillan.

Gardner, H. (1983). *Frames of mind: The theory of multiple intelligences.* New York: Basic Books.

Geller, E., Yokota, A., Schroth, P., & Novak, P. (1984). Study of fenfluramine in outpatients with the syndrome of autism. *Journal of Pediatrics, 105,* 823–828.

Gerbino, L., Oleshansky, M., & Gershon, S. (1978). Clinical use and mode of action of lithium. In M.A. Lipton, A. DiMascio, & F.K. Killam (Eds.), *Psychopharmacology: A generation of progress.* New York: Raven Press.

Gittelman-Klein, R., Klein, D.F., Abikoff, H., Katz, S., Gloister, A.C., & Kates, W. (1976). Relative efficacy of methylphenidate and behaviour modification in hyperkinetic children: An interim report. *Journal of Abnormal Child Psychology, 4,* 361–379.

Gleitman, H. (1986). *Psychology* (2nd Ed.). London: Norton.

Gleitman, H. (1987). *Basic psychology* (2nd Ed.). London: Norton.

Goldberg, L.R. (1981). Language and individual differences: The search for universals in personality lexicons. In L. Wheeler (Ed.), *Review of Personality and Social Psychology, 2,* 141–165.

Gordon, H. (1923). *Mental and scholastic tests among retarded children.* Educational Pamphlet, no. 44. London: Board of Education.

Gray, J.A. (1973). Causal theories of personality and how to test them. In J.R. Royce (Ed.), *Multivariate analysis of psychological theory.* New York: Academic Press.

Gray, J.A. (1982). *The neuropsychology of anxiety.* Oxford: Oxford University Press.

Gross, R.D. (1992). *Psychology: The science of mind and behavior* (2nd Ed.). London: Hodder and Stoughton.

Guilford, J.P. (1967). *The nature of human intelligence.* New York: McGraw-Hill.

Hall, C.S. (1953). A cognitive theory of dream symbols. *Journal of General Psychology, 48,* 169–186.

Hampson, S.E. (1988). *The construction of personality: An introduction* (2nd Ed.). London: Routledge.

Hampson, S.E. (1992). The emergence of personality: A broader context for biological perspectives. In A. Gale & M.W. Eysenck (Eds.), *Handbook of individual differences: Biological perspectives.* Chichester: Wiley.

Hare, R.D. (1965). Temporal gradient of fear arousal in psychopaths. *Journal of Abnormal Psychology, 70,* 442–445.

Harris, E.L., Noyes, R., Crowe, R.R., & Chaudhry, D.R. (1983). Family study of agoraphobia: Report of a pilot study. *Archives of General Psychiatry, 40,* 1061–1064.

Heston, L.L. (1966). Psychiatric disorders in foster home reared children of schizophrenic mothers. *British Journal of Psychiatry, 112,* 19–25.

Hibbert, G.A. (1984). Ideational components of anxiety: Their origin and content. *British Journal of Psychiatry, 144,* 618–624.

Hirschberg, N. (1978). A correct treatment of traits. In H. London (Ed.), *Personality: A new look at metatheories.* New York: Macmillan.

Hodges, W.F. (1968). Effects of ego threat and threat of pain on state anxiety. *Journal of Personality and Social Psychology, 8,* 364–372.

Holley, J.W., (1973). On the validity of some clinical measures. *Psychological Research Bulletin, Lund University, 13,* 1–9.

Holroyd, K., Penzien, D., Hursey, K., Tobin, D., Rogers, L., Holm, J., Marcille, P., Hall, J., & Chila, A. (1984). Change mechanisms in EMG biofeedback training: Cognitive changes underlying improvements in tension headache. *Journal of Consulting and Clinical Psychology, 52,* 1039–1053.

Howarth, E., & Browne, J.A. (1971). An item-factor-analysis of the 16PF. *Personality, 2,* 117–139.

Howe, M.J.A. (1989). The strange achievements of idiots savants. In A.M. Colman & J.G. Beaumont (Eds.), *Psychology survey, No. 7.* Leicester: BPS.

Howe, M. (1990a). Does intelligence exist? *The Psychologist, 3,* 490–493.

Howe, M. (1990b). Useful word but obsolete construct. *The Psychologist, 3,* 498–499.

Hunt, E.B. (1978). Mechanics of verbal ability. *Psychological Review, 85,* 109–130.

Hunt, E.B., Lunneborg, C., & Lewis, J. (1975). What does it mean to be high verbal? *Cognitive Psychology, 7,* 194–227.

Irwin, M., Lovitz, A., Marder, S.R., Mintz, J., Winslade, W.J., Van Putten, T., & Mills, M.J. (1985). Psychotic patients' understanding of informed consent. *American Journal of Psychiatry, 142,* 1351–1354.

Jamison, K.R. (1984). Manic-depressive illness and accomplishment: Creativity, leadership, and social class. In F.K. Goodwin & K.R. Jamison (Eds.), *Manic-depressive illness.* Oxford: Oxford University Press.

Jensen, A.R. (1969). How much can we boost I.Q. and scholastic achievement? *Harvard Educational Review, 39,* 1–123.

Jessup, G., & Jessup, H. (1971). Validity of the Eysenck Personality Inventory in pilot selection. *Occupational Psychology, 45,* 111–123.

Kanner, L. (1943). Autistic disturbances of affective contact. *Nervous child, 2,* 217–250.

Kaul, T.J., & Bednar, R.L. (1986). Experiential group research: Results, questions, and suggestions. In S.L. Garfield & A.E. Bergin (Eds.), *Handbook of psychotherapy and behaviour change* (3rd Ed.). Chichester: Wiley.

Kelly, G.A. (1955). *The psychology of personal constructs.* New York: Norton.

Kelly, G.A. (1964). The language of hypothesis: Man's psychological instrument. *Journal of Individual Psychology, 20,* 137–152.

Kety, S.S. (1974). From rationalization to reason. *American Journal of Psychiatry, 131,* 957–963.

Keuthen, N. (1980). *Subjective probability estimation and somatic structures in phobic individuals.* Unpublished manuscript, State University of New York at Stony Brook.

Kirigin, K.A., Braukmann, C.J., Atwater, J.D., & Wolf, M.M. (1982). An evaluation of teaching-family (Achievement Place) group homes for juvenile offenders. *Journal of Applied Behavior Analysis, 15,* 1–16.

Klein, D.F., & Davis, J.M. (1969). *Diagnosis and drug treatment of psychiatric disorders.* Baltimore: Williams and Wilkins.

Klein, D.F., & Gittelman-Klein, R. (1975). Are behavioural and psychometric changes related in methyphenidate treated, hyperactive children? *International Journal of Mental Health, 14,* 182–198.

Kline, P. (1991). *Intelligence: The psychometric view.* London: Routledge.

Kline, P. (1992). The factor structure in the fields of personality and ability. In A. Gale & M.W. Eysenck (Eds.), *Handbook of individual differences: Biological perspectives.* Chichester: Wiley.

Kostlan, A. (1954). A method for the empirical study of psycho-diagnosis. *Journal of Consulting Psychology, 18,* 83–88.

Krause, M.S. (1964). An analysis of Carl Rogers' theory of personality. *Genetic Psychology Monographs, 69,* 49–99.

Kurland, H.D., Yeager, C.T., & Arthur, R.J. (1963). Psychophysiologic aspects of severe behaviour disorders. *Archives of General Psychiatry, 8,* 599–604.

Laing, R.D. (1967). *The politics of experience.* New York: Ballantine.

Lazarus, A.A., & Davison, G.C. (1971). Clinical innovation in research and practice. In A.E. Bergin & S.L. Garfield (Eds.), *Handbook of psychotherapy and behaviour change: An empirical analysis.* Chichester: Wiley.

Lewinsohn, P.M., Steinmetz, J.L., Larsen, D.W., & Franklin, Y. (1981). Depression related cognitions: Antecedents or consequences? *Journal of Abnormal Psychology, 90,* 213–219.

Lick, J., (1975). Expectancy, false galvanic skin response feedback and systematic desensitization in the modification of phobic behaviour. *Journal of Consulting and Clinical Psychology, 43,* 557–567.

Lick, J., & Bootzin, R. (1975). Expectancy factors in the treatment of fear: Methodological and theoretical issues. *Psychological Bulletin, 82,* 917–931.

Liebowitz, M.R., Gorman, J.M., Fyer, A.J., Levitt, M., Dillon, D., Levy, G., Appleby, I.L., Anderson, S., Palij, M., Davies, S.O., & Klein, D.F. (1985). Lactate provocation of panic attacks: II. Biochemical and physiological findings. *Archives of General Psychiatry, 42,* 709–719.

Loehlin, J.C., Lindzey, G., & Spuhler, J.N. (1975). *Race differences in intelligence.* San Francisco: Freeman.

Losonczy, M.F., Song, I.S., Mohs, R.C., Mathe, A.A., Davidson, M., Davis, B.M., & Davis, K.L. (1986). Correlates of lateral ventricular size in chronic schizophrenia: II. Biological measures. *American Journal of Psychiatry, 143,* 1113–1117.

Lovaas, O.I. (1987). Behavioural treatment and abnormal education and intellectual functioning in young autistic children. *Journal of Consulting and Clinical Psychology, 55,* 3–9.

Lovaas, O.I., Koegel, R., Simmons, J.Q., & Long, J.S. (1973). Some generalization and follow-up measures on autistic children in behaviour therapy. *Journal of Applied Behavior Analysis, 6,* 131–166.

Luborsky, L., & Spence, D.P. (1978). Quantitative research on psychoanalytic therapy. In S.L. Garfield & A.E. Bergin (Eds.), *Handbook of psychotherapy and behavior change: An empirical analysis* (2nd Ed.). New York: Wiley.

MacKinnon, D.W. (1962). The nature and nurture of creative talent. *American Psychologist, 17,* 484–495.

Maddux, J.E. (1991). Self-efficacy. In C.R. Snyder & D.R. Forsyth (Eds.), *Handbook of social and clinical psychology.* Oxford: Pergamon.

Marks, I.M. (1969). *Fears and phobias.* New York: Academic Press.

Marks, I.M. (1987). *Fears, phobias, and rituals: Panic, anxiety, and their disorders.* Oxford: Oxford University Press.

Maslow, A. (1970). *Toward a psychology of being* (3rd Ed.). New York: Van Nostrand.

Mayo, C.W., & Crockett, W.H. (1964). Cognitive complexity and primacy: Recency effects in impression formation. *Journal of Abnormal and Social Psychology, 68,* 335–338.

McCrae, R.R., & Costa, P.T. (1985). Updating Norman's "adequate taxonomy": Intelligence and personality dimensions in natural language and in questionnaires. *Journal of Personality and Social Psychology, 49,* 710–721.

McGuigan, F.J. (1966). Covert oral behaviour and auditory hallucinations. *Psychophysiology, 3,* 421–428.

McKeon, J., Roa, B., & Mann, A. (1984). Life events and personality trait in obsessive-compulsive neurosis. *British Journal of Psychiatry, 144,* 185–189.

Mead, M. (1935). *Sex and temperament in three primitive societies.* New York: Morrow.

Mednick, S.A., Gabrielli, W.F., & Hutchings, B. (1984). Genetic influences in criminal convictions: Evidence from an adoption cohort. *Science, 224,* 891–894.

Mendlewicz, J., & Rainer, J.D. (1977). Adoption study supporting genetic transmission in manic-depressive illness. *Nature, 268,* 327–329.

Mischel, W. (1968). *Personality and assessment.* New York: Wiley.

Mischel, W. (1973). Toward a cognitive social learning reconceptualization of personality. *Psychological Review, 80,* 252–283.

Mischler, E.G., & Waxler, N.E. (1968). Family interaction and schizophrenia: Alternative frameworks of interpretation. In D. Rosenthal & S.S. Kety (Eds.), *The transmission of schizophrenia*. New York: Pergamon.

Morgan, C.D., & Murray, H.A. (1935). A method of investigating fantasies: The thematic apperception test. *Archives of Neurological Psychiatry, 34*, 289–306.

Morrison, J.R., & Stewart, M.A. (1971). A family study of the hyperactive child syndrome. *Biological Psychiatry, 3*, 189–195.

Nagpal, M., & Gupta, B.S. (1979). Personality, reinforcement and verbal operant conditioning. *British Journal of Psychology, 70*, 471–476.

Nash, E.H., Hoehn-Saric, R., Battle, C.C., Stone, A.R., Imber, S.D., & Frank, J.D. (1965). Systematic preparation of patients for short-term psychotherapy. II. Relation to characteristics of patient, therapist and the psychotherapeutic process. *Journal of Nervous and Mental Disorders, 140*, 374–383.

Nesse, F.M., Cameron, O.G., Curtis, G.C., McCann, D.S., & Huber-Smith, M.J. (1984). Adrenergic function in patients with panic anxiety. *Archives of General Psychiatry, 41*, 771–776.

Newmark, C.S., Frerking, R.A., Cook, L., & Newmark, L. (1973). Endorsement of Ellis' irrational beliefs as a function of psychopathology. *Journal of Clinical Psychology, 29*, 300–302.

Norman, W.T. (1963). Toward an adequate taxonomy of personality attributes: Replicated factor structure in peer nomination personality ratings. *Journal of Abnormal and Social Psychology, 66*, 574–588.

O'Leary, K.D., & Wilson, G.T. (1987). *Behaviour therapy: Application and outcome* (2nd Ed.). Englewood Cliffs, NJ: Prentice-Hall.

Oltman, J., & Friedman, S. (1967). Parental deprivation in psychiatric conditions. *Diseases of the Nervous System, 28*, 298–303.

Paul, G.L. (1966). *Insight vs. desensitization in psychotherapy: An experiment in anxiety reduction*. Stanford, CA: Stanford University Press.

Pervin, L.A. (1989). *Personality: Theory and research* (5th Ed.). Chichester: Wiley.

Quay, H.C., Routh, D.K., & Shapiro, S.K. (1987). Psychopathology of childhood: From description to validation. *Annual Review of Psychology, 38*, 491–532.

Quay, L.C. (1971). Language, dialect, reinforcement, and the intelligence test performance of Negro children. *Child Development, 42*, 5–15.

Rachman, S.J., & Hodgson, R.J. (1980). *Obsessions and compulsions*. Englewood Cliffs, NJ: Prentice-Hall.

Reinhardt, R.F. (1970). The outstanding jet pilot. *American Journal of Psychiatry, 127*, 732–736.

Rescorla, R.A. (1967). Pavlovian conditioning and its proper control procedures. *Psychological Review, 74*, 71–80.

Rogers, C.R. (1951). *Client-centred therapy*. Boston: Houghton Mifflin.

Rogers, C.R. (1959). A theory of therapy, personality, and interpersonal relationships as developed in the client-centred framework. In S. Koch (Ed.), *Psychology: A study of a science*. New York: McGraw-Hill.

Rosekrans, M.A., & Hartup, W.W. (1967). Imitative influences of consistent and inconsistent response consequences to a model on aggressive behaviour in children. *Journal of Personality and Social Psychology, 7*, 429–434.

Rosenhan, D.L. (1973). On being sane in insane places. *Science, 179*, 250–258.

Rosenhan, D.L., & Seligman, M.E.P. (1989). *Abnormal psychology* (2nd Ed.). London: Norton.

Rosenthal, D. (1970). *Genetic theory and abnormal behaviour*. New York: McGraw-Hill.

Roskies, E., Seraganian, P., Oseasohn, R., Smilga, C., Martin, N., & Hanley, J.A. (1989). Treatment of psychological stress responses in healthy Type A men. In R.W.J. Neufeld (Ed.), *Advances in the investigation of psychological stress.* Chichester: Wiley.

Rutter, M. (1979). Maternal deprivation. 1972–1978: New findings, new concepts, new approaches. *Child Development, 50,* 283–305.

Sarason, I.G., Smith, R.E., & Diener, E. (1975). Personality research: Components of variance attributable to the person and the situation. *Journal of Personality and Social Psychology, 32,* 199–204.

Saville, P., & Blinkhorn, S. (1981). Reliability, homogeneity and the construct validity of Cattell's 16PF. *Personality and Individual Differences, 2,* 325–333.

Scarr, S., & Weinberg, R.A. (1976). I.Q. test performance of black children adopted by white families. *American Psychologist, 31,* 726–739.

Scheff, T.J. (1966). *Being mentally ill: A sociological theory.* Chicago: Aldine.

Seligman, M.E.P. (1971). Phobias and preparedness. *Behavior Therapy, 2,* 307–320.

Shaw, L., & Sichel, H. (1970). *Accident proneness.* Oxford: Pergamon.

Shields, J. (1962). *Monozygotic twins.* Oxford: Oxford University Press.

Smith, M.L., & Glass, G.V. (1977). Meta-analysis of psychotherapy outcome studies. *American Psychologist, 32,* 752–760.

Snyder, S.H. (1976). *Madness and the brain.* New York: McGraw-Hill.

Spearman, C. (1923). *The nature of intelligence and the principles of cognition.* London: Macmillan.

Spitzer, R.L., & Fleiss, J.L. (1974). A re-analysis of the reliability of psychiatric diagnosis. *British Journal of Psychiatry, 125,* 341–347.

Sprague, R.L., & Berger, B.D. (1980). Drug effects on learning performance: Relevance of animal research to pediatric psychopharmacology. In R.M. Knights & D.J. Bakker (Eds.), *Treatment of hyperactive and learning disabled children.* Baltimore: University Park Press.

Stern, S.L., Rush, J., & Mendels, J. (1980). Toward a rational pharmacotherapy of depression. *American Journal of Psychiatry, 137,* 545–552.

Sternberg, R.J. (1982). A componential approach to intellectual development. In R.J. Sternberg (Ed.), *Advances in the psychology of human intelligence,* Vol. 1. Hillsdale: Lawrence Erlbaum Associates.

Sternberg, R.J. (1985). *Beyond IQ: A triarchic theory of human intelligence.* Cambridge: Cambridge University Press.

Sternberg, R.J., & Frensch, P.A. (1990). Intelligence and cognition. In M.W. Eysenck (Ed.), *Cognitive psychology: An international review.* Chichester: Wiley.

Szasz, T.S. (Ed.) (1974). *The age of madness: The history of involuntary hospitalization.* New York: Jason Aronson.

Teasdale, J.D. (1986). *Non-pharmacological treatments for depression.* Unpublished manuscript. Cambridge: MRC Applied Psychology Unit.

Tellegen, A. (1985). Structures of mood and personality and their relevance to assessing anxiety, with an emphasis on self-report. In A.H. Tuma & J. Maser (Eds.), *Anxiety and the anxiety disorders.* Hillsdale: Lawrence Erlbaum Associates.

Temerlin, M.K. (1970). Diagnostic bias in community mental health. *Community Mental Health Journal, 6,* 110–117.

Thurstone, L.L. (1938). *Primary mental abilities.* Chicago, IL: University of Chicago Press.

Tobacyk, J.J., & Downs, A. (1986). Personal construct threat and irrational beliefs as cognitive predictors of increases in musical performance anxiety. *Journal of Personality and Social Psychology, 51,* 779–782.

Torgersen, S. (1983). Genetic factors in anxiety disorders. *Archives of General Psychiatry, 40,* 1085–1089.

Truax, C.B., & Mitchell, K.M. (1971). Research on certain therapist interpersonal skills in relation to process and outcome. In A.E. Bergin & S.L. Garfield (Eds.), *Handbook of psychotherapy and behaviour change.* Chichester: Wiley.

Wachtel, P.L. (1977). *Psychoanalysis and behaviour therapy: Toward an integration.* New York: Basic Books.

Wagner, R.K., & Sternberg, R.J. (1986). Tacit knowledge and intelligence in the everyday world. In R.J. Sternberg & R.K. Wagner (Eds.), *Practical intelligence: Nature and origins of competence in the everyday world.* New York: Cambridge University Press.

Walters, J., & Gardner, H. (1986). The crystallizing experience: Discovering an intellectual gift. In R.J. Sternberg & J.E. Davidson (Eds.), *Conceptions of giftedness.* New York: Cambridge University Press.

Watson, D., & Clark, L.A. (1984). Negative affectivity: The disposition to experience aversive emotional states. *Psychological Bulletin, 96,* 465–490.

Watson, J.B. (1913). Psychology as the behaviourist views it. *Psychological Review, 20,* 158–177.

Watson, J.B., & Rayner, R. (1920). Conditioned emotional reactions. *Journal of Experimental Psychology, 3,* 1–14.

Wender, P.H., Kety, S.S., Rosenthal, D., Schulsinger, F., Ortmann, J., & Lunde, I. (1986). Psychiatric disorders in the biological and adoptive families of adopted individuals with affective disorders. *Archives of General Psychiatry, 43,* 923–929.

Wheeler, L.R. (1942). A comparative study of the intelligence of East Tennessee mountain children. *Journal of Educational Psychology, 33,* 321–334.

Winch, R.F., & More, D.M. (1956). Does TAT add information to interviews? Statistical analysis of the increment. *Journal of Clinical Psychology, 12,* 316–321.

Wittgenstein, L. (1958). *Philosophical investigations.* New York: Macmillan.

Wolpe, J. (1958). *Psychotherapy by reciprocal inhibition.* Stanford, CA.: Stanford University Press.

Zentall, S.S., & Zentall, T.R. (1983). Optimal stimulation: A model of disordered activity and performance in normal and deviant children. *Psychological Bulletin, 94,* 446–471.

Zubin, J., Eron, L.D., & Shumer, F. (1965). *An experimental approach to projective techniques.* New York: Wiley.

Glossary

Abnormal psychology: an approach to psychology which focuses on people suffering from psychological disorders

Acquiescence response set: the tendency to answer "yes" to items presented in self-report questionnaires (q.v.)

Adrenergic functioning: relating to the hormone adrenaline and other adrenaline-like substances; thought to be involved in panic disorder

Aetiological validity: one measure of the validity or value of a system of classifying mental disorders; the extent to which any given mental disorder typically has the same cause in different individuals

Aetiology: the cause or causes of a disease

Anxiety: a dimension of personality proposed by Gray, involving a combination of neuroticism and introversion; see also Neuroticism-stability, Introversion-extraversion, and Punishment

Arbitrary inference: drawing a conclusion which is not supported by the evidence; characteristic of depressed patients

Attention-deficit hyperactivity disorder: children with this disorder are very active, concentrate poorly, and are unable to concentrate

Autism: a severe condition in children in which there are very poor relationships with other people and poor language learning

Autonomic nervous system: part of the physiological system underlying individual differences in neuroticism in H.J. Eysenck's theory of personality; see also Neuroticism-stability and Visceral brain

Aversion therapy: a form of treatment in which undesirable behaviour is eliminated by associating it with severe punishment

Barbiturates: depressant drugs which used to be used extensively in the treatment of anxiety disorders; see also Benzodiazepines

Behaviourist: an approach to psychology in which it is assumed that behaviour is determined by environmental factors; see Situationism

Benzodiazepines: drugs such as Valium and Librium often used in the treatment of anxiety disorders; see also Barbiturates

Biofeedback: a method of treatment in which patients are given information about their physiological functioning (e.g., heart rate) in order to facilitate changes (e.g., lowering blood pressure in anxious patients)

Classical conditioning: a basic form of learning in which simple responses (e.g., salivation) are associated with new stimuli

Code: a summarised form of information used to remember the actions of a model within Bandura's theory

Cognitive processes: the processes of attention, perception, learning, reasoning, and so on, often neglected by personality theorists

Cognitive psychologists: psychologists who study mental activities such as attention, thinking, and memory in order to identify the processes and structures involved

Cognitive skills: abilities associated with the various cognitive processes (q.v.)

Cognitive triad: According to Beck, the negative thoughts about the self, world, and the future, characteristic of depressed patients

Combinations: As applied to H.J. Eysenck's theory of personality, the notion that many personality traits reflect a mixture of two or all three of his personality dimensions

Compulsions: repetitive, stereotyped rituals found in patients suffering from obsessive-compulsive disorder; see also obsessions

Concordance: the similarity in psychiatric diagnosis of pairs of twins

Concurrent validity: assessing whether a test is measuring what it is designed to measure by comparing test performance to information about an external criterion which is available at the time of test administration; see also Predictive validity

Conditioned reflex: the new association between a stimulus and a response formed in Classical conditioning (q.v.)

Conditioned response: the response which is produced as a result of Classical conditioning (q.v.)

Conditioning: basic forms of learning exhibited to a greater extent by introverts than by extraverts in H.J. Eysenck's theory

Conduct disorders: disorders of childhood involving aggressive and anti-social behaviour

Conflicts: rows and difficulties within families; prevalent in the families of children and adolescents with Conduct disorders (q.v.)

Conscious awareness: as applied to Conditioning (q.v.), the assumption that conditioned learning and extinction require awareness of what is happening

Consensual validity: assessing whether a personality test measures what it is designed to measure by comparing scores from self-report questionnaires (q.v.) with those from ratings (q.v.) provided by other people

Construct: an abstract notion (e.g., intelligence)

Construct validity: assessing whether a test measures what it is designed to measure by using it to test theoretical predictions

Contrast pole: within Kelly's Repertory Grid Test, the way in which one person differs from two other people; see also Similarity pole

Controls: normal groups against whom patient groups can be compared

Core constructs: those constructs which are of fundamental importance to the individual as revealed by Kelly's Repertory Grid Test

Cortical arousal: in H.J. Eysenck's theory of personality, activity in the brain is said to be greater in introverts than in extraverts; see Introversion-extraversion

Counterconditioning: a key ingredient in Systematic desensitisation (q.v.) involving the substitution of a relaxation response for the fear response to feared stimuli

Delusions: severely distorted thought patterns; often found in Schizophrenia (q.v.)

Denial: According to Rogers, a reaction to a discrepancy between a child's actual experiences and its self-perceptions in which the existence of the experience is denied; see also Distortion

Description: a simple account of the findings of research; see also Explanation

Descriptive validity: one measure of the validity or value of a system for classifying mental disorders, based on the extent to which patients assigned to different categories differ from each other

Distortion: According to Rogers, a reaction to a discrepancy between a child's actual experiences and its self-perceptions in which reality is distorted; see also Denial

Dizygotic twins: fraternal twins deriving from two fertilised ova; see also Monozygotic twins

Dopamine: a chemical neurotransmitter thought to play a part in schizophrenia (q.v.); see also Phenothiazines

Dynamic lattice: in Cattell's theory of motivation, the connections between basic biological motives or Ergs (q.v.,) and ways of satisfying those ergs (Sentiments; q.v.)

Dysthymia: long-lasting or chronic depression

Echolalia: meaningless repetition of what someone else has said; characteristic of Autism (q.v.)

EEG: see Electroencephalography

Electroencephalography: a technique for measuring brain-wave activity

Emotional arousal: the negative effects of high levels of arousal on feelings of self-efficacy in Bandura's theory

Empirical validity: assessing whether a test measures what it claims to measure by correlating test performance with some external criterion (e.g., correlating extraversion scores with the number of friends people have)

Equivalent forms method: assessing the reliability of a test by administering two comparable forms of it to a group of people

Ergs: in Cattell's theory, the basic biological goals of motivation (e.g., food-seeking); see also Sentiments

Expectations of help: one of the factors not of direct relevance to treatment which can facilitate recovery

Experimental extinction: disappearance of a Conditioned Response (q.v.) when the Unconditioned stimulus (q.v.) is no longer presented

Explanation: a detailed account involving an understanding of the findings of research; see also Description

External: in Bandura's theory, those environmental factors which influence behaviour; see also Internal

External world: in Sternberg's theory, the application of intelligence to the outside world is dealt with in his contextual sub-theory; see also Internal world

Extinction: a form of treatment involving Operant conditioning (q.v.), in which unwanted behaviour is not followed by reward or positive reinforcement in order to reduce its incidence

Factor analysis: a statistical technique designed to ascertain the number and nature of factors contained in a test

Fantasy': According to Rogers, a process whereby an individual resolves a discrepancy between his or her behaviour and self-concept by fantasising about himself or herself and denying any experiences which are inconsistent with those fantasies

Fixed-role therapy: a form of therapy devised by Kelly, in which the patient pretends to be someone else

Flooding: a form of treatment for obsessive-compulsive disorder and phobia in which there is prolonged exposure to the feared stimulus

General factor: the broad, general factor of intelligence identified by Spearman; see also Group factors

Genotype: an individual's genetic potential; see also Phenotype

Group Factors: fairly broad factors of intelligence (e.g., verbal; spatial) originally identified by Spearman; see also General factor

Guidelines: as applied to factor analysis, the suggestive evidence it provides about the structure of intelligence or personality

Hallucinations: visual and auditory perception in the absence of a stimulus; a symptom of schizophrenia (q.v.)

Humanistic psychology: an approach to psychology in which the focus is on subjective experience and the individual's major life goals; there is a reliance on phenomenology (q.v.)

Idiots savants: mentally handicapped individuals who have developed specific skills as a result of prolonged practice

Impulsivity: in Gray's theory of personality, a major dimension of personality combining neuroticism and extraversion; see also Neuroticism-stability and Introversion-extraversion

Intelligence: capacity for abstract reasoning, problem-solving, and other high-level cognitive activities

Intelligence quotient: a measure of general intellectual ability which can be calculated by dividing mental age by chronological age; abbreviated as IQ

Interactionism: an approach in which it is assumed that behaviour depends jointly on the person and on the environment

Internal: in Bandura's theory, those internal factors (e.g., what an an individual has learned) which influence behaviour; see also External

Internal world: in Sternberg's theory, the application of intelligence to the internal processes involved is dealt with in his componential subtheory

Introjection: According to Rogers, a process in which children incorporate other people's values into their own ways of thinking

Introversion-extraversion: a personality dimension identified by H.J. Eysenck, with extraverts being much more sociable and impulsive than introverts

IQ: see Intelligence quotient

Irrationality and incomprehensibility: one of the criteria of abnormality proposed by Rosenhan and Seligman; behaviour which appears to be poorly motivated

Labelling theory: according to this theory, attaching a psychiatric label a patient may lead to him or her being perceived as mentally ill, thus worsening his or her condition; initially proposed by Scheff

Latent dream: in Freud's theory of dreams, the underlying meaning of a dream; see also Manifest dream

Long-term memory: a part of the memory systems in which memories are stored indefinitely

Magnification and minimisation: the exaggeration of minor negative events and minimising of major positive events found in depressed patients

Maladaptiveness: one of the criteria of abnormality proposed by Rosenhan and Seligman; behaviour which prevents the individual from reaching his or her goals

Manic-depressive psychosis: a severe condition in which there are large mood swings between mania and depression

Manifest dream: in Freud's theory of dreams, the apparent meaning of a dream; see also Latent dream

Medical model: an approach to psychological disorders based on the assumption that there are important similarities between mental and physical illness

Misinterpret: as applied to panic disorder, the notion that there is exaggeration and distortion of physical symptoms

Modelling: learning by means of vicarious experiences (q.v.)

Monozygotic twins: identical twins derived from the same fertilised ovum; see also Dizygotic twins

Neuroanatomy: the structure of the nervous system

Neurosis: a broad category of mental disorders, including the anxiety disorders; see also Psychosis

Neuroticism-stability: a personality dimension identified by H.J. Eysenck, with those high in neuroticism being characterised by anxiety, depression, and tension

Neurotransmitters: chemical substances involved in transferring nerve impulses between neurons

Noradrenaline: a neurotransmitter (q.v.) which seems to be involved in clinical depression; see also Serotonin

Objective tests: a method of assessing personality under laboratory conditions in an unobtrusive fashion

Oblique solutions: an approach to factor analysis in which the personality factors identified are allowed to correlate with each; see also Orthogonal solutions

Observer discomfort: one of the criteria of abnormality proposed by Rosenhan and Seligman; generally produced by behaviour which breaks one or more of the unspoken rules of behaviour

Obsessions: recurring intrusive and irrational thoughts found in patients suffering from obsessive-compulsive disorder; see also Compulsions

Operant conditioning: a form of learning in which behaviour is controlled by appropriate administration of reward or reinforcement

Oppositional defiant disorder: a childhood disorder in which there is hostile, negative, and defiant behaviour

Orthogonal solutions: an approach to factor analysis in which all of the personality factors identified are uncorrelated with each other; see also Oblique solutions

Outcome expectancies: expectations as to whether producing the appropriate behaviour will be followed by reward

Outcome value: the perceived value of the reward for successful performance

Over-generalisation: sweeping conclusions about one's own worth based on limited evidence; characteristic of depressed patients

Peripheral constructs: minor constructs as assessed by Kelly's Repertory Grid Test; they can be changed with only small effects on the Core constructs (q.v.)

Personalisation: wrongly taking responsibility for negative events; characteristic of depressed patients

Personality: semi-permanent internal predispositions that make people behave consistently, but in ways that differ from those of other people

Personality types: small number of types or categories into which people can be allocated; see also Traits

Phenomenology: an approach in which the focus is on the individual's direct experiences rather than on his or her behaviour

Phenothiazines: drugs which block the chemical neurotransmitter Dopamine (q.v.), and which have proved useful in the treatment of Schizophrenia (q.v.)

Phenotype: an individual's observable characteristics; see also Genotype

Phobias: anxiety disorders in which there is strong fear of some object or situation; examples are agoraphobia (fear of open spaces) and claustrophobia (a fear of enclosed spaces)

Phrene: a Greek word meaning mind; the word schizophrenia derives from that word and from schizo (q.v.)

Predictive validity: assessing whether a test is measuring what it claims to measure by comparing performance on the test against some external criterion which is obtained subsequently; see also Concurrent validity

Previous experiences: past successes and failures that influence current level of self-efficacy—Bandura's theory

Projective tests: a method of assessing personality in which people are given an unstructured task to perform (e.g., describing what can be seen in an inkblot)

Psychoanalysis: a form of treatment lot psychological disorders proposed by Freud in which the focus is on providing patients with insight into their major unresolved conflicts

Psychopathology: see Abnormal psychology

Psychosis: a broad category of mental disorder, covering those who have a partial or total loss of contact with reality, for example, patients with Manic-depressive psychosis (q.v.) and Schizophrenia (q.v.); see also Neurosis

Psychotherapy: a general term to describe forms of treatment (e.g., Psychoanalysis, q.v.; Cognitive therapy, q.v.) involving attempts to change patterns of thought

Psychoticism-normality: a personality dimension identified by H. J. Eysenck, with those high in psychoticism being aggressive, hostile, and uncaring

Punishment: in Gray's theory of personality, individuals high in the personality dimension of anxiety are especially susceptible to punishment

Ratings: a method of assessing personality in which observers indicate the extent to which those being rated display various forms of behaviour

Rationalisation: According to Rogers, the process of an individual misinterpreting his or her behaviour to make it consistent with his or her self-concept; see also Fantasy

Reciprocal determinism: the two-way influence of person on environment and of environment on person emphasised by Bandura

Reinforcement: according to Skinner's law of reinforcement, the probability of a response occurring depends on whether it is followed by reinforcement or reward; see Operant conditioning

Reliability: the extent to which a test provides consistent findings

Repression: the process of forcing very threatening thoughts and memories out of the conscious mind in Freudian theory; motivated forgetting

Response prevention: when combined with Flooding (q.v.), a form of treatment for Phobias (q.v.) in which the patient is exposed to the feared stimulus and prevented from escaping from it

Reward: within Gray's theory, the personality dimension of Impulsivity (q.v.) depends on individual differences in susceptibility to reward

Schizo: a Greek word meaning split; the word schizophrenia derives from this word and from phrene (q.v.)

Schizophrenia: a severe condition in which there is loss of contact with reality, including distortions of thought, emotion, and behaviour

Selective abstraction: thinking in which one aspect of a situation is accorded exaggerated importance; characteristic of depressed patients

Selective placement: the attempt by adoption agencies to place adopted children into families which resemble those of their biological parents in terms of educational and social backgrounds

Selective positive reinforcement: a form of treatment involving Operant conditioning (q.v.), in which specified adaptive behaviour is followed by reward

Selective punishment: a form of treatment involving Operant conditioning (q.v.), in which specified unwanted behaviour is followed by punishment

Self-regulation: According to Bandura, a process of self-reward if a given standard of performance is achieved

Self-report questionnaires: a method of assessing personality by asking people to answer a series of standard questions

Sentiments: in Cattell's theory, the ways in which basic needs are satisfied within a given culture; see also Ergs

Separation: a child living apart from one of its parents; prevalent in children with Conduct disorders (q.v.)

Serotonin: a neurotransmitter (q.v.) which is involved in clinical depression; see also Noradrenaline

Shaping: in Operant conditioning (q.v.), using Reinforcement (q.v.) to produce progressive changes in behaviour in a desired direction

Similarity pole: within Kelly's Repertory Grid Test, the way in which two people resemble each other but differ from a third person; see also Contrast pole

Situationism: a Behaviourist (q.v.) approach to individual differences, in which it is assumed that behaviour is determined by the environment rather than by internal personality factors

Social desirability response set: tendency to give socially desirable (but not honest) answers on self-report questionnaires (q.v.)

Social persuasion: see Verbal persuasion

Somatic therapy: a form of treatment involving manipulations of the body (e.g., drug treatment)

Split-half method: assessing the reliability of a test by dividing it into two halves and then comparing subjects' performance on these two halves

Standard deviation: a measure of the spread of scores in a normal distribution

Standard score: a measure of an individual with respect to some group, based on his or her difference from the group mean in standard deviations

Standardised tests: tests (e.g. of intelligence) which have been administered to large representative groups of people, so that an individual's performance can be evaluated against that of others

Stimulus generalisation: the strength of the Conditioned response (q.v.) in Classical conditioning (q.v.) is determined by the similarity between the presented stimulus and the original training stimulus

Structure: as applied to intelligence, the notion that human intelligence is hierarchically organised

Subordinate constructs: those towards the bottom of the hierarchy of constructs identified by Kelly's Repertory Grid Test; see also Superordinate constructs

Suffering: one of the criteria of abnormality proposed by Rosenhan and Seligman

Superordinate constructs: those towards the top of the hierarchy of constructs identified by Kelly's Repertory Grid Test; see also Subordinate constructs

Syndromes: a set of symptoms which are generally found together; often used as the basis for the classification of mental disorders

Systematic desensitisation: a form of therapy for phobias (q.v.), in which the fear response to feared stimuli is replaced by a different response (e.g., relaxation); see also Counterconditioning

Taxonomy: a comprehensive system of classification (e.g., in abnormal psychology)

Test-retest method: assessing the reliability of a test by administering it twice to the same subjects

Test validity: assessing whether a test is measuring what it is designed to measure by correlating scores on that test with those on a well-established test

Token economy: institution-based application of Operant conditioning (q.v.) to criminals or mental patients

Traits: relatively long-lasting broad characteristics which jointly form Personality (q.v.)

Transference: in Psychoanalysis (q.v.), the transfer of the patient's strong feelings for one or both parents onto the therapist

Unconditioned reflex: a well-established association between an Unconditioned stimulus (q.v.) and an Unconditioned response (q.v.)

Unconditioned response: in an Unconditioned reflex (q.v.), the well-established response (e.g., salivation) to a given Unconditioned stimulus (q.v.) such as the sight of food

Unconditioned stimulus: in an Unconditioned reflex (q.v.), the stimulus which produces a well-established response; see also Unconditioned response

Unpredictability and loss of control: one of the criteria of abnormality proposed by Rosenhan and Seligman, in which behaviour is inappropriate to the situation

Validity: the extent to which a test measures what it is claimed to measure

Verbal persuasion: the effects of the arguments of others on an individual's feelings of self-efficacy

Vicarious experiences: the effects of observing the experiences of others on an individual's feelings of self-efficacy

Violation of moral and ideal standards: one of the criteria of abnormality proposed by Rosenhan and Seligman; breaking commonly held moral standards of behaviour

Visceral brain: the hippocampus, amygdala, hypothalamus and other parts of the Autonomic nervous system (q.v.) underlying individual differences in Neuroticism-stability (q.v.) in H.J. Eysenck's theory of personality

Vividness and unconventionality: one of the criteria of abnormality proposed by Rosenhan and Seligman, characterised by unusual and distinctive behaviour

Author index

Subject index

abnormality *see* psychopathology

"Achievement Place", 135

acquiescence response set, 45

activity raising, 160

adolescence, conduct disorders, 134

adoption studies
and intelligence, 16–17
and mental disorder
anti-social personality disorder, 126
attention-deficit hyperactivity disorder, 133
depression, 118, 119
schizophrenia, 115

adrenergic functioning, 122

aetiological validity, DSM, 99, 101–2

aetiology of disorder, 97, 102–3, *see also* psychopathology, causes

age, mental and chronological, 7–8

agoraphobia, 119, 121

alcoholism, aversion therapy for, 144

amnesia, 105

anthropology, and psychoanalysis, 154

anti-depressant drugs, 118, 165

anti-social personality disorder, 124–7

anxiety
dimension of personality, 57–8
disorders, 102, 119–23
and cognitive therapy, 122, 160–1
and drug therapy, 166
obsessive-compulsive disorder, 103–4, 123
panic disorder, 121–2
phobias, 84–5, 119–21, 142–4
"hierarchy", 143–4
trait, 45, 63–4
assessment of, 89–90

arousal, cortical, 55–6, 133

assessment *see* testing

attention-deficit hyperactivity disorder, 132–4
and drug therapy, 133, 166–7
and operant conditioning, 133–4, 166–7

autism, 128–30

aversion therapy, 144–5

Bandura, Albert
and cognitive therapy, 149–50, 157, 158
social cognitive theory of personality, 81–6
basic processes, 82–4
evaluation, 85–6
self-efficacy and clinical therapy, 84–5

barbiturates, 166

Beck, Aaron, 117, 157–60

behaviour, abnormal, 92–3, *see also* psychopathology

behaviour therapy, 3, 104–5, 140–50, 172
classical conditioning, 141–5
evaluation of, 148–50
and obsessive-compulsive disorder, 123
operant conditioning, 145–8
phobias, 120, 142–4, 149

behavioural model, 104–5, 108, 120, 142

behaviourism, 62–3, 81–2, 104

benzodiazepines, 166, 167

Binet, Alfred, 6–7, 20

biochemistry, see brain

biofeedback, 147–8

bipolar depression (manic-depression), 102, 118–19

brain, and mental disorder, 105
anti-social personality disorder, 126–7
anxiety disorders, 122, 123
childhood disorders, 130, 133
depression, 118, 165
schizophrenia, 105, 115, 164, 165

Burt, Sir Cyril, 22–3

Cattell, Raymond
theory of crystallised and fluid intelligence, 23–4

evolution, theory of, 1
experience
  openness to, 78, 79
  subjective, 80, 83
extinction of conditioning,
  141, 142, 146
extreme environments, 16–
  17
Eysenck, H.J.: trait theory of
  personality, 53–6, 61
  Personality Questionnaire
  (EPQ) and Inventory
  (EPI), 43–4, 51, 54, 56

factor analysis, 11, 20–1, 50–
  1
factor theories
  of intelligence, 19–27
  of personality, 2, 50–62
families, and mental disorder, 105, see also adoption studies; twin studies
  anti-social personality
  disorder, 127
  conduct disorders, 134
  schizophrenia, 116
fenfluramine, 130
fixation, 150–1
fixed-role therapy, 74
flooding therapy, 120, 123,
  142–3
fostering studies, 16–17
fraternal twins see twin
  studies
free association, 152
Freud, Sigmund, 103, 106–
  7, 150–6 passim

"g" factor (Spearman), 22,
  24–5
Galton, Sir Francis, 1, 6, 19–
  20
Gardner, Howard: theory of
  multiple intelligences,
  33–5

"general paresis", 163
genetics see heredity vs. environment
genotype, 13
graded task assignment, 160
Gray, Jeffrey: trait theory of
  personality, 57–8
Guilford, J.P.: structure-of-intellect theory, 23

hallucinations, 113
heredity vs. environment
  and intelligence, 12–19
  fostering studies and
  extreme environments,
  16–17
  group differences, 17–19
  twin studies, 14–16
  and mental disorder,
  104–5, 108, 135–7
  anti-social personality
  disorder, 125–7
  anxiety disorders, 120–1,
  121–2, 123
  childhood disorders,
  129–30, 131, 133, 134
  depression, 117–18
  environmental factors,
  136–7
  genetics, 135–6
  schizophrenia, 114–16
homosexuality, 90
humanistic psychology, 80
Hunt, Earl: cognitive theory
  of intelligence, 28–9
hyperactivity see attention-
  deficit hyperactivity disorder
hypnosis, 151–2

ideal self (Rogers), 75–6
identical twins see twin
  studies
idiots savants, 4, 26–7
impulsivity, 57

incongruence (Rogers), 77–9
Index of Self-Actualisation,
  75–6
"insight", 3, 106, 151, 155,
  157
intelligence, 1–2, 4–37
  definition of, 4–6
  contemporary theories of,
  27–35
  Gardner's theory of
  multiple intelligences,
  33–5
  Hunt's cognitive theory,
  28–9
  Sternberg's triarchic
  theory, 29–33
  factor theories of, 19–27
  Cattell's theory of
  crystallised and fluid
  intelligence, 23–4
  early factor theories, 22–3
  factor analysis, 20–1
  Guilford's
  structure-of-intellect
  theory, 23
  group differences in, 17–19
  heredity vs. environment,
  12–19
  normal distribution, 8–9
  quotient (IQ), 5, 7–8
  testing, 6–12
interactionist theory of personality, 63–5
introjection (Rogers), 77
introversion-extraversion
  dimension of personality
  (Eysenck), 54–5, 57, 59, 61

Kelly, George: personal construct theory, 70–5
  clinical applications, 72–4
  evaluation, 74–5
  Role Construct Repertory
  Test, 70–2
Kraepelin, Emil, 98

Kwakiutl Indians, 90

labelling theory, 94, 95–6
learning *see* behaviourism;
    conditioning; modelling
lexical access, and intel-
    ligence, 28–9
lie scales, 44–5
life events, and mental disor-
    ders, 103–4, 106, 117–8,
    135
lithium drugs, 102, 165–6
logic, errors of, 159–60, 161
loosening of constructs , 73

mania, 73, 165–6
manic-depression (bipolar
    depression), 118–19
medical model of mental dis-
    order, 96–8, 105–6, 108,
    162–3, *see also* somatic ther-
    apy
mental age, 7–8
mental disorder *see* psycho-
    pathology
mental retardation, 130–2
Minnesota Multiphasic Per-
    sonality Inventory
    (MMPI), 42–3
modelling, 83–5
mongolism, 131
monoamine oxidase (MAO)
    inhibitors, 118, 165
monozygotic twins *see* twin
    studies
motivation
    Bandura's theory, 86
    Cattell's personality
        theory, 52–3
    Rogers' theory, 76, 81
multiple intelligences, the-
    ory of (Gardner), 33–5
myth, mental illness as, 94

neo-Freudian psychoana-

lysis, 154–6
neuroanatomy, and mental
    disorder, 105, 115
neurosis, 111
neuroticism-stability dimen-
    sion of personality (Ey-
    senck), 54–5, 57, 59, 61
neurotransmitters, 118, 130,
    165
New Guinea, 154
noradrenaline, 118, 164, 165
normality, 94
Norman, W.T., 58–9

objective tests of person-
    ality, 41, 47
obsessive-compulsive disor-
    der, 103–4, 123
occupational selection, and
    personality testing, 59–61
operant conditioning, 145–8
    and attention-deficit
        hyperactivity disorder,
        133–4, 166–7
    and autism, 130
    and conduct disorders, 135
    and mental retardation,
        131–2
oppositional defiant disor-
    der, 132
outcome value and expecta-
    tions (Bandura), 84

panic disorder, 121–2
partial reinforcement, 145
Pavlov, I.P., 141
permeability of constructs
    (Kelly), 73
personal construct theory *see*
    Kelly
personality, 2, 38–85
    anti-social behaviour, 61
    assessment, 40–9
    cognitive approaches to,
        69–88

Bandura's social
    cognitive theory, 81–6
Kelly's personal
    construct theory, 70–5
Rogers'
    phenomenological
    theory, 75–81
constructivism, 65–6
and creativity, 26
definition of, 38–9
disorders, 100, 124–7
factor theories of, 2, 50–62
    Cattell's trait theory, 51–3
    Eysenck's trait theory,
        53–6
    Gray's trait theory, 57–8
    compromise theories,
        58–62
    interactionism, 63–5
    situationism, 62–3
    traits and types, 39–40
pervasive development dis-
    orders, 128–30
phenomenological theory of
    personality *see* Rogers
phenomenology, 69, 75, 80–1
phenothiazines, 115, 164–5
phenotype, 13
phenylketonuria, 131
phobias, 119–21
    behavioural explanation
        of, 120, 142
    flooding therapy, 120,
        142–3
    and self-efficacy, 85
    systematic desensitisation,
        143–4, 149
placebo effect, 169–70
positron emission tomo-
    graphy (PET) scan, 123
predictive validity
    DSM, 99, 102
    tests, 11, 41
predisposition to disorder
    see diathesis